Library Management
for the Digital Age

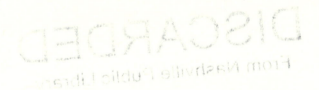

Library Management for the Digital Age

A New Paradigm

Julie Todaro

ROWMAN & LITTLEFIELD
Lanham • Boulder • New York • Toronto • Plymouth, UK

Published by Rowman & Littlefield
4501 Forbes Boulevard, Suite 200, Lanham, Maryland 20706
www.rowman.com

10 Thornbury Road, Plymouth PL6 7PP, United Kingdom

British Library Cataloguing in Publication Information Available

Library of Congress Cataloging-in-Publication Data

Todaro, Julie, 1950–
  Library management for the digital age : a new paradigm / Julie Todaro.
    pages cm
  Includes bibliographical references and index.
  ISBN 978-1-4422-3069-9 (cloth : alk. paper) — ISBN 978-1-4422-3015-6 (pbk. : alk. paper) — ISBN 978-1-4422-3016-3 (ebook)
  1. Library administration. 2. Library administration—Case studies. I. Title.
  Z678.T63 2014
  025.1—dc23
                                                   2014001672

♾™ The paper used in this publication meets the minimum requirements of American National Standard for Information Sciences—Permanence of Paper for Printed Library Materials, ANSI/NISO Z39.48-1992. Printed in the United States of America

Contents

Preface

The profession of library and information science has changed so dramatically in the last two decades that content about libraries in general as well as content about managing libraries, library employees, services, and resources is often too quickly out of date. Historical, classic, or even recent content is helpful in outlining directions and identifying how processes may be accomplished but, once applied to an environment, may no longer match the reality.

In my over thirty-five years in the profession in all types and sizes of libraries, the most challenging aspects of my job included the general management of the organization and the management of the myriad of employees working in the organization. Other "most challenging" aspects on my list include the management roles and responsibilities of working across lines of the organization with peers and colleagues as well as managing "up" to my immediate supervisors and other administrators and stakeholders.

In the search for content and techniques to assist me in creating contemporary structures to better manage activities, issues, and people in my own libraries, I realized that the best techniques were those that identified context in the workplace, meaningful connections of issues and activities to individual employee roles and responsibilities, and, most importantly, managing change and the identification of specific management issues and activities changing or being introduced into the workplace.

While each workplace is unique, my experience in a variety of types and sizes of libraries and my commitment to a focus on all types and sizes of libraries, has provided me with a unique perspective that has enriched all of my positions and given me an appreciation not only of the extent of differences among libraries and librarians, but also of the similarities within the profession and among professionals. This book is my attempt, therefore, to capture the breadth of the profession and to identify techniques and processes for managing that breadth. I would hope that readers both in educational settings and in practice will be able to recognize themselves or their workplaces in this content and/or use the techniques and processes to identify their own solutions.

Recommending the best professional management literature (books, journals, website content) of today to accompany this book content, however, is a book in and of itself. In sorting through recommended resources, I struggled to define general vs. specific types of management as well as management by size and type of organization, profit vs. nonprofit, and nonlibrary vs. library content, and use-in-practice vs. education and training. Instead of adding hundreds of titles, I identified what I considered to be indispensable for a manager's "bookshelf." This general annotated list is located in the appendices; however, recommended sources for each chapter are located at the end of the chapter.

The title of a nonfiction book should communicate to readers an idea of not only context but also general content and, if possible, application of content. *Library Management for the Digital Age: A New Paradigm* offers readers an opportunity to find themselves within the text or make their own application of content rather than telling readers "this is the only way." As such:

- content includes information on all types and sizes of libraries
- content includes a wide variety of management situations
- readers will find themselves on either or both sides of paradigms and can also decide to create new paradigms
- readers from the lowest to the highest tech library environment not only will be able to find, identify, or locate "themselves" and their libraries, but also will be able to find multiple ways (both classic and new) to articulate issues as well as multiple ways (both classic and new) to identify solutions

BOOK ORGANIZATION: PART I

Library Management for the Digital Age: A New Paradigm introduces library managers and librarians who wish to be managers to the "new management" within the twenty-first-century library environment; the content is intended to be analyzed in a variety of ways including the use of case method. In addition, in part I, content is also illustrated and analyzed through the use of Paradigm Shifts, which are used to compare and contrast the old, "classic" management style with new, "contemporary" management practices. The sixteen chapters are as follows:

Chapter 1. Classic Management vs. New Management

Library managers must be able to understand not only their workplace environment but also the practice of management and the role of change in management.

Chapter 2. Preparing and Maintaining the New Manager

Learning how to manage has changed and learning opportunities include education, training, professional development, and/or continuing education.

Chapter 3. "Managing" New Employees/Staff/ Human Resources/Stakeholders

A major part of learning a workplace environment is getting to know the organization's employees including how they have changed, how they have stayed the same, and how to choose appropriate methods of managing, directing, and coordinating.

Chapter 4. New Management of Change

Today's managers must be able to define change and assist others in issues surrounding change as well as techniques for dealing with resistance to change and embracing change.

Chapter 5. New Managers Designing New Organizations

Managers must assess organizations to determine if structures and practices need to be changed to meet the needs created by changing work environments.

Chapter 6. Management Infrastructure Documents in New Organizations

An organization's management documents must be continuously assessed to determine if they keep up with the dramatic rate of change found in work environments today.

Chapter 7. Managing New Services and Resources

Library managers manage and market a hybrid of classic as well as newer resources and services such as one-stop, distance, or remote access, and constituent-driven programs, resources, and services.

Chapter 8. Managing Those Outside the "Sphere"

Much attention should be paid to relationships that provide support for the library such as peer organizations, partners, and the library's umbrella institution.

Chapter 9. New Management "in Action" Communication

Managers should audit their communication practices, identify skills set, and employ best practices to implement exemplary communication techniques.

Chapter 10. New Managers within Classic and New Organizations

Library managers need successful coordinating and directing relationships with governing and advisory groups as well as stakeholders and supporters.

Chapter 11. New Managers in Classic and New Facilities and Environments

Today's managers must be prepared for maintaining, renovating, designing, and building library facilities that range from historic to the newest environments.

Chapter 12. New "Landscapes" for Library and Information Settings

Library managers must be aware of and in tune with not only local, regional, or state issues and changes but also national and global societal changes and issues.

Chapter 13. Managing the Balance to Meet New Constituent/Customer Expectations

Library managers must keep up with changing constituents (users and potential users) for library resources and services to remain relevant and essential to constituent communities.

Chapter 14. Accountability, Measurement, and Assessment in New Management Organizations

Library managers must be well versed in assessment and measurement, as well as accountable to their umbrella organizations and communities for expenditures, resources, and the impact of those expenditures on constituents.

Chapter 15. New Budgeting with (Mostly) Classic Budgeting Issues

Library managers are responsible for organizing, tracking, and spending dollars and must be able to justify and account for all public and private dollars, library services and resources, and the library's physical and digital infrastructure.

Chapter 16. Emergency Management Roles and Responsibilities of New Managers

Libraries have long been involved in disaster planning to protect services and resources and today's work environments demand that employees are prepared at the highest levels for handling critical issues and risk and emergency management.

BOOK ORGANIZATION: PART II

The management content described in part I is complemented by the sixteen cases in part II. Each case matches up with the chapter of the same number (e.g., case #1 matches with chapter 1). The cases are intended to be analyzed using the ten-point case method that is described in the introduction to part II. Cases can be analyzed in conjunction with part I content, or can be utilized independent of part I. For each case, the focus and uses within various types of libraries is given.

THE DIGITAL AGE AND PARADIGM SHIFT

Finally, a reasonable question might be, however, can or *how* can low- or lower-tech environments make significant use of a management book presenting "digital age" paradigms and paradigm shifts? The answer to this question lies *not* in library funding levels or the identification of the type or size of the library or management style of the librarian—rather in the definition of *digital age*.

Many terms change or morph as they "age" or progress through their context or continuum. And, of course, things are relative. That is, three to four decades ago, a "high-tech" library might have been one with a card catalog converted to a high-speed microfilm reader and by no stretch of the imagination would that "high-tech" environment with the same reader (and some might say *with any* microfilm!) be considered "high tech" today.

Such is the term *digital age*. With almost dozens of definitions and interpretations of *digital age*, one can find a literal definition of the difference between analog and digital as well as phrases many consider to be synonymous with *digital age* such as *computer age*, *information age*, or the *new media age*. *Digital age* is a perfect categorization of our current "state" in *all* library and information settings because not only does the phrase mean the changes in technology that have and continue to occur, but it also includes new ways of doing business, different ways of looking at things, changing processes and procedures, and the speed with which things change and become different. The reality is that libraries today are different, and *Library Management for the Digital Age: A New Paradigm* offers ideas not only on *what is* different and new that includes technology, but also different ways of looking at the usual, classic, or familiar for not only "what is now" but also "what is next."

Acknowledgments

Acknowledgments are the author's chance to identify those who inspired content but—because of my breadth of experience and, therefore, because the content in this book comes from both good and bad managers I have worked for, worked with, and observed—it's hard to acknowledge specific individuals who may represent one, the other, or—actually—aspects of both. Instead I choose to thank my infrastructure of support for life, which includes family, friends, professional acquaintances, and dogs—a wide range of purebred, mixes, and rescues! In addition, I have to thank Charles Harmon for this opportunity and his support.

Introduction

Most introductions are designed to describe what's in the book. For this work, however, it's equally important to identify what doesn't seem to be included in the content, why some terminology is used or not used, as well as how and when the book might be used. To this end, this introduction includes what is in the book but also answers questions about what isn't in the book and why some things are identified as they are.

What *Is* Included in the Book?

This book includes descriptions of libraries, employees, services, and resources but does so specifically in the context of how they have changed. Rather than providing historical contexts, paradigms describe what is happening or has just happened in many contemporary settings, and then Paradigm Shifts and management cases provide the bigger picture of how the profession, libraries, employees, and services and resources are changing and define what is "new." To keep content from stagnating, however, I've provided information in terms of what is contemporary, what is new, as well as how to use techniques in the workplace to continue to define what is changing and what is not only new but also next.

"New" management education and training curriculum and content, within the context of a contemporary workplace, should:

- identify contemporary management definitions
- focus on management issues
- illustrate how management definitions, issues, etc., apply to today's and tomorrow's environments and specifically nonprofit environments such as libraries

- illustrate how management definitions, issues, etc., apply to all types and sizes of libraries
- identify best practices, benchmarks, and examples
- provide techniques and tools for managers to learn and apply the discipline of management

Just as this content can be used in teaching, learning, and training settings, the *practitioner* should embrace this content and the techniques used to introduce content. That is, managers in the field should explore these techniques for the transition from management theory to the application of management content for employees, ancillary groups, umbrella organization employees, institutional partners, and vendors. New management managers must bring this content and these techniques into the workplace to illustrate management excellence and provide a rationale for data-driven decision-making and problem-solving. To this end, each chapter provides an overview of content, one or more Paradigm Shifts, and questions for discussion; cases that complement each chapter are included in part II, to be analyzed with the case method. Although a number of areas in the library and information *profession do* routinely use the case method technique for teaching and learning certain issues in academic settings (e.g., intellectual freedom, human resources, ethics), techniques such as the design of Paradigm Shifts and the case method should be integrated into workplace operations at all levels and for all types and sizes of libraries.

What Constitutes Contemporary Management Education and Training?

Decades of "old management" education and training curricula have outlined the study of management in similar if not identical ways beginning with a historical look at theory, and types and styles of management. While the "history of management" approach is the older or more classic way of providing context for contemporary management, the reality is that studying management theory, and older or classic types and styles, is not a critical or required *initial* step in learning how to manage or—more importantly—how to excel at management. Instead, identifying aspects of management and management definitions, focusing on successful, contemporary management issues, illustrating how historical or more classic types and styles apply to today's and tomorrow's nonprofit environments, illustrating how types and styles apply to current library settings, and providing techniques and tools for managers to learn and apply the discipline of management is the more successful curriculum for educating and training the *new* management manager. In addition, more typical management learning tools and techniques for managers have been used in educational settings or classrooms rather than in the workplace, and although these techniques are critical for learning how to transition from theory to the application of management content, new management managers must bring these techniques into work environments for efficiency, effectiveness, and more successful communication, as well as data- and information-driven decision-making and problem-solving.

For example, there are a variety of ways to use a Paradigm Shift as a technique in studying management. These ways include:

• study relevant curriculum, read or review the Paradigm Shift, and answer questions in group or classroom settings with guided discussions
• read or review the Paradigm Shift, answer questions in group or classroom settings, study relevant curriculum, and answer questions again through a guided discussion, and in the second discussion, compare answers to see if application of the management techniques altered answers or the suggested resolutions to the situation

Using Paradigm Shifts as management techniques in a new management workplace, however, is highly recommended. This technique—in group or classroom settings—is helpful in addressing issues and assists in decision-making and problem-solving, as well as teaching other managers and potential managers how to manage. Using Paradigm Shifts in the workplace can include:

• interview those involved; identify facts and issues; design a paradigm; provide a forum (ad hoc or ongoing group) for discussion; review the Paradigm Shift with the group and address, discuss, and answer questions; and then complete a Paradigm Shift and/or choose from among alternatives
• interview those involved; identify facts and issues; provide a forum (ad hoc or standard) for discussion; design a paradigm with those involved and other employees appropriate to the situation; review the Paradigm Shift and address, discuss, and answer questions; and/or choose from among alternatives

Although a number of areas in the *profession do* use Paradigm Shifts routinely, such as intellectual freedom and emergency management, this management technique should be integrated into operations at all levels if possible.

How Does This Book's Style or Content Delivery Work for Teaching and Learning Settings as Well as in the Workplace or Practice?

Although almost all content about using paradigms, Paradigm Shifts, and case method techniques place their use in education and in training classrooms, the use of these techniques in the practice of management can be a manager's best tool for modeling behavior, discussing issues, solving problems, and orienting, training, and retraining. Education and training uses include:

- read the content, read the case or review the Paradigm Shift, and answer questions in group or classroom settings with guided, group discussions
- read the case, following practices for reviewing cases individually, have group discussion, and compare approaches and opinions on case handling and solutions
- review the Paradigm Shift in a group setting and answer questions, read content and answer—in the group—questions again, have guided discussion, and compare and contrast answers to see if content altered discussion, answers, or the resolutions
- read content, break group into small groups, have discussion, and compare and contrast approaches of smaller groups in larger group

Uses in practice include, for example, using tools for problem-solving:

- select a problem, interview those involved, identify facts and issues, prioritize, speculate on outcomes, share/discuss with those involved, propose solutions in team meetings, choose solutions based on data gathered, and create a Paradigm Shift for how the situation, activity, and problem were before and are now after the solution
- select a Paradigm Shift related to an organizational issue (new space, new service, changing resources), create a third column, gather a group, and complete the third column as a team
- select a Paradigm Shift related to an organizational issue (new space, new service, changing resources), create a third column, ask individuals involved to complete the third column by themselves, gather a group, compare third column as a team to identify difference and similarities, and create a third column after discussions
- select a problem, interview those involved, identify facts and issues, provide a forum (ad hoc or standard) for discussion, design a paradigm with those involved and other employees appropriate to the situation, ask others such as departments or small groups to take the paradigm and create a Paradigm Shift, gather a group of those smaller groups, compare shifts,

have groups defend shift elements chosen, and create the Paradigm Shift created by all involved

Who Are the Manager's "Employees" in Libraries Today and How Should They Be Identified?

All types and sizes of libraries have varieties of people working in them at any given time. There are too many variations and categories of individuals to accurately characterize each situation in, for example, paradigms, cases, and general content specifically; therefore, for this book, the term *employees*—typically used to refer to only paid or salaried individuals—will be used to encompass full- and part-time workers, student workers, volunteers, interns, etc. While library managers need to have overarching policies for everyone for whom they are responsible, they need to ensure that every category of employee be covered (whether included or excluded) when considering human resource issues (insurance, benefits, performance, etc.) as well as management issues (communication, roles and responsibilities, etc.). Although it is not possible—given the range of types and sizes of libraries and their umbrella organizations, to provide specifics for the many different levels and types of employees for each situation, it is important to identify how these categories and levels of employees might be addressed by managers. A basic list is most easily done by identifying categories of employees by type of library.

Questions that managers need to have asked and answered for their employees include:

- Which employees are covered by which policies and procedures of the organization and/or umbrella organization?
- Who speaks for the library and library management, including in general communication and in decision-making, for public presentations, in formal and informal group meetings, and in written communication? And in a related issue, who is allowed to use library letterhead in communications?
- Who enters into agreements or is allowed to sign contracts? And what levels or types of contracts?
- How do organizational benefits apply to categories and levels of employees and, if applicable, what other benefits might apply such as umbrella organization, related entities, partnership benefits, or local, state, or federal infrastructure such as worker's compensation?

Public Libraries

Public libraries can have permanent full- and part-time employees who are paid (hourly, salaried, on contract or subcontract, etc.); temporary (seasonal or grant) full- and part-time employees who are paid (hourly, salaried, on contract or subcontract, etc.); supporters who are directly involved with the library such as governing or advisory board members; workers from umbrella organizations; individuals from library partnerships; individuals present due to shared spaces; as well as volunteers (Friends, from the courts, law enforcement, those giving back to the community such as Rotarians, church groups, youth organizations, and internships).

Academic Libraries

Academic libraries can have permanent full- and part-time employees who are paid (hourly, salaried, on contract or subcontract, etc.); temporary (seasonal or grant) full- and part-time employees who are paid (hourly, salaried, on contract or subcontract, etc.); supporters who are directly involved with the library such as advisory group members; internships; volunteers from the university, college, or library Friends group; student services or student government; from museum or archival enthusiasts; or content specialists from disciplines or departments. Others can include college or university employees such as the institutional or instructional technology support department whose employees support library technology, the college or university public relations and marketing department, and/or academic fundraising or development.

School Libraries

School libraries can have permanent full- and part-time employees who are paid (hourly, salaried, on contract or subcontract, etc.); temporary (seasonal or grant) full- and part-time employees who are paid (hourly, salaried, on contract or subcontract, etc.); supporters such as PTA, adult, and youth advisory group members; internships; volunteers from the friends, students, parents, and/or student government. Other employees can include those involved in development and fundraising and/or annual book sale or book fair and school district- or building-level employees including institutional or instructional technology.

Special Libraries

Special libraries can have permanent full- and part-time employees who are paid (hourly, salaried, on contract or subcontract, etc.); temporary (seasonal or grant) full- and part-time employees who are paid (hourly, salaried, on contract or subcontract, etc.); internships; supporters such as the business's governing or advisory group; and employees from within the organization such as content specialists or employees from institutional technology or the marketing department. Other individuals could include experts for collection management and the design and delivery of print and web services and resources.

Where Should Managers Identify Types and Levels of Employees?

Rather than identifying or naming employees in each policy and procedure, managers can:

- add a legend with all employee categories possible in the organization to each general policy and procedure and management document, and indicate coverage on the legend
- define categories and types and levels in general and refer to categories (with subheadings, footnotes, etc.) in policies and procedures and management documents
- create categories of policies and procedures and management documents for each type of employee

Managers must remember that anyone who "operates" within or for a library structure should be identified and categorized as to how they fit into or work for the organization. For purposes of this book, however, all categories of "employees and workers" are referred to generally as "employees."

Why Didn't I Include a Chapter in the Book on Technology or a Chapter on Planning?

The short answer is because technology and planning are infused and integrated throughout the content, just as they are infused and integrated throughout today's libraries. The long answer is . . . twenty-first-century managers lead exciting lives. The world around them and their libraries is changing at an exponential rate (a rate of change I identify as "dog-year change"), and they have opportunities for providing resources, services, facilities, and access that previous managers were only able to dream of. Great opportunities, however, bring great challenges, and to approach these challenges, managers design directions that are articulated in the library's vision and mission statements and in goals, objectives, and outcomes.

Reviewing vision, mission, and goals and objectives statements and how they have changed throughout the years illustrates the issue of viewing technology by itself. That is, for many years libraries created technology goals for automating services, planning, and facilities. Today's approach is to design an *access* goal with objectives that focus on automation, hardware, software, and infrastructure as a means to an end of achieving access. So readers will find technology throughout paradigms, cases, content, and in questions and recommended resources.

Are Techniques and Process All I Need to Be a Good Manager?

The appendixes provide resources for content and additional techniques and processes and these resources include dynamic content-rich environments for professionals to use for keeping up with their profession. These recommended resources include association websites as unique sources of continuing education and professional development as well as online professional support provided by education, training, and content-delivery providers (such as WebJunction) and support structures for major library and information science vendor providers (such as Online Computer Library Center Inc.).

Finally, the debate for management content is always, "What are the major functional areas of management?" or more specifically, "How should one study management?" While there is no perfect way, this book divides content into sixteen areas that include basics such as "what is management?" and the management of library functions such as human resources and facilities. A few areas that are more prevalent in the literature now as well as more unique to the competency set critical to contemporary library managers, such as the management of emergency and critical incident issues, are covered in their own chapter.

Part One

TWENTY-FIRST-CENTURY MANAGEMENT IN LIBRARIES

Chapter One

Classic Management vs. New Management

- Definitions: What makes "classic management" "classic" and "new management" "new"
- New managers: Definitions, profiles, competencies, roles, and responsibilities

A case method is intended to be used in conjunction with this chapter. The case designed to be used with this chapter is case 1, "A Difficult Path of Moving Up and Out," located in part II, p. 239. The case can be read and discussed before and/or after reading the chapter content.

MANAGING IN THE CHANGING WORKPLACE

In my (very!) long career, I have had the very best managers and—frankly—the very worst managers. From experience, I have learned "how to manage" and "how not to manage" through observation, by studying examples and reviewing models, and through research and application. But very often observation, study, research, and application are *not* clear cut—that is, I have observed excellent project managers who were not good employee or "people" managers. I have observed more traditional, non-techie managers successfully manage tech-savvy, millennial employees *and* high-tech managers who could not manage their digital/virtual employees either in person or remotely. I have observed successful employee or "people" managers who could not manage their budgets or their projects. And I have observed good employee *and* good budget *and* good project managers who could not manage external partners.

I can also easily say I have learned from both good and bad management education in undergraduate classes, graduate-level classes, continuing

3

education, and professional development. I have taken both good and bad management workshops *and*—with hindsight—I now realize I have sat through webinars and in classrooms while instructors presented basic and advanced management content yet didn't understand how to apply their content, knowledge, or experiences to practice in contemporary work environments. In addition, I have had my share of management instructors who did not distinguish between leadership and management, were not aware that different types and sizes of organizations often need different types and styles of management, and did not include discussions on the need to change styles of management given a diverse employee population and—most importantly—the need to change elements of style given individual in-person and digital work activities and situations.

So can every library manager have the perfect mix of technology knowledge, skills, and abilities? Can every manager be aware of how to manage diverse employees who include traditionalists, boomers, millennials, generation X (or Y), or today's techie, social media–driven workers? Can every manager have knowledge of all of their constituents' needs and wants? Can every manager be aware of, anticipate, and then get out in front of societal trends that shape the selection and access to resources as well as the design of in-person and digital environments and service delivery?

More than likely, no. What is clear, however, is that library managers must focus on a number of things that they *do* need to be aware of, understand, and be committed to, and that those elements, coupled with observations, research, study, and use of examples and models, will prepare them for success. These elements include the following.

- *Whether or not change is good or bad, it's the way of life in the workplace.* Pervasive and rapid change is so much a part of the workplace today; managers have no choice but to understand "change" in and of itself, the issues of fast-moving, changing environments, and, specifically, tools and techniques for dealing with change in the workplace.
- *Technology and technological concepts are integrated into the infrastructure of society.* Technology is so infused into the profession of library and information science that managers today must have knowledge of the basics of technology for their profession as well as technological applications for their library resources and services and those technological applications specific to their workplace. Most importantly, however, is the need for managers to recognize *how* technology has changed the workplace.
  - Technology moves quickly and the timeline for "doing business" in technologically driven environments is profoundly different. What used to

change once or twice a year may change monthly or—given the dynamic nature of technology driven by the web—weekly or daily.
  ○ Constituents used to technology expect the newest and the latest.
  ○ For constituents not as used to technology, librarians must recognize what they need to be successful and provide it as well as teach it.
  ○ New technologies drive new terminology and new literacy, and thus dictate new terminology and new literacy for librarians and library services and resources.
  ○ New technology-driven resources and services need new technology-ready infrastructure and spaces.
  ○ New technology-driven libraries need employees who are ready to design, support, and deliver new resources and services.
  ○ New libraries need management structures and styles with maximum flexibility to respond to the new timeline for "doing business."

• *One size does* not *fit all employees, partners, stakeholders, and so on.* Today's managers must be aware of and embrace the fact that their employees, colleagues, partners, vendors, and upper-level administrators are a highly diverse blend of individuals with vast ranges of knowledge, skills and abilities, and attitudes as well as divergent opinions and commitments to the profession. This knowledge—along with the knowledge that these individuals must be tech-ready to work in contemporary libraries—must be accompanied with the approach that managers must take diversity into account in designing and maintaining successful workplaces.
• *Again, one size does not fit all constituents.* Today's managers must be aware of and embrace the fact that their constituents are a highly diverse blend of individuals with vast ranges of knowledge, skill, and abilities and attitudes as well as diverse wants and needs. Managers must take this diversity of knowledge levels, skills and abilities, and attitudes as well as wants and needs into account in designing and maintaining successful library facilities, programs of service, and choice and delivery of resources.

It *is* appropriate to explore different ways to manage—to explore the wide variety of solutions to management problems as well as to identify completely different approaches to dealing with the same or similar issues with employees and constituents. At the core of a successfully managed environment in today's libraries is the realization that, while there are different ways as well as both right ways and wrong ways and different conclusions, there are *preferred* solutions to these management issues. Once a manager realizes that the process of change must be managed, technological changes will drive many, and often most, decisions, and a variety of directions will

need to be provided to accommodate diversity of employees and constituents. Managers should consider:

- the use of a variety of data and techniques for illustrating and visualizing
  data for deeper levels of understanding to meet administrator, umbrella organization, stakeholder, supporter, and legislative needs and requirements
- the use of case methods and models for illustrating and explaining issues
  to match the breadth and diversity of learners and employees for planning,
  decision-making, and problem-solving
- the use of a variety of data, techniques, case methods and models for explaining, illustrating, visualizing, and so on, issues for planning, decision-
  making, and problem-solving to match the breadth and diversity of user and
  nonuser (constituent) situations
- carefully chosen and well-designed management styles and approaches both
  in general and specifically those that fit or match diverse employees in both
  in-person and digital work environments and by type and size of library

"CLASSIC MANAGEMENT" AND "NEW MANAGEMENT"

Anyone who has been a library manager for years will acknowledge that the
field has changed more rapidly and dramatically in the last two decades than
it has in previous decades and continues to change—often weekly and sometimes daily. Trying to successfully manage today's "in-person" and digital
libraries without identifying new ways to manage is difficult. Although some
traditional techniques may still work because of the blend of old and new in
the workplace, new techniques must be integrated into a manager's repertoire
and adapted to both traditional and new environments, and to changing employees and constituents.

For managers, learners, and employees, the discussion of "why" and "how
to" can begin by illustrating change within the context of the "way it used to
be" with a Paradigm Shift from old workplaces to new workplaces as well
as old management vs. new management. Changes, visualized through Paradigm Shifts, can include differences such as:

- the integration of technology and computerization into all business practices
- the design of new, remodeled, and reorganized physical facilities
- the delivery of resources and services
- the changing nature of communication through use and impact of technology and social media in business practices

- the presence of varying generations in the workplace with the newest members of the workforce such as millennials or generation X not only working in but also *managing* the workforce as well as the delivery resources and services
- the integration/coordination of remote work locations and nonwork locations (e.g., virtual or telecommuting employees, colleagues, partners, vendors, etc.)
- global concerns and perspectives in the workplace
- the type and rate of change for resources and formats of research and information
- the individual and collaborative use and design of content and materials (in all formats) in in-person and online library and learning environments

Although these many and diverse general changes dictate changes throughout the organization, the first set of changes critical to management success is an outline of changes in management roles and responsibilities—looking at the classic vs. the new workplace (see Paradigm Shift 1.1).

PARADIGM SHIFT 1.1.
Management in Classic vs. New Workplaces

Although not all libraries today look different to constituents or even individuals in umbrella organizations, in general, the majority of workspaces and structures that house, support, maintain, and deliver resources and services are different. Hardware and software, facilities, formats of resources, services, and communication within these environments are different in contemporary libraries and are continuously changing. General issues for all types and sizes of libraries include:

Classic Management in Classic Workplaces	New Management in New Workplaces
• Library and information resources, infrastructure, and facilities are located in primarily traditional umbrella environments such as municipal, county, for-profit/special, and academic (K–12 and higher education).	• Library and information resources, infrastructure, and facilities are now in traditional and nontraditional umbrella environments, 501c3 libraries, other not-for-profit, and for-profit or corporate.
• Technology is not new in library settings and is one of the most critical, complex, and rapidly changing elements in management roles and responsibilities, but management of technology and of technological environments and employees is typically not included in formal and informal management and training.	• Technology is integrated into all library settings and remains one of the most critical, complex, and rapidly changing elements for managers. Management of technology functions and the technology is an area less frequently included in formal and informal library management and training. Managers seek external education and training.
• Workplaces have unique or stand-alone computerization or technology-	• Technology and computerization of internal business operations and library

(*continued*)

PARADIGM SHIFT 1.1.
(continued)

Classic Management in Classic Workplaces	New Management in New Workplaces
supported or -provided business practices and operations, resources, and services. Office productivity, infrastructure, public services finding tools, and digital resources exist in individual software packages and on different platforms and hardware.	resources and services for constituents is networked, integrated, online, dynamic, and available onsite, online, 24/7.
• Federal, regional, state, and local policies impacting libraries are complex and far-reaching and monitoring, understanding, and applying these policies is a primary responsibility.	• Rapidly changing federal, regional, state, and local policies impacting libraries are a primary role and responsibility of contemporary library managers and are complex, far-reaching, and greatly expanding in numbers and types of required and preferred oversight.
• Economic issues greatly effect ongoing and new funding and "cutback, downsize, and/or change management" nonprofit content is often not a part of management education and/or training.	• Economic issues (often poor or with a focus on technology spending primarily) greatly affect ongoing, new funding and "cutback, downsize and/ or change management" content is in profit and nonprofit management education and training illustrated through the case method.
• Libraries form partnerships with other organizations and institutions as well as with for-profit entities.	• Expanding partnerships for libraries and information settings challenges managers who have both knowledge of general management as well as knowledge of managing entities not like their own. They must have knowledge of these new environments to be successful.
• Facilities are retrofitted to connect and provide access to a variety of resources and services in public spaces.	• Facilities are designed new or redesigned or renovated for integration of technology into both support and public spaces.
• Communication is top-down, across, and bottom-up in the organization but along standardized channels including memos; in-person discussion; phone calls and conference calls; and—in the last three decades—institutional electronic mail packages and—in the last two decades—standalone "e" or digital mail for the global audience.	• Communication is throughout the organization with diverse channels including print memos; in-person discussion; phone (individual and conference calls); e-mail; online discussion boards; real-time, online communication packages and simulation environments; social media; and texting. Communication has

Classic Management in Classic Workplaces	New Management in New Workplaces
Communication opportunities have elements of standardization for use, terminology, and retention.	standards for use, terminology, timing, retention, and labeling.
• Resources and services are delivered onsite through technology and user interfaces with diverse protocols. Users require assistance.	• Resources and services are delivered onsite and online/digitally through online interfaces with a reduced number of access points or one access point with standardized protocols.
• Libraries select library materials based on constituent population–identified needs, and expressed preferences articulated in collection-development policies, and community and federal and state public policy. Formats are varied and include hardback, paperback, CD, and DVD. Formats are altered in cycles that include annual or semi-annual timelines.	• Libraries provide access to more than what they "select" for target populations and this "global rather than local issue" must be addressed continuously, is often controversial, and is subject to community, state, and federal as well as partnership standards. Formats are print and media and include hardback, paperback, DVD, streaming media, and online content.

New Managers—Definitions, Competencies, Roles, and Responsibilities

If today's library managers are questioned about their workplace and whether or not it has changed in the last two decades, the vast majority would acknowledge that almost every aspect of their work world has changed and thus every aspect of the concept and practice of management has changed. In the professional literature, *management* is defined in many different ways; however, newer *management* definitions focus on process and product—both in person and remotely or virtually, and accomplishing goals through employees both individually and in teams. New management managers in today's organizations—whether they are being retrained, bring updated, or new to the management in general—must be aware of the expectations placed on yesterday's more "classic" management managers and must be prepared to commit to and implement a transition to new roles and responsibilities to handle changing workplaces, programs and services, and employees.

Changing or new roles and responsibilities dictate new competencies or changing or new knowledge(s), skills and abilities, and attitudes. Elements of today's definitions, roles and responsibilities lists, and lists of competencies may often, and appropriately, change based on organizational goals, administrative expectations, constituent needs, the type and size of libraries, organizational structure, and a constantly changing workplace. Competency lists for new management managers are diverse and long.

COMPETENCIES FOR "NEW MANAGEMENT" MANAGERS

Knowledge of:
- twenty-first-century technology and technological applications
- diverse digital and virtual modes and methods used to promote excellent communication skills—oral, written, nonverbal
- the global workplace
- management of nonprofit and not-for-profits
- both classic and new formats of resources and supporting technology
- the organization's resources including today's owned as well as accessed resources
- changing work patterns such as employees working individually as well as collaborating through in-person, remote, digital, and virtual work teams
- social media and the application of social media to communication among employees and an organization's external communication plan for constituents
- an organization's constituents and internal and external audiences
- how the organization's constituents use resources and perform research individually and collaboratively with other constituents, including in-person and digital or remote teams
- how the organization's constituents work individually and collaboratively to create content and products
- how the library organization fits into the umbrella organization as a whole
- how employees learn, their learning preferences, and the process of unlearning in both traditional/classic and nontraditional/contemporary ways
- how to maintain a positive political climate
- how to maintain a positive and productive organizational culture
- concepts of leadership vs. management
- practices for remote management
- practices for remote leadership
- practices and the importance of conflict resolution with a focus on win/win strategies

Skills/abilities for:

- the application of technological theory to practice in general and to specific sizes and types of libraries
- the organization and coordination of other people and activities including digital or virtual and in-person employees
- motivating employees for commitment to organization goals and to be responsible citizens of the organization
- the design and implementation of an organization-wide digital or remote and in-person communication plan for internal and external target audiences
- the design, implementation, and maintenance of operational, short-term, and long-term plans within the process of strategic planning
- flexibility
- budgeting and financial management
- the creation of measurements and accountability processes including performance processes for in person, digital, and remote
- recognizing, confronting, and resolving issues and difficult situations

- anticipating and solving problems
- managing complexity
- managing the change process
- managing ones' own time, timing for employees, and timing critical to organizational success
- the use of contemporary modes and methods of communication, management, and leadership such as social media and smart technologies
- the design, implementation, and management of small and large projects

Attitudes for:

- a commitment to global thinking and action for the workplace including employees and constituents
- a commitment to identifying the changing nature of employees and articulating profiles by age, place in one's career, and work location such as millennials, mid-career managers, remote employees, and digital employees
- a commitment to the practice of integrity and honesty in oneself, employees, and internal and external partners, peers, and colleagues
- a commitment to ensuring constituent satisfaction/loyalty
- a commitment to building consensus
- a commitment to empowering employees
- a commitment to innovation and transformation
- a commitment to being proactive rather than reactive
- a commitment to building a network of employees who support each other and the goals of the organization
- a commitment to encouraging and setting expectations for individual excellence as well as excellence in digital, remote, and in-person team behavior
- a commitment to leading by example with vision, enhancing leadership skills of others, and supporting "followership"
- a commitment to promoting understanding among people with different points of view
- a commitment to seeking, appreciating, and maximizing diversity
- a commitment to developing talent and encouraging and supporting mentorship opportunities

While general lists of competencies assist in, for example, the design of position descriptions, performance evaluations, and position advertisements as well as the determination of the best match of a manager to an organization, it is critical to define the specific contemporary roles and responsibilities of contemporary managers.

ROLES AND RESPONSIBILITIES

New management roles and responsibilities can be expressed within the context of classic management function lists or can be outlined in more contemporary language. Classic management functional lists with new or contemporary roles and responsibilities include those shown in Table 1.1.

Table 1.1. New Management Functions

Management Functions	New or Contemporary Management Manager Roles and Responsibilities
Planning—Annual or Operational, Short-Term, Long-Term, and Strategic	New/contemporary management managers: • implement and manage change • dynamically and strategically plan and implement ideas in low-tech, hybrid, and high-tech environments • lead in designing and carrying out longer-term, strategic plans as well as operational or annual/short-term plans • coordinate operational with long-term/strategic plans • ensure employee goals, activities, and initiatives coordinate with other (institutional, umbrella organization, regional, state, community, city, county, system, consortia) plans and with operational and strategic plans • collect data to research, assess, and measure all plans • work with upper-level managers, administrators, and other internal and external employees to gather input into planning • educate and train planning participants (internal, external) • coordinate planning participants (internal, external) • communicate planning progress or problems • analyze plans for continuous planning revisions
Staffing/Human Resources/Personnel—Coordinating and Managing or Directing the Activities of Others	New/contemporary management managers: • are able to assess their workforce to determine skills sets, preferences, and employee knowledge bases • focus first on people rather than work product • commit to providing opportunities for work product and processes from self-directed employees • commit to an organization that includes self-directed teams • model (for all employees) a commitment to professionalism • manage and lead employees including motivation and performance management with a focus on both rewarding good behavior and correcting bad behavior • commit to appropriate orientation and training • commit to education, training, and professional development

Management Functions	New or Contemporary Management Manager Roles and Responsibilities
	• commit to integrating partners into the organization • commit to establishing and integrating external oversight and advisory groups into the organization • commit to addressing change • problem-solve and make decisions • manage conflict
Accountability	New/contemporary management managers: • commit to and guide data-driven decision-making for organizations and match data to goals, strategies, and tasks • gather and analyze data for resources and services • continuously scan and maintain constituent usage data • integrate and implement diverse methods of assessment to illustrate value, impact, and accountability • appropriately expend public and other funding
Budgeting/Controlling	New/contemporary management managers: • acquire diverse funding streams through justification and negotiation for expenditures with management • ensure appropriate and ethical use of public and private funding streams • track dollars for operational, short-term, and long-term activities • justify and negotiate with external, commercial entities
Communicating	New/contemporary management managers: • articulate vision/mission and big-picture ideas to employees, partners, and constituents • design and maintain a communication plan for internal and external information and communication needs (out to the community and upward to umbrella organizations) • articulate employee/organizational needs to administrators and partners and other internal and external relationships • design content (print and media) for marketing, public relations, publicity (including signage), instructions, general instructional content, and so on. • advocate at local, regional, state, and national levels • facilitate communication among employees and teams

(continued)

Table 1.1.   (Continued)

Management Functions	New or Contemporary Management Manager Roles and Responsibilities
	• are skilled in public speaking/presentation • are skilled at and committed to teaching and instruction • integrate technological solutions into the organization's communication plan and processes
Reporting	New/contemporary management managers: • articulate task and strategy completion monthly, quarterly, annual, and on-demand annual • monitor and track projects, grants, activities, and the creation of post-activity reports • establish protocols for reporting data within and external to the organization • create and maintain structures for partnerships

Just as society *and* the workplace have changed, it stands to reason that employees and all those who work in or support the library, or in partner libraries, have changed as well. Managers must not only scan those who work in libraries for changes but also alter the environment and structures around them not only to meet needs but also to provide the tools and training needed to make employees and others successful. Employee changes include those shown in Paradigm Shift 1.2.

PARADIGM SHIFT 1.2.
Managers and Employees in the Workplace

Classic Workplaces	New Workplaces
• Employees are a mix of ages, experience, and education. Managers choose a management style based on their own experience, expertise, preferences, the organization's functions, resources and services, and employee roles and responsibilities.	• Employees are a diverse mix of ages, experience, education, and preferences for work environments. Managers need a flexible management style based on experience, expertise, library functions, resources, services, employees, colleagues, umbrella organizations, and partnerships.
• Employees, as well as colleagues, partners, and vendors, etc., conduct business in person, onsite, at partner or colleague locations, and by fax, phone, phone conferencing, teleconferencing, and by mail.	• Employees, as well as colleagues, partners, and vendors, etc., conduct business in person, onsite, at partner locations, by fax, phone, conferencing, e-mail, synchronous or asynchronous online forums, and chat.
• Managers are typically older than employees or—at the very least—have greater or different expertise in the	• Managers are a diverse mix of ages and experience and "generations" of society with—possibly—more "classic"

Classic Workplaces	New Workplaces
profession or in the type and size of library environment.	employees managed by—for example—millennials or those newer to the profession and possessing different education or experience.
• Budget and finance competencies are needed but often lacking in "old management" managers due to the lack of formal management education and training in general and specific to this basic but critical role and responsibility. This lack of knowledge and skills and abilities extends to acquiring and managing dollars that come through organizations as well as identifying and acquiring outside funding through development, grant opportunities, and entrepreneurial activities.	• Budget content is included in management education and training, is available in stand-alone education and training opportunities, and is critical to success at basic and advanced levels. Managers must be knowledgeable about outside funding including development, grant opportunities, entrepreneurial activities, and budgeting for partnerships. • Contemporary managers must be well versed in accountability, justification, and negotiation. The study of finance and budgeting for nonprofits must include techniques for development and "growing" the budget through alternative avenues and the application of tools for dealing with cutbacks, downsizing, the process of change, and the human factor in changing or shrinking organizations.

As is typical with contemporary organizations and especially libraries, no organization "finds themselves" completely on one side of the Paradigm Shift or the other. Instead, organizations, workplaces, employees, and managers will recognize practices and processes on either side of the Paradigm Shift and sometimes find themselves and their practices on *both* sides of the Paradigm Shift. Shifts—no matter the topic—illustrate actual changes, possible changes, and—in many cases—needed changes for managers. Shifts provide managers with snapshots of organizations to aid them in defining where organizations are and where they need to be. Managers use paradigms and Paradigm Shifts as tools to assist in defining contemporary organizations, management of contemporary organizations, and data to supplement data gathered for operational and strategic planning. In addition, paradigms and Paradigm Shifts can be used to educate managers, employees (new and those from different organizations) as well as administrators, stakeholders, vendors, partners, and supporters in general as well as external decision-makers.

Along with tools to illustrate specifics of organizations, resources provide validation, trends, and benchmark data. Managers should gather indispensable resources for their ongoing use as well as to share with others involved with the organization.

INDISPENSABLE RESOURCES REGARDING CLASSIC MANAGEMENT VS. NEW/CONTEMPORARY MANAGEMENT

The following sources provide content on management definitions, sets of management competencies, basic management training, lists of roles and responsibilities, and basic management training. More in-depth information on managers of all types and sizes of libraries is available on the following websites:

"Alison." Accessed September 10, 2013. http://alison.com.

"American Library Association (ALA)." Accessed September 23, 2013. www.ala.org.

"American Society for Training & Development." Accessed August 10, 2013. www.astd.org/Search?q=management.

"Big Dog's & Little Dog's Performance, Learning, Leadership and Knowledge." Accessed October 27, 2013. http://nwlink.com/~donclark.

"Free Management Library." Accessed October 24, 2013. http://management help.org.

"Ken Haycock & Associates Inc. Blog." Accessed June 23, 2013. http://ken haycock.com/blog.

"OCLC." Accessed October 27, 2013. www.oclc.org.

"Resources for School Librarians." Accessed October 27, 2013. www.sldirec tory.com.

"Special Library Association (SLA)." Accessed September 23, 2013.www .sla.org.

"WebJunction." Accessed October 21, 2013. www.webjunction.org.

"Workforce." Accessed October 27, 2013. www.workforce.com.

DISCUSSION QUESTIONS FOR CHAPTER 1

1. Is it reasonable to apply management issues and techniques we learn from profit environments to nonprofit environments?
2. Is it possible for a manager to motivate employees and organizational supporters, and so on, to look to the future in poor economic times? Is it worth it? And if it is worth it, why?
3. Do managers need different management techniques to manage in-person and digital or virtual employees?
4. What are elements of a flexible management style?
5. What do contemporary managers need to know about their employees and other constituents to be successful?

Readers are reminded that a case method is intended to be used in conjunction with this chapter. The case designed to be used with this chapter is case 1, "A Difficult Path of Moving Up and Out," located in part II, p. 239.

Chapter Two

Preparing and Maintaining
the New Manager

- Teaching and learning management
- Education, professional development, training, and continuing education

> A case method is intended to be used in conjunction with this chapter. The case designed to be used with this chapter is case 2, "Building Your Own Management Training Program," located in part II, p. 248. The case can be read and discussed before and/or after reading the chapter content.

APPLYING LEARNING TO APPLICATION AND PRACTICE

One of my most gratifying experiences as a presenter came at the end of a program that teamed a well-known author/speaker with a panel of new librarians. Panel members represented a variety of types and sizes of libraries and were there to absorb the speaker's message—specifically the spirit and content—and then expand or enrich the context of the speaker's message using their education and experience. We only had a morning to make a difference but we felt the design and presentation of the program provided the opportunity to present a complicated but not altogether new set of ideas to our profession but in a new context.

During the event there was standing room only with great attention paid to all of the content. At the close of the program we had much applause as well as a standing ovation. Those responses indicated for me—a more jaded and well-worn presenter and educator—that we had made a great deal of sense to audience members, but that's never the only thing I want. Capturing the imagination of an audience is always what I want and *is* a major feat, but quite possible. For me, the real reward came during accolades and included "Great job!," "Best program ever!," and "He's wonderful; they were great!" At that point, however, someone said to me: "Honestly, this changed my life. Not only do I know exactly how I am going to apply this at work, but I also know how I am going to use this in general. I am looking at data completely differently! I now know how to attract and connect my users to my resources!"

Little did this person know how perfect an assessment they made of the program content and the impact it had on them. In just a few sentences they articulated that: it caught their attention; they realized (almost immediately) how it applied to them and their work; they learned how to change what they were doing or—better yet—introduce the new, valued topic into their workplace; *and* they had a specific approach for applying what they learned in general and specifically for their user.

The process of the program and presentation—for this participant—"became" both an "art" and a "science." They saw the big picture of the idea; they experienced not only an enthusiasm for the idea but also an awareness of the importance as well as a deeper understanding—on the road to knowledge—of the topic by absorbing and then identifying how the content applied to them and their organization and user. In addition, their takeaway was an immediate application of value and potential constituent or user outcomes.

For an educator, trainer, presenter, and so on, it's the "trifecta" of learning outcomes with all competencies (attitudes, skills/abilities, and knowledge) included as well as a value of the topic and understanding of application and an approach for that application. For me it was the reminder that management processes can be successfully taught and learned (!) with diverse audiences of nonmanagers, managers, and potential managers in such a way as to have an immediate impact for work. In subsequent presentations, I have dissected and redissected this successful approach and applied it to many situations for teaching my own employees as well as general audience participants.

This process of moving learning to understanding and application is accomplished through identification of issues or elements of the situation (such as a paradigm) and then identification and application of context to unique or defined situations, such as "new" or "contemporary" or type or size of organization, such as the Paradigm Shift. This level of learning can be achieved for employees, new managers, managers interested in retooling, administrators, and stakeholders—to name just a few groups (see Paradigm Shift 2.1).

PARADIGM SHIFT 2.1.
Preparing Classic vs. Contemporary Library Managers in Educational Programs

Management education has long been focused on identifying context and application and—when no context or application is possible (ex., students, employees, others with no knowledge of the environment)—the use of techniques that invent context such as case method and when explained and discussed—can be applied to other work situations. How managers or potential managers learn to be managers or experience successful management are issues for nonprofits in general and libraries specifically.

Classic Management Education	New/Contemporary Management Education
• General management education typically focuses on profit environments and has little content on nonprofit and not-for-profit organizations.	• There is increasing nonprofit and not-for-profit content in management education including nonprofit, not-for-profit, formal and informal coursework, and continuing education.
• Few formal graduate programs exist for those interested in nonprofit and not-for-profit management.	• There is an increasing number of formal master's programs such as public policy master's degrees and MBAs with content and experiences available in nonprofit and not-for-profit environments.
• Some library and information science master's degrees have internship programs in partnership with higher education with focuses on both academic content and management positions.	• Library and information science master's degrees have more field experiences (general and management) available in a variety of types and sizes of libraries.
• Most school library certification library and information science programs include and require management coursework and many standard programs include management and leadership content in the core curriculum.	• Most school library certification programs in library and information science graduate programs include and require management coursework, and standards for school library certification require both management and leadership content.
• Library and information science graduate education for school librarian certification requires school library field experience that includes management experience.	• Library and information science requires school library field experience, and—given newer standards at both national and state levels—more management content and experience is available through coursework, experience, and project management.
• A number of management education and training programs exist that go beyond more typical workshop length and provide immersion content on management.	• A reduced number of management immersion programs exist overall, while those remaining struggle with increasing costs for sponsors and hosts. Their content remains relevant and recommended; however, participants should identify curriculum that best suits their needs.

Classic Management Education	New/Contemporary Management Education
• Management content is offered primarily through in-person credit coursework. • Some library and information science graduate programs require management courses.	• Management content is offered through both in-person and online credit coursework. • Significantly more library and information science programs require management curriculum. It is integrated into basic core content and delivered in required individual management courses—some general in focus and some with a type of library focus.

TEACHING AND LEARNING MANAGEMENT

There are a myriad of ways people learn. Identifying learning issues includes identifying how people like to learn work or work-related content; how people like to learn leisure or recreational content; how much time people have to learn the content; how much time people have to learn and then apply what is learned; how best people learn; and how best to deliver the content to be learned.

In addition, there are many factors that influence learning. These factors are ones that today's managers as well as trainers, educators, and developers work with to determine what is the best way to teach for the best possible learning experience and include: comfort levels with learning; the time of day people are learning; the stress related to the teaching and/or learning situation; the environment in which people are learning; the environment people have to practice or reflect on content; the environment where people apply the content; past education, training, professional development, and continuing education successes as well as past failures; the background of the learner (age, gender, ethnic, culture, education, experience in general as well as prior education, training, and so on, given the specific content being learned); whether or not the people have to learn or want to learn the content; consequences of *not* learning; and feelings of the learner, such as if they are frightened of what they need to learn, concerned about the technology such as the hardware, the software, the process itself, the presenter, and/or the consequences of not learning. Other issues include does the learner like/dislike change given that the odds are that there *is* change surrounding what they need to learn?

Learning and the role of teaching and learning in twenty-first-century organizations today play a pivotal role for new management managers. The importance of identifying these roles in workplaces cannot be minimized and includes:

- the realization and commitment of management to the integration of teaching and learning into the organization
- the inclusion of the role and importance of teaching and learning in the organization's internal management documents, including more big-picture statements (such as organizational vision, mission, strategies), communication and reportage (such as marketing and public relations and annual reports), and operational documents (such as hiring content, manager expectations of employees, performance evaluations, job descriptions, and both departmental and individual goals and objectives)
- the inclusion of the role and importance of teaching and learning in the organization's external management documents, including contracts, partnership agreements, and any other consortial or collaborative documents
- the identification and commitment to determining styles of and preferences for teaching and learning for employees
- the identification and commitment for matching content to be learned to employees' styles and preferences
- the identification of and commitment to matching content or area for learning and study to recommended pedagogy for that specific area

This recognition of the importance and role of teaching and learning should permeate the organization to include the process of advertising for, interviewing, and selecting employees; employee orientation; training employees for their primary roles and responsibilities; the design of employee professional development plans for both primary and secondary roles and responsibilities; the organization's education initiatives; and providing general content for continuing education (see Paradigm Shift 2.2).

PARADIGM SHIFT 2.2.
Preparing Classic vs. Contemporary Library Managers in Library Workplaces

Classic Management Managers/Education, etc.	New Management Mangers/Education, etc.
• Organizations have career ladders and promote into management from within but typically only hire for jobs as advertised.	• Organizations have career ladders and provide a learning infrastructure for career ladder participants to be able to promote for management from within. Succession management is prevalent in many organizations where both internal and new hires can be hired for the position advertised but also identified, then internally prepared for their "next" position—in management.
• Some library and information science graduate management programs	• More internships are available in general in for-profit environments, and

Classic Management Managers/Education, etc.	New Management Mangers/Education, etc.
include internships for managerial roles in for-profit environments.	many nonprofits and not-for-profits have internships available as well.
• Management education includes a wide range of continuing education workshop and class opportunities.	• Management education includes diverse workshops and class opportunities; however, much leadership and management content is combined.
• Library and information science associations provide a number of both leadership and management conference programs as well as workshop and extended-length programs.	• Library and information science associations continue to provide a number of both leadership and management conference programs as well as workshop and extended-length programs and now also offer a program of advanced study in management and leadership.
• Some libraries hire professionals with management degrees for mid- and upper-level management positions rather than library and information science degrees.	• More libraries hire professionals with library and management degrees as well as just management degrees for mid- and upper-level management positions rather than only library and information science degrees.

PARADIGM SHIFT: CLASSIC VS. NEW MANAGEMENT EDUCATION

In-Person Learning vs. Online Learning

One additional and primary twenty-first-century issue regarding teaching and learning is the impact of technology on the design and delivery of teaching and learning. Not only do new or contemporary managers have to identify general styles and preferences for learning for employees, but they must also ensure that discussions about styles, preferences, and pedagogy include on-line vs. in-person styles, preferences, and pedagogy. Given that much content today may *only* be delivered in online format, today's managers must weigh employee issues, availability, and cost. In addition, today's managers must determine the appropriateness to general organizational content. For example, should an employee's orientation to an organization always be in person? Or can a mix of in-print and online or a hybrid of orientation content suffice? Should employees being introduced to new, primary responsibilities in the organization always have initial training in person or will hybrid do?

"It depends" is often the answer. In contemporary libraries—given the number of full-time, part-time, and temporary employees and often "turn-over" of these part-time or "nonpermanent" employees, the number of managers, and the amount of time managers have today—managers need to seek other solutions. Given the amount and type of information that must be delivered in very specific terms (e.g., legal content) and the reality that much content is *only* available online, today's managers must find ways to integrate online content and hybrid learning into organizational teaching and learning.

In addition to the general "hybrid" discussion, a hybrid approach should be expanded beyond the mix of in-person vs. online, to a mix of in-person only, to a guided online discussion that can be synchronous or asynchronous. That is, online content can be viewed by individuals for their own information or as train-the-trainers, by small or larger groups or teams; by individuals or groups of all sizes with facilitated or guided learning; by individuals or groups of all sizes with pre- or post-required learning; by individuals or groups of all sizes with discussion by experts; or by those with different education or experience. Other combinations could include in-person and/or online content; in-person and/or online with specific opportunities such as mentors and mentees; and panel discussions, as well as active learning techniques.

In-Person vs. Online Management Learning

Another "appropriateness" issue for in-person vs. online teaching and learning is whether or not the specific content and the goal of teaching the content are appropriate for online delivery. That is, can teaching or retraining managers how to manage *or* can teaching or retraining employees what to expect from their new managers be successfully completed in person? Online? Both or a hybrid?

Just as discussions on teaching and learning always include "it depends" as an acceptable answer, "it depends" is the first answer for the question, "What works better, in-person or online management learning?" When looking at management teaching and learning and in-person or face-to-face vs. online pedagogy, however, recommendations include:

- new management curriculum is best delivered with pre-study or preparation for learners
- new management curriculum can be delivered in a wide variety of ways; however, establishing context for application early in the educational process is critical
- active learning techniques are critical to the illustration of management application and context and assist in curriculum being learned and applied quickly and successfully
- since retraining in general often necessitates changes in opinion and attitudes for the learners, teaching new management is more successful when active learning as well as techniques such as the case method are used to instruct

LEARNING MANAGEMENT FOR LIBRARIES

To maximize teaching and learning new management for managers and employees in libraries, general management should be taught but specifically nonprofit and/or not-for-profit management should be a content focus. In addition, active learning should be employed with a focus on libraries and specifically the type and size of libraries. Using case method is recommended for individual or group learning and serves to illustrate the issues for levels of employee, types of patrons or constituents, and those issues specific to the type and size of libraries and the variety of umbrella organizations such as counties, cities, educational structures, and businesses.

In addition, case method is successfully used for introducing and educating regarding the profession's vision, mission, and values statements and for introducing modes and methods for their application and role in practice. Case method is also successfully used for awareness, articulation, and recognition of differences of opinion and attitudes and changing opinions and attitudes.

Learning Management at the Beginning of vs. Midway or Throughout a Library Career

Although many librarians come to libraries with management experience, many do not. Twenty-first-century managers should identify new management needs for organizations; that is, should new employees have prior management education? Should new employees have management experience? Should education and/or experience be in any management setting? Nonprofit or not-for-profit only? Libraries only? Specific type and size of library only? Should retraining or updating managers or employees in regards to management be formal education? Should it be professional development and/or training? Should it be general continuing education or specific continuing education based on specific organizational need?

Managers should assess each opening and management-related learning opportunity to identify specific need and then:

- alter job descriptions to add or rephrase management content for education and/or experience
- alter job ads/marketing of positions to identify management issues, education, and/or experience
- revise job interview questions to identify education, experience, and so on
- alter employee selection criteria to match identified management needs
- revise teaching and learning management content for existing employees to match education and experience as well as institutional goals

- revise teaching and learning management content for retraining existing employees to be specific based on education and experience of each employee

Learning from Others—Mentor Programs and Mentor Programs for Managers

Mentor programs in organizations are increasing in number and are considered one of the primary ways to introduce, educate, and train contemporary manager content and practices into all sizes and types of libraries. Because of the increase of use of technology in both communication and education delivery, mentors can be onsite or in person but also can be at remote locations, at other libraries of the same type and size, and at other libraries of different types or sizes. In addition, mentors can work through umbrella structures, external partners and consortia, associations, or other businesses and organizations and can be formal and informal.

Mentoring to retrain new managers or orient or educate new managers in new management can provide a focus on becoming oriented and acculturated to the management of the organization; can provide in-depth content for existing employees on learning primary and secondary management roles and responsibilities; and can assist existing managers in learning new management roles and responsibilities within the organization. In addition, mentors can be more successful than a variety of educational opportunities because mentors can provide feedback for employees from managers other than their own, thereby creating a safe space for trial and error.

Mentoring for twenty-first-century management can be virtual, digital, or e-mentoring with the mentor process existing in person, online, or a combination and specifically can be:

- informal with a relationship—typically short term—created spontaneously and maintained informally by the pair
- formal—with an articulated process in place and relationships facilitated and supported by the organization
- short term—specifically with an identified process but with, for example, project-management relationships
- facilitated—with an articulated workplace process but an additional program layer that involves groups external to the immediate organization and significant, required process, program, and performance documents
- groups—for departments or groups involved in similar experiences (a reference department of one library can mentor another reference department as they move through the integration of a new statistics program; a group

of summer reading club volunteers mentoring a group of new volunteers through the summer reading club program)
- co-mentoring—for two or more specific mentors with different expertise for the specific program to work with individual new to an activity (one mentor could have preparation experience and the other could have process or evaluation experience)

REQUIRING AND/OR PREFERRING MANAGEMENT CONTENT

In trying to decide if management education and/or development and/or training for new management managers should be required or preferred, it is obvious that whether or not one feels that managers are only born and not made, it is logical that no matter the inherent talent, by whatever means, managers need to stay current and should find out what management styles work best in organizations. In addition, employees need to learn about how they should be managed as well as how to meet the expectation of managers and how to work with new management managers. When deciding what must or should be learned, how much to learn, or what content is required or preferred, we return to the "it depends" question. With the breadth of content available, many different opportunities for identifying and delivering content are available. These areas, however, do not have definitive, unique, or discrete processes or content. That is, there are no or few clear-cut paths to selecting content for library managers. Identified paths, however, include:

- institutions that offer both formal and informal opportunities with delivery methods that include in-person, digital, and virtual as well as hybrid modes and methods
- content that includes only profit as well as both profit and nonprofit; a focus on management and leadership; and a focus on management rather than supervision, or supervision rather than management
- audiences such as diverse target audiences for both managers and potential managers; target audiences for both managers and their employees; and target audiences for all types and sizes of libraries

Specifically, management teaching and learning opportunities include hybrid, in-person, and digital and virtual modes; and modes in formal and informal undergraduate education, nonlibrary graduate programs, and graduate programs in library and information science; association content available through formal courses of study that result in certifications; and association content available through informal delivery as well as both formal and informal independently offered coursework. In addition to management content, there is significant content for teaching mentors how to "mentor" and work with mentees, and there is a growing body of content on mentoring specifically for managers as well.

In any study of management (including content and processes to use in educating, training, and developing employees to change how they manage, to become new managers, and/or to learn how new managers acculturate into the workplace), there is debate over management concepts and definitions. Although the classic debates are "Is management an art or a science?" as well as "What is management?" vs. "What is leadership?," there are a variety of definitions for management vs. supervision that need to be discussed at the institutional level in order to put the correct content and/or curriculum in place.

While some individuals and organizations use *management* and *supervision* interchangeably, the more commonly agreed-upon definitions define *management* as the more overarching and broader function of the two. Specifically managers establish goals, plan for goal completion and implementation, identify resources needed and expended during the process, and measure and assess goal completion. Although planning work flow, identifying who completes the work, and identifying resources are management functions, the supervisor would oversee individuals assigned the work to direct work through to completion.

Although most libraries are not typically large enough to have multiple levels or layers of management and supervision, examples of this issue in libraries would be the circulation desk supervisor who "runs the desk" and reports to the manager who is the head of public services, and the collection or shelving/stack supervisor who directs the work of hourly workers and reports to the head of reference.

In addition, the classic definitions of *management* vs. *supervision* state that one can be a manager without supervision responsibilities or managing any supervisors, and supervisors can also manage goals and functions and plan, organize, assign, and evaluate. In libraries, this is more common as positions can include collection development managers who don't manage people but coordinate activities of professionals as they build collections; supervisors who manage individuals, for example, at reference and establish goals, plan for goal completion and implementation, and identify resources for the reference department as well; and a technology manager in a small to medium-sized library where there is only one technology specialist who runs the network or technology infrastructure.

Finally, in many contemporary environments that require employees hired for management positions to have management experience, *management experience* is defined only as someone who has "signed timesheets." This requirement, therefore, combines the requirements for managers along with requirements for supervisors.

DECIDING ON EDUCATION, TRAINING, PROFESSIONAL DEVELOPMENT, AND/OR CONTINUING EDUCATION

After discussing whether or not the content should be required or preferred and for whom, it is important to determine not only the pathways but also the focus of the content. While there is never agreement on the best way for content to be identified and delivered, teaching and learning can be categorized in a variety of ways that include: education (considered a change in knowledge of content that is the foundation of the profession as well as primary work roles and responsibilities); training (considered a change in skills and abilities and specifically related to primary roles and responsibilities); development/ professional development (considered a change in attitude or values related to work and applying content to work); and/or continuing education (content often considered external to work—the opposite of training—but is designed to be applied to work).

Education

Library managers should have foundation knowledge for management and specifically management of nonprofit or not-for-profit environments. In addition, education that not only teaches theory but also establishes context and the relationship between management and the library is important as well as basic education that illustrates ways to apply theory to the practical, organizational setting.

- Although most organizations do not require undergraduate education, at the very least undergraduate content introduces theory and practice, and other content can build on that knowledge base.
- Graduate content, either through graduate library and information science programs or through management graduate programs, is preferred. (Management coursework in library programs includes general management courses as well as management functions and management of types of libraries as well as library functions. Examples of course titles offered

in graduate programs include: Managing Information Services and Organizations; Management of Special Libraries and Information Services; Professional Communication; Human Resource Management; Library Administration and Management Core Course; Financial Management; Management and Administration for the Information Professional; and Leadership and Management Principles for Library and Information Services.)

• Graduate programs in areas related to management provide solid foundations for library managers, especially when they allow students to focus on nonprofit and/or not-for-profit environments.

Today's management education can be offered in person and/or online or a hybrid of both, and many programs offer or require internships and field experiences that provide opportunities for applying theory and immersion in nonprofit or not-for-profit environments. Although some library director positions do require management education, many or most do not. Research on management education for librarians has identified management education integrated into only 50–60 percent of library graduate programs. Additional surveys seeking opinions of graduates on whether or not they wish they had management content in graduate school results in overwhelming "yes" answers from librarians who either sought to be or "ended up" as library managers.

Training

Management training typically includes practical application of management tips, tools, and techniques. Training opportunities for library managers are shorter in length and often one-shot or single focus and are designed to be related to work environments either specifically or geared to type or size of organization. There are many online synchronous and asynchronous management training environments for self-directed work as well as small- or large-group work. Existing managers wishing to retool or retrain for "new management" often seek the "newest" management tips, tools, and techniques.

Professional Development

Although "professional development" is used in a variety of ways in organizational teaching and learning for management competencies, this approach to professional growth is focused on the design of a personalized plan of study and learning designed to meet individual, specific needs. Managers new to organizations, existing managers in organizations seeking retooling or retraining, as well as those seeking to move into management should identify strengths and weaknesses and prepare their individualized plans of—given individual needs—the perfect combination of education, training, and professional development. In addition, many plans are designed to build individual growth for a specific job as well as for the next job. For example, professional development plans are used in succession planning when an individual is hired for a management position, but is identified for a higher level or different management position. Because the higher or "next" job is available within a specific period of time, these plans are specialized to meet the timing of both the organization and individual career plans. Mentorship opportunities are often built in to professional development plans.

Continuing Education

Many argue that continuing education (CE) is not unique from, for example, training. Others use the CE term as an umbrella term for all education, training, and professional development that is not a formal education program ending with a credential. Many definitions, however, identify continuing education as a program of skill-building for organizations where the content is broad in delivery (e.g., customer service), but the plan is to customize content to meet specific organizational needs.

Managers' "bookshelves" used to be primarily print resources, and print or classic materials continue to be critical to learning the basic tenets of professions, including the history of the profession and the wisdom of library and information professionals. However, the online world has changed a manager's bookshelf, which is now a mix of print and online content, covering both classic and contemporary topics for teaching and learning.

INDISPENSABLE RESOURCES FOR LIBRARY MANAGERS REGARDING PREPARING THE NEW MANAGER

There are a variety of ways to educate library managers. The following resources provide links to basic education and training for general management as well as for library management. In addition to general library management content, a number of resources, such as association resources, contain specific content on basic management for types and sizes of libraries. In addition to basic management training and education, several websites include basic information about librarianship and related areas such as library design and library law. Also, the following websites (e.g., state agencies, state associations) provide training and education on basic management for types and sizes of libraries unique to that state or region:

"Alison." Accessed September 10, 2013. http://alison.com.

"American Library Association (ALA)." Accessed September 23, 2013. www.ala.org.

"American Society for Training & Development." Accessed August 10, 2013. www.astd.org/Search?q=management.

"Designing Libraries." Accessed October 27, 2013. www.designinglibraries .org.uk.

"EDUCAUSE." Accessed September 15, 2013. www.educause.edu.

"Free Management Library." Accessed October 24, 2013. www.freemanage mentlibrary.org.

"The Future of Libraries." Accessed September 12, 2013. www.davinciinsti tute.com.

"Ken Haycock & Associates Inc. Blog." Accessed June 23, 2013. http:// kenhaycock.com/blog.

"Library and Information Science—A Guide to Online Resources." Accessed October 27, 2013. www.loc.gov/rr/program/bib/libsci/guides.html.

"Librarylawblog." Accessed September 30, 2013. http://blog.librarylaw.com/ librarylaw.

"Library Networking: Journals, Blogs, Associations and Conferences." Accessed October 27, 2013. www.interleaves.org/~rteeter/libnetwork.html.

"Library Research Service (LRS)." Accessed September 23, 2013. www.lrs .org.

"Library Technology Guides." Accessed October 27, 2013. www.librarytech nology.org/LibraryTechnologyReports.pl.

"OCLC." Accessed October 27, 2013. www.oclc.org.

"The Pew Charitable Trusts." Accessed October 27, 2013. www.pewtrusts.org.

"Resources for School Librarians." Accessed October 27, 2013. www.sl directory.com.

"State Libraries." Accessed October 27, 2013. www.publiclibraries.com/ state_library.htm.

"State and Regional Chapters." Accessed October 27, 2013. www.ala.org/ groups/affiliates/chapters/state/stateregional.

"Top Technology Trends." Accessed September 21, 2013. http://litablog.org/ category/top-technology-trends.

"Urban Libraries Council." Accessed October 27, 2013. www.urbanlibraries .org.

"WebJunction." Accessed October 21, 2013. www.webjunction.org.

"Workforce." Accessed October 27, 2013. www.workforce.com.

DISCUSSION QUESTIONS FOR CHAPTER 2

1. Can someone be trained to be a manager if they have never managed?
2. Many feel management students and employees can learn from negative examples as well as from positive examples. How can negative examples be introduced into management teaching and learning in the classroom or in a work setting?
3. Where is contemporary professional development for library managers "coming from"? That is, can managers find education and training unique to library management through their own institutions? Through library education? Through associations? From the commercial training sector?
4. Is it possible to learn all one needs to know about becoming a good library manager from on-the-job training? Is it possible to learn all one needs to know about becoming a good library manager from education and training only?
5. Can (and if so, how can) someone advance to a library management position without any management experience?

Readers are reminded that a case method is intended to be used in conjunction with this chapter. The case designed to be used with this chapter is case 2, "Building Your Own Management Training Program," located in part II, p. 248.

Chapter Three

"Managing" New Employees/Staff/ Human Resources/Stakeholders

- "New" employee roles and responsibilities in organizations
- "New" internal stakeholders (board, foundation, Friends, etc.)
- "New" external stakeholders (partners, vendors, etc.)

A case method is intended to be used in conjunction with this chapter. The case designed to be used with this chapter is case 3, "Rumor Has It," located in part II, p. 253. The case can be read and discussed before and/or after reading the chapter content.

HUMAN RESOURCES ROLES AND RESPONSIBILITIES

While Human Resources (HR) roles and responsibilities remain among the most time-consuming roles and responsibilities for *all* managers, they are often the least "embraced" and often the least enjoyed by managers. In fact, besides the usual or more typical HR work of managing, supervising, and coordinating employees, managers are often responsible for managing employees and other stakeholders, both internal and external, but specific to the organization such as library Friends, foundation boards, advisory groups, as well as partners, supporters, decision-makers, and library vendors. These roles and responsibilities include identification of contemporary, new roles and responsibilities, coordinating activities, and designing work production and work flow in support of the library.

Besides the general management activities of these groups, a primary responsibility of managers is motivating employees and both internal and external stakeholders. Motivating factors in libraries and library environments, however, are often problematic, since more typical factors such as salary, benefits, "territory" (e.g., offices), and equipment and tools (e.g., computers, personal technology devices) are not readily available and often not even possible due to cost and institutional guidelines.

The reality is that HR roles and responsibilities are often identified by non-managers as the reason why many don't seek management positions in that they fear legal issues; the time spent on HR responsibilities, which removes them from their primary profession of library and information science; the continuously changing landscape of federal, state, and local laws and legislation; and dealing with institutional rules, regulations, and guidelines. To complicate matters, many HR networks and information resources, training, and educational opportunities emanate from profit content; even when nonprofit content is identified as adjacent or at least appropriate, content is seldom as specific as needed. Because there are so many types and sizes of libraries with a myriad of umbrella organizations that have their own HR departments, library managers are constantly challenged to become proficient and, once initially prepared, to keep up with human resources issues. The following Paradigm Shifts show changes between classic and contemporary employee roles/responsibilities and performance, behaviors, and issues.

PARADIGM SHIFT 3.1.
Classic vs. Contemporary Employee Roles and Responsibilities

While more specific information on classic and changing roles and responsibilities is outlined in this chapter, a paradigm shift on overall changes best illustrates how library positions have changed.

Classic Employees/Human Resources/Personnel	New/Contemporary Employees/Human Resources/Personnel
• Time away/time off from the organization is governed by workplace policies and procedures on professional leave, workload, continuing education (including professional development), and vacation and sick leave for the librarians. Other library staff, however, are only privy to time away from the organization that includes vacation, sick leave, and some continuing education.	• Time away/time off from the organization is governed by workplace policies and procedures on professional leave, workload, continuing education (including professional development), and vacation and sick leave for librarians and many other library staff whose roles and responsibilities are broad and need different types and levels of support from the organization such as clearly defined policies and procedures on working from home. Some organizational documents may also include appropriate access to work and work tools by partners and support group members.

(continued)

PARADIGM SHIFT 3.1.
(*continued*)

Classic Employees/Human Resources/ Personnel	New/Contemporary Employees/ Human Resources/Personnel
• Librarians and library employees have worked on committees, groups, and on some projects where some decision-making is part of the process.	• Librarians and library employees work on teams (and other work groups) distinguished from committees by their self-directed approach to work that includes design of goals and outcomes, work plan, and decision-making. This includes membership by partners and support group members.
• Librarians and library employees possessed and maintained more traditional technology competencies such as knowledge of productivity software and basic instructional design such as overheads.	• Librarians and library employees must maintain all traditional and also add twenty-first-century toolbox competencies for staff such as high-end productivity software, web design ware, social media, and so on. Partners and support group members may also be included in required or preferred competencies for "doing business."
• Open positions for librarians and library employees are filled with the same or similar organizational information, but with a review for position description accuracy of position roles and responsibilities.	• Open positions of librarians and library employees trigger assessments of departments and position roles and responsibilities. Assessment results are used to revise—as appropriate— position descriptions and departmental organization, goals, roles and responsibilities, and so on, as well as team goals and outcomes.
• Librarians, library employees, and some partners identify internal and external as well as formal and informal communication processes for disseminating information about library services, resources, programs, and activities.	• Librarians, library employees, partners, and support group members identify internal and external as well as formal and informal communication processes for disseminating information about library services, resources, programs, and activities. Social media is now considered part of formal and informal communication processes for "connecting" and communication, and many organizations have guidelines for identifying and managing personal work from professional work.
• Librarians and library employees work on individual workstations— possibly assigned to them—as well as networked hardware for general use in the workplace.	• Librarians and library employees work on individual workstations, networked hardware, and personal technology that is purchased for and can be checked out or assigned to librarians and employees, partners, and supporters.

Classic Employees/Human Resources/Personnel	New/Contemporary Employees/Human Resources/Personnel
• All librarians and library employees are aware of their roles and responsibilities through job descriptions and individual goals and outcomes as well as team and committee and departmental goals and strategic plans.	• All librarians, library employees, partners, and support group members are aware of their roles and responsibilities through job descriptions and individual goals and outcomes as well as team and committee and departmental goals and strategic plans. Additional roles and responsibilities are outlined in management expectation of employee behavior.

PARADIGM SHIFT 3.2.
Managing Classic vs. Contemporary Employee Performance, Behaviors, and Issues

Not only have changes in the overall structure of organizations changed the way work is done including how employees are assigned work, how they do their work, what tools they use, timelines for work and training, and education needed for work, but also changes have dramatically impacted employee performance. Organizations must consider not only performance itself but also how performance is tracked, measured, and reported, and how employee work life is integrated with work performance.

Classic Employee and Human Resources Issues	Contemporary Employee and Human Resources Issues
• Library managers' and employees' communications concerning personal issues such as health and home life are openly and broadly discussed.	• Library managers' and employees' communications concerning personal issues such as health are held confidential in the workplace to ensure privacy. Discussions of personal life are discouraged in work settings.
• All library managers and employees should expect fair and equitable treatment from managers. This treatment emanates from the policies and procedures of the organization as well as other documents of the organization including job descriptions and where appropriate contracts and agreements.	• Library managers and employees as well as partners, stakeholders, and so on, should seek and expect fair and equitable treatment from managers. This treatment emanates from the policies and procedures of the organization and other documents including job descriptions, contracts, and agreements. In addition, partners and stakeholders may outline employee expectations.
• Librarian and library employee work behaviors are identified for job roles and responsibilities and committee and/or team descriptions.	• Organizations maintain extensive work behavior guidelines for librarian, employee, partner, and support group member job roles and responsibilities, and committee or team descriptions as well as work with hardware, software,

(continued)

PARADIGM SHIFT 3.2.
(continued)

Classic Employee and Human Resources Issues	Contemporary Employee and Human Resources Issues
	and related resources such as the Internet. In addition to work behaviors outlined for individuals, work behaviors may also be outlined for work groups, teams, projects, and so on.
• Management and employee discord and disagreements between and among all employees and between employees and constituents are managed primarily by internal processes and include problem-solving techniques.	• Management and employee disagreements between and among employees and constituents are managed by internal and external processes and include problem-solving techniques as well as specific avenues for dealing with conflict and grievances. Disagreements may be referred to external sources including umbrella organization units or external third parties who have contracts to manage issues of employees (mediation and/or arbitration).
• Librarians and library employees have been working together in person for primary and secondary job responsibilities and on—for example—committees and other projects.	• Librarians and library employees work together in person and virtually (asynchronous and synchronous) for primary and secondary job responsibilities, on teams and projects. Additional individuals who work in new environments with great ease—based on new technology—partner and support group members.

Dramatic changes in performance and how work is done have caused the profession to identify not only "new" or "contemporary" roles/responsibilities but also what new roles and responsibilities are needed and ultimately what new types of employees are needed in contemporary organizations.

"NEW" EMPLOYEES?

There are many schools of thought about employees and workplace human resource issues. While some propose that today's and tomorrow's employees are dramatically different individuals and need significantly different organizations, management styles, leadership styles, and roles and responsibilities, there are many others who propose that people are the same as they have always been; it's just the environments and tools that have changed. In fact, if low performance is considered an issue for an employee, managers are encouraged to clarify—for employees who might use excuses that "their job has changed and therefore their performance has changed"—that employee jobs haven't changed but the tools with which they do their job have changed.

It's almost impossible, however, to accept either one proposal exclusive of the other. Instead, the reality is that so much has changed both in the world and in the workplace in the last ten years, that one could argue for both a dramatically different twenty-first-century employee and workforce with different competencies, changed expectations, diverse education required and preferred, different organization designs, different learning styles, and varied preferences for both management and leadership styles.

When looking at a "new" or "today's" workforce in general, however, there are a number of human resources and/or people elements and issues for managers to consider for "new" management. They include:

- an increasingly older workforce due to fewer retirees
- wide ranges of ages of employees working together, given the greater number of older employees
- newer employees having more tech competencies, less fear of technology
- employees seeking more diverse work schedules and opportunities for working offsite through new technology
- generational gaps in work values in library employees as well as gaps in experiences and ethics
- increasingly diverse lifestyles of employees—"brought into the workplace" by the employees themselves
- an increasing number of women in higher levels of management
- an increasing number of younger employees in management
- an increasing number of women working in technology-driven areas
- wide variances in how employees can/prefer to learn—affecting orientation, training, continuing education, and professional development
- 24/7 access to people to maintain 24/7 access to resources, services
- employees working with and moving among different types of library environments and community environments
- employee job or functional work descriptions needing revision and/or updating
- varying employee roles and responsibilities that need to be reviewed and balanced as technology is integrated and changes
- employees needing managers to set performance expectations
- all employees seeking training/professional development dollars to keep up

- employee privacy—both of workspace and work content as well as manager/employee interactions—being harder to maintain
- employee workplace wellness and health—given the reality that technology encourages a physically inactive lifestyle—threatening workplace wellness

In order to be successful in new workplace environments, librarians and library employees need both typical and more standard workplace competencies, diverse additional competencies, and different categories of competencies. New competencies and categories of competencies include (often overlapping) academic, personal and interpersonal, and organizational competencies as well as civil competencies. Specifically, librarians and library employees need the following academic competencies critical to success:

- writing skills to communicate effectively through all modes and methods of communication
- comprehensive reading and understanding skills
- use of math, logic, and reasoning skills; functional and operational mathematical literacy; an understanding of statistics
- a scientific knowledge base, including applied science
- skills in the use of computers and other technologies such as smart, personal technology products
- effective information-accessing and -processing skills
- the ability to conduct research and interpret and apply data
- the ability to design outcomes and set and assess goals

Specifically librarians and library employees need the following personal and interpersonal competencies:

- self-discipline
- adaptability
- flexibility
- listening skills

Specifically librarians and library employees need the following organizational competencies:

- the ability to work independently
- the ability and commitment to be self-directed
- the ability to apply ethical principles to information issues
- an ability to be a team player
- an ability to be a team leader
- respect for the values of effort, understanding the work ethic

- commitment to the profession
- commitment to lifelong learning
- commitment to the institution/work environment (successful "citizen" of the institution)

Specifically librarians and library employees need the following civil competencies:

- multicultural understanding including insights into diversity and the need for an international/global perspective
- conflict-resolution and negotiation skills
- understanding and practicing honesty, integrity, the "golden rule"
- understanding and respect for those not like oneself—an appreciation of diversity
- the ability to take increased responsibility for one's own actions
- commitment to intellectual freedom

While the list of competencies seems almost impossible to expect, require, or even prefer for any and all levels of employees, expectation of level of competencies provides the needed variance. For example, librarians might be expected to have a deep understanding of intellectual freedom as well as a commitment to intellectual freedom, while circulation desk staff might be expected to have an awareness of intellectual freedom.

EMPLOYEE ROLES AND RESPONSIBILITIES IN ORGANIZATIONS

Professions have a variety of levels of employees, and while some professions have clear-cut roles and responsibilities between and among levels of employees, many do not. Library and information science is one such profession with many gray areas between and among employee roles and responsibilities. Areas of roles and responsibilities in libraries include user services, technology infrastructure, technical services, and administrative and management services. Within these areas are specific functions including reference services, age-level services, instruction through information literacy, and acquisitions and cataloguing in technical services.

In addition, administrative services roles and responsibilities of managers and supervisors as well as higher-level administrators include the management and planning of libraries; management of business services such as handling contracts for services, materials, and equipment; supervision of library employees; supervision—where appropriate—of volunteers; marketing and public-relations; development, fundraising, and other entrepreneurial activities such as 501c3 budgeting; managing food services for constituents; and basic and advanced budgeting. Although employees have had a variety of types of input into management activities, in today's library environments employee roles and responsibilities and management expectations for employees include: responsibility for data-gathering and interpretation; budget requests and some basic budget management; input into organizational, departmental, and individual annual and strategic planning processes; coordination and sometimes supervision of frontline employees and volunteers; committee and team coordination; project work as well as some project management; work with umbrella organization peers, partners, and constituents; and work with external peers, partners, and constituents. Issues include the following.

- Although the American Library Association typically identifies "librarians" as professionals who possess a master's degree from an ALA-accredited institution, educational degrees for "librarian" titled positions vary by type and size of library. Roles and responsibilities, therefore, are not specifically defined by "title" or "type" and/or size of library.
- There are many types and levels of employees in libraries, many of whom are not librarians or have the title "librarian." They include circulation desk employees, a variety of collection-maintenance and collection-management positions, youth specialists, and technology positions. Roles and responsibilities vary dramatically and many think that the roles are blurring between and among librarians and, for example, library assistants or technicians, and librarians and tech-support roles, to name but a few areas.
- Libraries often have unique services and functions within the organization, and thus the individuals who work in these areas have unique roles and responsibilities. These more unique, or nontraditional, library services include areas such as museum functions, volunteer functions, genealogy functions, educational services such as tutoring, adult education, and other general community functions.
- Librarians and library employees today are blending more traditional or typical roles and responsibilities with diverse new roles and responsibilities. Consequently it means that employees do more as they add new roles and responsibilities to existing roles and responsibilities.
- Librarians must maintain a knowledge base for their roles and responsibilities in the selection and organization of information and resources. This knowledge base has always included the range of popular to scholarly materials but now includes diverse formats and the broader world of publishing and technology, to name but a few areas.

- Although librarians have always maintained knowledge of "what's current" and "what's new," new roles and responsibilities include the process of identifying and tracking trends and trending to determine "what might be next."
- Librarians and/or library employees in one-person or small libraries (all types) have multiple types of, as well as blended, roles and responsibilities.
- Librarians and library employees must maintain a knowledge base for their roles and responsibilities in the building and maintenance of the library and technology infrastructure. This knowledge base includes library and general commercial technology for employees and library operations, and the delivery of electronic resources and delivery modes and methods for constituents.
- Librarians and library employees must be knowledgeable in the variety of types and sizes of libraries (public, academic, school, special, unique such as museum environments) for relationships such as formal and informal partnerships, collaborations, and consortia. Depending on the location and needs of the library, additional partnerships with other libraries can include environments such as government agency information environments; unique content environments such as medical, legal, and research environments; religious environments; and smaller environments in the private sector such as ad agencies. With the myriad of nonprofits in communities, libraries and library employees must also have basic knowledge of community needs, nonprofit constituent needs, and the vision and mission of these organizations in their role of serving the community.
- Recommended roles and responsibilities for librarians and library employees include customer service; basic library operations; working in a team; literacy services; keeping up with cutting-edge/future issues; teaching and learning for training other employees; information literacy and instruction; personalizing services based on customer needs; searching/locating and instruction in searching and locating; organizing digital information for best access; and designing user interfaces.

One major issue in libraries today focuses on roles and responsibilities of librarians vs. library employees identified as paraprofessionals. This issue is one of the most complicated issues in library human resources, however, since the title "paraprofessional" varies in definition by type of library, by size of library, by job category, by job function, based on the geographic location, and sometimes based on a combination of the above.

In general, the title "paraprofessional" can be characterized as a nonlibrarian and/or a library employee without a master's degree from the profession of library and information science. Departments and/or job functions in libraries more typically performed by paraprofessionals include circulation desk services, technical services (basic copy cataloging), information services (as opposed to or vs. more in-depth reference services), media services, and age-level programming such as children's and youth services. The issue is a complex one because:

- in some environments, position roles and responsibilities are identified as a librarian position, while the identical position roles and responsibilities in another library might be identified as a paraprofessional
- some libraries identify paraprofessional roles and responsibilities as those that are more routine, while in other libraries paraprofessionals perform a variety of nonroutine roles and responsibilities
- some paraprofessionals assume responsibilities that are typically taught/ learned in graduate library programs; these assignments bring into question the role of the master's degree professional in the organization vs. individuals who are taught aspects of graduate education on the job or in libraries
- paraprofessional salaries are typically less and often much less than librarian salaries; this proves frustrating for paraprofessionals—obviously—as they make less money while working at job functions where librarians are paid more; additional frustration, however, is often felt by managers who seek equity and consistency in staffing roles and responsibilities
- paraprofessionals typically have positions that are not identified as self-directed since they are not considered professional; however, they may well be performing roles and responsibilities identical to self-directed professional, librarian positions; this leads to inconsistent organizational structure, job identification, and dissatisfaction by many in the workplace when individuals are treated unequally and seemingly "not trusted" to perform roles and responsibilities on their own

Unclear designations of roles and responsibilities in many libraries raise questions such as: "What should librarians be responsible for in the workplace vs. what should paraprofessionals be responsible for in the workplace?" "What standards are available to define roles and responsibilities?" "What should graduate program curriculum include?" "How does graduate curriculum differ from professional development and continuing education in institutions?"

Finally, the majority of management positions in libraries include relatively standardized roles and responsibilities for managing and supervising people. While managing and supervising people can be rewarding, the reality is that the descriptive phrase, "It was the best of times; it was the worst of times," could be used to explain a manager's job functions. Certainly dealing with people can be among the most enjoyable as well as the most disliked management role/responsibility, and whether or not a manager supervises one or one hundred people, the joys and the problems are the same.

So why are human resources roles and responsibilities NOT enjoyable?

Managing people takes much and sometimes *most* of a manager's time, and although a goal of any manager is to organize and structure employees' work time, time spent managing people cannot easily be controlled. In addition, managing employees includes not only coordination of work activities but also employees "fighting" with other employees, employees fighting with managers, employees disagreeing with customers, employees who inappropriately bring their problems into the workplace, motivating employees during both good and bad times, and customers in negative interactions with other customers, to name just a few areas of a manager's focus.

The business of management can be satisfying for librarians and library employees. Those who enjoy managing and motivating people and managing money, projects, resources, and services find rewards from meeting constituent needs, creating successful organizations, maintaining well-run institutions, creating growth opportunities for employees, and realizing visions and missions.

"NEW" INTERNAL STAKEHOLDERS (BOARD, FOUNDATION, FRIENDS, ETC.)

Library board members (advisory and governing), foundation board members, Friends group members, volunteers, advisory council members, and a variety of other internal stakeholders have been committed to the support and success of all types of libraries for decades. While significant numbers of dedicated people continue to step up to serve on the multitude of boards, councils, and groups, the reality is that the nature of volunteering for these roles and responsibilities has changed significantly in the past two decades. As the economy shifts, as opportunities for this type of volunteering expands, and as volunteer roles and responsibilities have changed as organizations change, the profile of the stakeholder has changed. "New" stakeholders must be comfortable with change; technologically astute or at least comfortable with technology; familiar with outreach and development in support of the library's funding; comfortable with and committed to advocating for the library in local, state, and possibly federal environments; and comfortable with the library's values, vision, and mission in twenty-first-century accessible environments. While librarians could argue that many of these roles are not *new* roles, the context of the blend of traditional and nontraditional roles and responsibilities is a twenty-first-century context. Given the "new" profile, however, how should "new" internal stakeholders be recruited and retained?

- Managers should consider changing stakeholder board makeup and memberships based on institutional needs such as a move from a generally appointed board to a competency-based board (e.g., a lawyer to vet library legal issues, an architect because the library needs renovating) and/or a giving board (required cash or in-kind giving for board service).
- Individual internal stakeholder group membership positions need to have position "descriptions" that clearly identify roles, responsibilities, projects, and/or activities as well as time commitments. The library's values and vision should be part of position descriptions.
- Managers should focus on building and maintaining a cohort of stakeholder group members that might include: extensive orientation; training (e.g., advocacy); ongoing professional development (leadership, team building); a unique group identity; a communication process; group environments (actual and virtual); consistent attention; and—as needed—mentor and mentee relationships.

"NEW" EXTERNAL STAKEHOLDERS (PARTNERS, VENDORS, ETC.)

Partners, vendors, collaborators, consortial members, and various other formal and informal relationships have been part of the library environment and community since its inception. Not only have libraries changed, but also doing business with libraries of all types and sizes has changed, and as business has changed, the roles and responsibilities have changed. "New" external stakeholders must be familiar with all types and sizes of organizations involved in relationships; knowledgeable about the library's business operations; comfortable with both traditional and new elements of the library; technologically astute; interested in supporting libraries by advocating for the library in local, state, and possibly federal environments; and comfortable with the library's values, vision, and mission in twenty-first-century accessible environments. While some might argue that many of these external roles—like the internal roles—are not NEW roles, the context of the blend of traditional and nontraditional roles and responsibilities is a twenty-first-century context. Given the "new" profile, however, how should "new" external stakeholders be recruited and retained?

- Managers should consider having external stakeholder group memberships to determine what the institution needs to "expand" or "increase" or realize their vision or mission. They need to answer the question, "Who do I need to partner with to better serve my constituents?"
- Individual external stakeholder group membership positions need to have position "descriptions" that clearly identify roles, responsibilities, projects, and/or activities.
- Benefits of group membership for *all* stakeholders as well as constituents should be identified.
- Managers should research the variety of relationships possible and best practices in these relationships.
- Managers should establish networks of external stakeholder group members that might include: a communication process, group environments (actual and virtual), consistent attention, and specific "point people" or liaisons.

Finally, given the broad range of human resources roles and responsibilities that contemporary managers have, supporting resources—both print and on-line and both internal and external—must be carefully maintained to ensure accurate up-to-date information.

INDISPENSABLE RESOURCES FOR LIBRARY MANAGERS REGARDING MANAGEMENT OF EMPLOYEES

Identifying content on managing employees includes the use of resources with basic information about employee roles and responsibilities, competencies, and legal issues—to name just a few areas—as well as basic and advanced training and education materials. In addition to general content, the resources below have content on specific types of employees—such as millennials—and on how the design of libraries supports both public and private spaces.

"American Library Association (ALA)." Accessed September 23, 2013. www.ala.org.
"Designing Libraries." Accessed October 27, 2013. www.designinglibraries .org.uk.
"Free Management Library." Accessed October 24, 2013. www.freemanage mentlibrary.org.
"Ken Haycock & Associates Inc. Blog." Accessed June 23, 2013. http:// kenhaycock.com/blog.

"OCLC." Accessed October 27, 2013. www.oclc.org.
"Top Technology Trends." Accessed September 21, 2013. http://litablog.org/
    category/top-technology-trends.
"WebJunction." Accessed October 21, 2013. www.webjunction.org.
"Workforce." Accessed October 27, 2013. www.workforce.com.

DISCUSSION QUESTIONS FOR CHAPTER 3

1. What are three contemporary twenty-first-century management responsibilities regarding library employees?
2. What organizational/management documents need to change to match contemporary human resources issues?
3. Has a manager's list of roles and responsibilities regarding external employees and/or supporters changed? If so, list three new roles and responsibilities.
4. How might managers identify, assign, and communicate roles and responsibilities that fall under the category of "other duties as assigned?"
5. Should managers include vendors as part of the organization's operational planning? If yes, why? Should they include them as part of the organization's strategic planning? If yes, why?

Readers are reminded that a case method is intended to be used in conjunction with this chapter. The case designed to be used with this chapter is case 3, "Rumor Has It," located in part II, p. 253.

Chapter Four

New Management of Change

- Getting to "new" (transition and change)
- Change in nonprofit, not-for-profit, profit management

A case method is intended to be used in conjunction with this chapter. The case designed to be used with this chapter is case 4, "Do You Have Any Change on You?," located in part II, p. 259. The case can be read and discussed before and/ or after reading the chapter content.

TWENTY-FIRST-CENTURY CHANGE ISSUES/CRITICAL NEED FOR CHANGE MANAGEMENT IN LIBRARIES

Although there are many recommended types and styles of management, some classic and some more "new" or contemporary, the real issue behind "new" management is not a style or type but what specific factors or elements direct someone to choose a new style or new type of management. In addition, today's important management issues include how managers *get* to "new" or how we "change" or transition ourselves and our organizations from one style or type to another. But what changes for libraries and, thus, library managers are out there?

A number of significant, dramatic changes in libraries impact librarians, library employees, and constituents. These changes are so pervasive in libraries in their impact on organizations and the design and delivery of resources and services that change-management techniques should be employed in the short term and—more than likely—in the long term as well. Changes requiring significant attention and application of change-management techniques include:

- initial and ongoing technology in both constituent resources and services
- technology for librarian and library employee work product
- technology for individual productivity
- constituent expectations
- constituent competency levels
- customer service
- employee competency levels
- stakeholder identification and commitment
- partner commitment and competency levels

GETTING TO "NEW" (TRANSITION AND CHANGE)

Not everyone is comfortable with change, and libraries historically have been organizations not necessarily associated with constant change. In fact, libraries and information environments have been changing in almost every way for the past two decades, and these constantly changing environments are comprised of some individuals who like change and many individuals who don't.

To realize the importance of change in general and, specifically, change in and of itself, change should be defined and examined for why some embrace and some resist change, and how people deal with change should also be identified. In addition, techniques for dealing with change play a critical role in the "toolbox" of managers. Finally, "change management," a recognized area of management since the early 1990s, should be studied and applied to library and information environments.

Defining Change

There are dozens of definitions of *change* and—depending on the source—definition elements can be positive or negative, with contexts including profit or nonprofit, or home, family, and/or one's personal life. Elements or parts of definitions include:

- to make different in some particular way
- to make radically different
- to give a different position, course, or direction
- to replace with another
- to make a shift from one to another to become different
- to pass from one phase to another
- to undergo transformation, transition, or substitution

- to make either an essential difference often amounting to a loss of original identity or a substitution of one thing for another
- to break away from sameness, duplication, or exact repetition
- to make a change that limits, restricts, or adapts to a new purpose

Change and words often associated with change include both positive and negative descriptors.

- Positive words to typify change can be *exciting, energizing, growth,* and *renewal.*
- Negative words to typify change can be *relentless* or *unrelenting, unprecedented, unmitigated, chaotic,* and/or *ill prepared.*

So, given the need to identify change in context in order to make the transition, how do we identify and illustrate change in libraries? Paradigm Shift 4.1 illustrates old vs. new ways of dealing with change.

PARADIGM SHIFT 4.1.
Focus on Change—Classic Management vs. Contemporary Management

Classic Management	Contemporary Management
• Libraries/library managers typically don't address things that "change" systematically.	• Libraries/library managers address functions/aspects/elements that are changing in a systematic fashion and have significantly more change in traditional areas as well as in areas where changes are driven by technology.
• Library graduate programs, continuing education, and professional development opportunities in libraries do not include much curriculum on change in and of itself.	• Library graduate programs, continuing education, and professional development opportunities in libraries include some curriculum on change in and of itself but have also expanded techniques for teaching change such as the use of case method, scenarios— especially future scenarios—paradigms, and paradigm shifts.
• Library managers typically do not integrate visual techniques for illustrating change issues.	• Library managers strive to integrate visual techniques for illustrating change issues into the organization.
• Nonprofit or not-for-profit organizations have typically limited dollars. Without substantial resources, "keeping up" is difficult. This inability to keep current means that change is not frequent and sometimes not possible.	• Nonprofit or not-for-profit organizations have typically limited dollars but cannot change or do business without the basic twenty-first-century infrastructure. Change is now frequent and approached consistently and as a function of the organization.

(continued)

PARADIGM SHIFT 4.1.
(*continued*)

Classic Management	Contemporary Management
• Libraries are not seen as change agents in institutions, organizations, or communities.	• Libraries strive to be change agents and are more frequently identified as such in communities, umbrella organizations, partnerships, and consortia.
• Change (updates to hardware, new software) occurs normally such as annually, or semi-annually.	• Change occurs significantly more often than in previous years, especially in the area of technology.
• Libraries are considered relatively static environments that do not change annually with any significance.	• Libraries are frequently changing environments in many areas including technology (hardware, software, online resources) and new collection formats to name just a few areas.

Because change has so many definitions and so many contexts, managers know that organizations include people who embrace change and people who resist change.

Resisting Change

It's typically *not* possible to guarantee that managers and/or leaders will be able to get employees to embrace change. It is more likely, however, that causes for resisting change can be addressed to the extent that employees will not only tolerate but also be able to deal with change and—ultimately—be successful in and plan for intermittent or constant change. Since general resistance to change is the primary reason why change is difficult, why *is* there such resistance to change? Reasons include:

• neither the reasons for change nor the benefits of the change are adequately or effectively communicated
• the goals and benefits regarding change are not accepted by the people who have to function with the change
• people don't understand or address change in and of itself
• people fear the unknown and can't predict the outcome
• people don't understand how/why they react to change
• people fear failure regarding changes they must make
• people like their current situation in general and specifically their own situation
• people think that change is happening due to trends or fads and consider these transitory
• the reason for and purpose of change is not clear or relevant

- people dislike the person recommending, announcing, or implementing the change
- people see change as an attack on their performance and react defensively
- people are not given time to adjust to change/learn new areas
- the coming change wasn't communicated at all or in a timely fashion
- the timing of announcing the change was wrong or perceived as wrong by the people involved in it
- people believe that the change will make a boss—or others—look good but not them
- a previous change was handled badly
- people have fear of having to work harder because of the change
- people have fear of loss of rights or status because of the change
- people do know why the change is coming but don't support or accept it or think they need it or understand the consequences as it relates to the organization or to them
- people think that things are working well and see no reason to change
- people have resistance to change just because it is change

Embracing Change

Although the image of librarians and library employees is not necessarily an image that conjures up individuals who love or embrace change, all libraries are changing—some slowly and some rapidly. Although we can't guarantee that all of our employees will embrace change, in twenty-first-century libraries, all staff need to be both familiar and comfortable with change as well as committed to working in a changing environment.

To bring employees closer to accepting and—if possible—*embracing* change, managers and leaders need to clearly articulate how organizations and employees benefit from change such as growth potential for employees and identifying and meeting new and changing constituent needs. To this end, managers should seek to:

- identify the general benefits of change
- establish context for the benefits of change for libraries
- establish context for the benefits of change for their specific libraries and functions
- integrate the concept and importance of change into the organization to include:

  ○ the identification of change language for position descriptions
  ○ the integration of change into orientation, training, and professional development

And most importantly:

- identify the benefits of change *specifically* for individual employees and their positions and job functions

TECHNIQUES FOR DEALING WITH CHANGE

Although choices for exact techniques should be matched to institutions and institutional needs, there are specific techniques that work better than others. They include general directions and specific ideas.

General

- Involve others in "changing," gathering data, and analyzing changes.
- Identify and inform (early) those who need to help carry out changes.
- Clearly define people's roles in change discussion, the goals of possible changes, and their achievement indicators.
- Disseminate the decision to change and the goals and objectives for the change in writing.
- Identify/assist others in identifying how the change will specifically affect them.
- Identify and address people's needs for dealing with change! Disrupt only what needs changing to accomplish your goals for the change.
- Design flexibility into the change process. Don't change too quickly.
- Allow people to complete current efforts and take adequate time to assimilate new skills, procedures, support mechanisms, and work behaviors that are needed to successfully institutionalize the change.
- Identify good and bad aspects of the change and address all sides and, whenever possible, focus on the data supporting, the need for, and the benefits of the change.
- Establish timelines and parameters and define the limits of the change.
- Design adequate training for change elements.
- Build in adjustment time for all people involved.

Specific

Specific techniques to carry out steps include the following.

- Address the issue of the change head on. Provide specific content on the change, how the change affects people, how people "see" and deal with the change, and how they get "through" the change. Establish standard visual images to communicate and educate such as flow charts and Paradigm Shifts.

- Establish broad organization/institutional calendars that specifically address the change amid standard issues and events. These workplace calendars should focus on managing events, activities, and issues and not just chronically when something occurs. Calendars should incorporate organizational functions into calendars so employees will be able to identify how their functions and responsibilities fit into the organization and the change as a whole (i.e., project management timelines).
- Define expectations for performance of employees and employers/administrators within the context of the change. This can be achieved by commenting on overall job descriptions such as "effect on all circulation positions" as well as comments on positions—where there is great change—with specific comments job by job.
- Establish learning mechanisms for organizations for existing practices and training and professional development for learning new areas and dealing with change as well as teaching others how to work/live with change (including constituents).
- Assess communication patterns and techniques and establish standards for dealing with ongoing practices and integrating the "new" including communicating changes relating to both employees and constituents.
- Design and implement a proactive plan for dealing with rapid change/information-sharing with umbrella organizations and constituents.
- Assess "anchor" organizational elements for their stability—that is, ensure that employee documents such as employee handbooks, job descriptions, performance expectation documents, and so on are dynamic and current.
- Articulate support mechanisms in place for librarians, library employees, and so on to deal with all change aspects including mechanisms for dealing with change such as stress relievers, sense of and area for play, respect for and outlets for reaching creative potential, and mechanisms (which can be temporary) for dealing with problems associated with the change and complaints concerning the change.
- Be specific on elements of the change including benefits, negative aspects, consequences, and perceptions.
- Identify librarians, library employees, stakeholders, or partners as well as other worker levels (in some libraries work-study workers, volunteers)—based on competency and commitment to change—as "change agents."
- Identify other librarians, library employees, stakeholders, or partners as well as other worker levels (in some libraries work-study workers, volunteers) who need to be involved as well as those who can lead (from the middle or the front line) in targeted change activities.
- Identify and integrate stakeholders and partners to define stakeholder and partner roles and responsibilities in change implementation.

• Identify and implement measurement and assessment of the process, impact, success, and communication of change.

CHANGE IN NONPROFIT/NOT-FOR-PROFIT ORGANIZATIONS, PROFIT MANAGEMENT

Although change is a fact of twenty-first-century life in all organizations, twenty-first-century change has had a much greater impact on the nonprofit and not-for-profit organization. Today's major change factors in these organizations have focused on changing visions and missions and changing clients, but specifically have been impacted by technology hardware and software opportunities as well as sliding scales in costs and implementation. Gone are the days of nonprofit and not-for-profits with significantly fewer opportunities for achieving a presence in the marketplace and serving and reaching clientele. The impact of self-directed approaches for designing products and services has forced major changes on these organizations. These changes include:

• managers and leaders have had to make significant changes in their competencies and, because there are typically fewer employees in these organizations, higher-level managers need to dramatically change their roles and responsibilities such as:
  ○ learning today's hardware and software
  ○ implementing new web-based technologies
• constituents for these organizations have many of the same needs but different elements such as access, delivery, and expectations
• advisory and governing board members need the same match and commitment to vision and mission but different competencies
• contemporary economic issues dramatically alter the dollars available for giving to organizations
• contemporary political issues dramatically alter many funding opportunities such as limits on successful grant recipients based on, for example, faith-based guidelines

INDISPENSABLE RESOURCES FOR LIBRARY MANAGERS REGARDING MANAGEMENT OF CHANGE

The most successful way to find content on "change" in libraries is to seek research, information, and opinion on a specific changing function, service, or resource such as the "evolution of e-readers." That content, paired with content on societal changes and/or information changing and/or libraries of the future will offer rich content on libraries as they change. Although information on "how to change a library" or "change" specifically is not as available, a growing body of learning objects, charts, graphs, and research on the rate of change of information is available and provides a context for library managers. The following resources have content on "change" in general and the changing nature of the workplace, and specifically the future of libraries and the impact of a changing society on libraries.

"EDUCAUSE." Accessed September 15, 2013. www.educause.edu.

"Free Management Library." Accessed October 24, 2013. www.freemanage mentlibrary.org.

"The Future of Libraries." Accessed September 12, 2013. www.davinciinsti tute.com.

"Ken Haycock & Associates Inc. Blog." Accessed June 23, 2013. http:// kenhaycock.com/blog.

"OCLC." Accessed October 27, 2013. www.oclc.org.

"The Pew Charitable Trusts." Accessed October 27, 2013. www.pewtrusts.org.

"Steven Bell's Resource Center." Accessed October 27, 2013. http://steven bell.info.

"Top Technology Trends." Accessed September 21, 2013. http://litablog.org/ category/top-technology-trends.

"WebJunction." Accessed October 21, 2013. www.webjunction.org.

DISCUSSION QUESTIONS FOR CHAPTER 4

1. Are there library managers "out there" who aren't interested in getting to "new"? If so, how does a librarian deal with more of a traditional manager?
2. What types and kinds of changes are taking place in libraries?
3. Are all types and sizes of libraries changing at the same time and in the same way? Some changing more slowly? Which ones and why?
4. What techniques do *you* use to deal with change/changes at work?
5. What are three ways managers can assist employees who are resistant to change?

Readers are reminded that a case method is intended to be used in conjunction with this chapter. The case designed to be used with this chapter is case 4, "Do You Have Any Change on You?," located in part II, p. 259.

Chapter Five

New Managers Designing
New Organizations

- Business structures (functions/strategic directions driving organizational design vs. facilities and disciplines driving organizational design, integrating in-person with digital/virtual, and actual)

A case method is intended to be used in conjunction with this chapter. The case designed to be used with this chapter is case 5, "Racking Up the Library Pool Table," located in part II, p. 265. The case can be read and discussed before and/or after reading the chapter content.

ORGANIZATIONAL STRUCTURES IN LIBRARIES

Although many professions and their entities have very standard, typical, or consistent organizational structures, libraries have a wide variety of organizational designs. In fact, libraries have as many different organizational models as they do types and sizes of libraries. Contemporary organizations include more traditional structures with managers, middle managers, and frontline employees, but they also have matrices with employees having multiple managers, and flat structures with few middle managers.

In addition, libraries can have a variety of types of organizational structures because the services and resources are/can be arranged in a variety of ways including by target population, by age level, by format, by genre, by location, based on access points and processes as well as in-person vs. remote location. In general, libraries tend not to have extensive management infrastructures and managers often have large spans of control.

Libraries also have a number of organizational positions where professionals manage a function or a service rather than manage people. These professionals are often identified as coordinators rather than managers and the areas can include resources management such as collection-development coordinator, target population/age-level services management, and/or coordinators such as the coordinator of children's librarians, and/or an age-level coordinator of just a service such as youth or young adult services coordinator.

This variety is due to libraries being dramatically different as to umbrella organization or governing entity, size of a library, and whether or not they are school, academic, public, or special libraries. The variety also adds to the difficulties of identifying best practices for organizing employees and workers into logical structures. Additional layers of problems with providing consistent or typical structures make standardizing communication as well as management documents a difficult task. Within this variety and no matter the umbrella organization:

- larger libraries—no matter the type—have more standard or typical bureaucratic management structures such as manager, director, dean or head; an associate or assistant to the primary manager, director or head; and a span of control that includes middle managers or department heads (head of reference, head of a branch or other location) and coordinators (collection development manager, budget officer, etc.) of functions
- smaller libraries—no matter the type—have significantly fewer employees, and thus typically no associate or assistant, and few "levels" of employees, creating less of a bureaucratic structure and sometimes a greater span of control

In general, in libraries:

- most library managers have larger spans of control, that is, more employees reporting directly to them, such as:
  - a head of reference with all full-time and part-time librarians reporting directly to the head of reference
  - the branch or department manager with no assistant or associate and all branch and department employees reporting directly to the branch or department manager
  - the head of technical services with all employees (acquisitions, system/automation, interlibrary loan/access) reporting directly to them
  - a preservation manager who coordinates preservation and conservator activities of all employees and manages two part-time librarians including a digital archivist

- many library organizations have employees who are managed directly by a library manager but also work with and report on some level about their work to a coordinator of, for example, age level or resource format functions such as:

  - a children's librarian directly supervised by the branch or department manager with children's services coordinated by the library or system-wide coordinator of children's services
  - a circulation desk assistant who provides—as their major responsibility—tech support for public service computers and is supervised by the head librarian, but whose tech support, training, budgeting, and so on, activities are coordinated by the institutional technology manager

Other factors that affect an organization's structure can include:

- the presence of unions throughout an organization
- the presence of unions at certain levels within an organization
- decentralized facilities with no main facility
- decentralized facilities with a main facility
- size of the institution (the larger the institution, the greater the number of divisions of functions, roles, and responsibilities; the smaller the institution, the fewer the number of divisions of functions, roles, and responsibilities)
- the design and/or floor plan of the building
- the role of technology in delivery of services and resources
- the number of employees in the organization
- the organization of the umbrella organization
- the management style of the umbrella organization
- the identification of a constituent group and subsequent needs of that group
- the number of constituents identified in a target group
- the management style of the library manager
- the presence and role of partners in the organization

Given the number and type of organizational structures and the number of types and sizes of libraries, library managers have to take great care to apply both general and specific management styles and preferences to the design of their library organization.

PARADIGM SHIFT 5.1.
Classic vs. Contemporary Organizational Design of Library Resources and Services

Area, Services, Resources	Classic Organizational Structures	Contemporary Organizational Structures
Services by Age Level	• Age-level services are organized and managed as separate departments. Employees "specializing" in serving age-level target populations are present in departments and are managed by, for example, the branch manager; however, age-level activities have an additional coordinator to ensure consistency among locations such as a youth services or seniors coordinator to ensure consistent delivery of services.	• Age-level services are organized and managed as departments—sometimes separate and sometimes merged with other age-level or related services such as resources for those constituents. Employees "specializing" in serving age-level target populations are present in departments, typically also support more general services at their location, and are managed by the manager of the location.
Resources by Age Level	• Age-level resources are acquired, organized, and managed from a single coordinator with employees "specializing" in serving age-level target populations present in departments and managed by, for example, the branch manager.	• Age-level resources are acquired, organized, and managed both from a single coordinator as well as—depending on the size of library—from the children's services employees within children's departments or rooms in larger libraries. Employees "specializing" in serving age-level populations are managed by the branch manager.
Hardware/ Software	• Libraries provide rooms or areas with concentrations of equipment (e.g., microfiche, microfilm, etc.) and hardwired workstations for public use such as "single focus" reference workstations. Spaces are typically identified by the content delivered and/or the technology used such as "Microfiche Reading Room" and "Reference Workstations." Initially equipment was individually "loaded" with software products, and then products were loaded onto local-area	• A number of technological advances make dispersion of hardware throughout all types and sizes of libraries possible. These include user interfaces with ease of searching, dispersed printing, wireless access, and a general increase in competencies of constituents who have access to technology both in other environments and in constituent homes. • Managers disband equipment-driven departments and spaces and integrate hardware now networked with web access into content areas. Therefore,

(continued)

PARADIGM SHIFT 5.1.
(continued)

Area, Services, Resources	Classic Organizational Structures	Contemporary Organizational Structures
	networks, then wide-area networks.	*research* workstations are located in reference. Workstations for youth are located in the children's area and in the Young Adult or Youth Services Department.
Resources by Format	• Libraries group materials by format and in larger libraries there are departments of formats such as the Film Department or the Media Department. These departments are managed by format librarians such as media librarians and film librarians. Additional formats or types include some specialized collections such as map collections and government documents. In smaller libraries formats are shelved together. • Libraries are organized by departments that represent both format and age level with some content differentiation.	• Materials' media, etc., formats are interfiled with print materials "in person" and—obviously—in online access with most being accessible in open stack areas. Library departments are merged, such as government documents are often split between reference and circulation; and media is interfiled. Unique, special collections requiring unique storage and climate control or needing assistance in viewing, such as map collections, are still managed by departments.
Resources by Depth/Level/ Discipline	• Libraries have collections divided by depth or level such as undergraduate and graduate as well as by discipline such as "the architecture library" or the health sciences collection. Additional divisions by department can include "popular" or "current reading" or "bestsellers" or by genre such as "westerns."	• Libraries merge depth and level into general collections both in reference and in circulation. While discipline-specific collections (with all formats) do remain primarily in law and medicine, many other discipline-specific collections are combined into general reference and circulating. This organizational structure may yield independent libraries (such as law and medicine) with separate managers—and often separate online catalogs—but for all other merged discipline collections, general managers manage.

Area, Services, Resources	Classic Organizational Structures	Contemporary Organizational Structures
Services and Resources by Location	• Libraries have a variety of locations within one structure such as main academic libraries and branch collections—some with specialized collections and some with general collections. • Larger public libraries and special library systems have one main location with satellite or branch locations, which for the most part are small, general collections that include some geographically necessary content such as languages represented, job, or career needs for underemployed areas. School libraries have libraries in each school that are general but tailored to meet the age-level constituent and curriculum. • Management of these organizations includes managers in each location much like managers of departments in larger libraries in one location.	• Increasing numbers of online resources have reduced the size of print collections needed in branch locations and have enriched small and often remote general collections. • Contemporary libraries continue to have a variety of locations within one structure such as main academic or public libraries and branch collections—some with specialized collections and some with general collections. • Larger public libraries and special library systems continue to have one main location with satellite or branch locations, which for the most part are small, general collections that include some geographically necessary content such as languages represented, job, or career needs for underemployed areas. School libraries are general but tailored to meet the age-level constituent and curriculum.

FACTORS AFFECTING ORGANIZATIONAL STRUCTURE IN LIBRARIES

A wide variety of other activities, issues, and entities affect an organization's structure. This variety can include employee organizations such as unions, the physical facility as well as the size of the institution, technology, and the employees—including the number, their expertise, and their roles and responsibilities.

Unions

Unions in organizations provide structures. While these structures aren't typically more rigid *or* more flexible, they are designed to clearly spell out roles and responsibilities, what people do and don't do, and activities such as communication between and among organization entities. Unions identify and protect employees through clear delineation. These articulated protections, or contracts, identify not only who does what and when (if relevant) but also who reports to whom and management roles and responsibilities. Union presence may dictate more structure, less job sharing, or cross training—elements that make management's role more structured with less flexible opportunities for change.

Facilities

While no entity wants to organize a management structure around building design, it is a reality in libraries. This reality contributes to the wide variety of management structures found in contemporary libraries—given the fact that library facilities are historic, new, and cutting edge, as well as exist in unusual retrofitted environments.

Design in an individual building can include: merged departments because of a lack of space, and departments being pulled apart because one department is on one floor and the other department is on another floor. One department manager may manage another department because they are contiguous rather than related in function. Additional management structures reflect the fact that the library buildings or areas of service are decentralized facilities with no main facility, and thus, branch or location managers report directly to a chief librarian, or they may be decentralized facilities that have a main facility, and therefore, parallel services in the largest location either manage or coordinate related services in smaller locations.

Floor plans may also dictate management structure as the types of furniture, the flexibility of the environment, and the placement of desks (that are fixed) can create a large circulation department, for example, with a number of services emanating from the department/area because they fit there, they are public services, and the floor plan has only one public service circulation desk. Again, while not ideal for data-driven decision-making, arrangements of furniture can, in fact, govern management structures.

Institution Size

Recommended spans of control vary per type of library and management text or expert. If a large institution has seventeen branches, typically organizational development consultants would say that seventeen people are too many to report to one manager, given that the managers have different projects, user populations, and so on. For example, the assumption is that bank managers may manage twenty-five people; however, those employees are all doing the same work. On the other hand, library managers have similar roles and responsibilities but can be managing employees with vastly different tasks, at different locations, using different materials, and so on. Obviously, the smaller the library, the fewer the number of divisions of functions, roles, and responsibilities, thus the fewer the number of departments and, therefore, the fewer the number of managers needed.

Technology

Technology plays a role in the designation of management structures. A retrofitted older space with tech access brought in can dictate that a tech department of hardware and support, for example, be located in a certain department and thus supervised by that department. Other technology issues include how the tech infrastructure is managed vs. how tech support for public-access computers is handled. That is, institutional technology is a different department than, for example, instructional technology in K–12 or higher education environments. In cities and counties, libraries may have a tech-support person or a paraprofessional for public access computers who reports to librarian in access services, while employee computers are supported by the city or county IT department. Technology is also an area where tech-support people, who are often not librarians, might report to a high-ranking manager who has a technology knowledge base.

Employees

The greater the number of employees (including workers such as work-study students and volunteers, etc.), the more middle management structures must be included to avoid large (over ten) spans of control. Whether or not the worker is a volunteer also dictates who might manage or how the workers might be arranged within the institution. Other employee issues occur when employees have specific expertise, and thus roles and responsibilities must be supervised by someone with similar expertise. Other factors include:

- the library's umbrella organization might be committed to one organizational chart given size, money available, and so on, and the library—wanting consistency—may well organize in a parallel manner
- target populations or constituent groups may need outreach and thus an age-level service might be connected to an outreach department. In addi-

tion, a large youth population might dictate that service points or departments be divided up into children, youth or young people, and young adults
• the presence of a variety of internal and external relationships or partnerships might dictate that management structures change to accommodate
partnership parity or employee expertise

Although libraries have both typical and atypical organizational structures, it
is often hard to find specific, matching examples in resources. This uniqueness makes it even more important for managers to identify best practices
to track. In addition, managers should seek resources with best practices for
more narrowly defined functions within organizations such as specific services and facility areas.

INDISPENSABLE RESOURCES FOR LIBRARY MANAGERS
REGARDING THE LIBRARY ORGANIZATION

Content on the nature and structure of organizations as well as on the variety
of structures available can be found in the general management literature. Association content is rich with structures and is found not only in "the future by
type of library" but also in—for example—association content on leadership
and management (e.g., LLAMA). "Future" discussions also contain content
on changing structures. Library managers should also use facilities content
for content on how "form follows function" or—in this case—how new design of buildings can dictate organizational structure.

"American Library Association (ALA)." Accessed September 23, 2013.
    www.ala.org.
"Designing Libraries." Accessed October 27, 2013. www.designinglibraries
    .org.uk.
"Free Management Library." Accessed October 24, 2013. www.freemanage
    mentlibrary.org.
"The Future of Libraries." Accessed September 12, 2013. www.davinciinsti
    tute.com.
"OCLC." Accessed October 27, 2013. www.oclc.org.
"WebJunction." Accessed October 21, 2013. www.webjunction.org.

DISCUSSION QUESTIONS FOR CHAPTER 5

1. Give two examples of how the design of a library building drives the management style of the organization.
2. Are organizations with employees in remote locations organized similarly to organizations in one building or in primarily one location? If so, why; if not, why not?
3. Are different types of libraries organized in significantly different ways? If so, how do they differ?
4. Identify two organizational structures where one employee might have two managers.
5. Have age-level services and departments changed in organizational structures in contemporary libraries? If so, identify two ways they have changed.

Readers are reminded that a case method is intended to be used in conjunction with this chapter. The case designed to be used with this chapter is case 5, "Racking Up the Library Pool Table," located in part II, p. 265.

Chapter Six

Management Infrastructure Documents in New Organizations

• Policies, procedures, rules, regulations, guidelines, manuals, handbooks, and so on, delivered in print and through wikis, blogs, and other online mechanisms

> A case method is intended to be used in conjunction with this chapter. The case designed to be used with this chapter is case 6, "Manuals, Handbooks, Policies, Procedures, Budgets, Minutes, and Plans, Oh My!," located in part II, p. 271. The case can be read and discussed before and/or after reading the chapter content.

MANAGEMENT OF DOCUMENTS

Management infrastructure should be supported with articulated, written content in policies, procedures, rules, regulations, guidelines, handbooks, manuals, reports, budgets, and a variety of plans including marketing, communication, and emergency and risk management, as well as more general strategic plans and operational plans. Although many libraries have extensive management document infrastructures, many do not, and many library documents that *do* exist in the organization are often not systematically updated. Other management document issues include the need for and difficulty of interpreting umbrella organization management documents for library use, the identification of best-practice documents that are often *not* the match or appropriate for library use, and the availability but lack of match of profit-management documents applied to nonprofit settings.

Contemporary documents—in print, digital, online/web based—are also published, disseminated, and maintained in a variety of ways in contemporary libraries including through internal networks using web pages, internal drives, blogs, wikis, and other web-delivered software such as proprietary software used for designing electronic pathfinders. Managers of these diverse new formats must decide which format they will maintain, how and who will update critical content, and what content needs to be available, for example, to limit users in general and/or to specific populations such as departments, levels of employees, locations, and so on.

PARADIGM SHIFT 6.1.
Classic vs. Contemporary Library Management Documents

Just as organizations, employees, and managers have changed, the documents that define and support the new or contemporary organizations must change. One of the most important roles of contemporary managers is that of design, implementation, and maintenance of all internal and external documents. Assessing what documents need to be revised or be significantly changed includes the comparison of what documents were within the organization and are no longer needed, what documents need to remain and be revised, and what documents need to be created and maintained.

Management Documents—Classic	Management Documents—Contemporary
• Documents reside in one or few locations for general reference.	• Documents reside online and are accessible by all within the organization, and many institutions have content accessible on the open web.
• Content from umbrella institutions and other areas (law, legislation, local ordinance) is available "as is."	• Content from umbrella institutions and other areas (law, legislation, local ordinance, and partner content) is available as is and includes interpretation that provides but is not limited to: context and application to institution and application to employees, library workers, and other primary and secondary audiences.
• Managers have files with content and—when necessary—interpretation and application on a case-by-case basis or for specific situations only.	• Manager files include content and interpretation and application in general and then further application on a functional and/or departmental level and on a case-by-case basis and for specific situations including employee group or title level.
• Vetting, review, and revision take place every few years and/or when foundation content (law, etc.) changes, events, activities and services, and resources change, or situations challenge content and lead to review and revision.	• Very specific timelines are in place for vetting, review, and revision including annual, event, or activity-specific and tracking to organizations and entities related to or responsible for content and intent changing. Vetting teams by function and/or title are included in organizational processes for continuity and consistency.

(continued)

PARADIGM SHIFT 6.1.
(*continued*)

Management Documents—Classic	Management Documents—Contemporary
• Content is created for institutional employees and some library workers.	• Content is created for institutional employees, some library workers, advisory and governing board members, as well as individuals in umbrella institutions, partners, and secondary audiences including vendors, and so on.
• Some content is integrated into employee orientation and training.	• All employee, worker, partner, and other related group content is integrated into orientation and training as well as into the organization's staff development plan. Content is vetted and identified as "in person," online, or actual, as well as online, self-directed, workshop, and so on. Content is matched to pedagogy, and necessary topics such as ethical issues are offered with follow-up discussion and analysis by trainees so application is clear. The process of verification of awareness of content and application understanding is included in the process.

The primary reason for discussing and outlining recommended content for manager "bookshelves" or "files" is that there are many elements that managers must be aware of immediately upon arriving at an organization, immediately upon assuming a management position, or—in the natural course of management activity—immediately in order to handle critical situations or issues. Important content includes not only the institutional information but also those reference documents from umbrella institutions, legal entities, and so on, and any interpretation or application of information for the institution for clarification. Examples include:

• legal and/or mandated content with any pending issues such as any internal or external legal issues (some of which may be human resources issues)
• human resources content in general including institutional interpretation of local, state, and federal guidelines, and basic files such as job descriptions, current/past evaluations, work plans, improvement plans, benefits information, and compensation information
• policies and procedures of the organization/institution related to constituents and their access and use

- any health, safety, and security documents related to employees, constituents, and institutional information

A manager must have a variety of institutional or organizational management documents on their "shelf" or at their fingertips or in their files. General categories of this content include for the library specifically:

- plans—strategic, long term, short term, building/facilities, communication, marketing and/or public relations, work plans of stakeholders such as board or Friends or foundation work plans, plan of action for programs/services, vision, mission, goals with strategies or objectives and tasks, assessment documents in general with specificity for outcomes, technology plans, and human resources plans to include hiring plans, and/or training or continuing education content
- budgets—line item requested/received and tracking content, justifications, and—based on the budgeting styles chosen by the institution—competitive packages, zero-based or zero-increase budgets, and/or planned programmed budgeting systems and other financial information such as documentation and accountability content as well as content related to fundraising, alternative financing, wills/estates, and bond funds
- grant content (which can include budget, assessment, etc.)—both funded and unfunded
- contracts, agreements, MOUs, and so on, for vendors and partners
- reports—organizational, partner, and/or stakeholder
- policies
- procedures

General categories of this content include for the umbrella institution specifically:

- plans of the overarching entities including umbrella organization plans, community plans, and plans of local, state, regional, and federal organizations and entities
- budgets including umbrella organization budgets, community budgets, and budget requirements of local, state, regional, and federal organizations and entities
- related umbrella institution or community contracts, agreements, MOUs, and so on, for vendors and partners
- policies and procedures of related groups

Other professional management documents include:

- benchmark or best-practice data
- professional content

- consultant reports
- curriculum from educational programs
- curriculum from continuing education
- network content (in person and/or online)

Online content—very prevalent in today's libraries—can be gathered and "stored" in organized and easily accessible environments; however, managers must be as careful about vetting online content as they are about vetting consultant information, and benchmark and best practice. In addition, managers must take great care in participating in all forums for discussion. Just as a manager must be careful about in-person networking or partner discussions, a manager must take great care in posting content and in discussions online. Why?

- Managers should take care in publicly sharing issues and problems and appearing to be unable to manage.
- Managers should be aware at all times that sharing problems publicly may compromise a manager's work environment and violate ethical practices.
- Managers should be aware that restricted online lists *are* part of the manager's communication and are part of public record.

Although managers should take care to post opinions, problems, and issues online, online forums are ideal for delivery of current information through RSS updates and web content notification systems.

When evaluating other documents for inclusion in the manager's bookshelf or in designing institutional management documents, managers should evaluate based on criteria and design using standard and recommended elements. Evaluating documents should include:

- a review of relevancy of the document to nonprofits in general, to specific profit elements, to the library in general, to the type of library, to the size of library, and/or to the goal of the issue or project at hand
- an assessment of accuracy of content
- an assessment of currency of content
- a match of the target audience of the document to the target audience

When designing documents such as reports, training materials, budget justification, and strategic plans as well as other major plans such as facilities, communication, and development plans, managers should include:

- a brand that identifies document intent or request
- an executive summary of the content geared to the target audience

- an introduction that identifies the purpose of the document, the audience, authorship, the design team, any unique aspects such as timeline, parameters of the content
- initial content with vision, mission, and goals of the organization as well as board, Friends, and foundation content as needed
- content delivered with narrative, data, stories, and so on
- emphasis on accomplishments, message, data, requests, and so on, through design or delivery
- visuals to enhance technical writing and narrative such as charts and graphs
- explanation or assistance in understanding as needing such as a detailed table of contents, a glossary, and so on
- additional content such as presentation media, a Q&A with anticipated concerns

Institutions, and most entities, in fact, have content that articulates the overall philosophy of doing business and the ways business should be conducted. Although institutions have created and operated on these statements for decades, in today's institutions these statements are:

- more readily accessible (e.g., online) and thus need to be more easily understood
- broader in that they may need to include more and different entities such as institutional partners and stakeholders
- reviewed more often given broader audiences and thus more diverse coverage
- reviewed following critical incidents that may warrant institutional or partner and/or stakeholder changes
- reviewed more frequently for legal compliance issues given broader audiences and more diverse coverage

POLICY DOCUMENTS

Today's content is organized in a series of statements that are identified in diverse ways and could be titled: rules, guidelines, policies, and/or principles. Just as there are different ways to identify content, there are a variety of definitions and descriptors, and it follows that this content—no matter how it is identified—means different things to different people in different settings. In general, however, these statements—most typically identified as policies—answer the question, "Why are you doing this?" and are guiding or governing principles that allow, constrain, and/or mandate action. General philosophical and managerial common elements of policies include:

- articulated values that underpin organizational vision and mission
- institution-wide application
- approval by—when applicable—legal counsel
- approval at the senior levels of the entity and/or the governing bodies
- institutional direction for the foreseeable future
- definition and assurance of necessary compliance with local, state, regional, and/or federal laws and legislation such as ADA/ADAAA, harassment, as well as local ordinances
- directives with clear-cut expectations, performance, and behaviors by job function, by title, and/or by process owner
- benchmark and/or best-practice content from general professional content, neighboring institutions, and partners, as appropriate
- fair, nondiscriminatory application and consequences, if applicable

Specific design and focus common elements of policies include:

- systematic and continuous review for currency and timeliness, but typically infrequent major changes
- critical incident review upon occurrence for determination of impact of major events and activities
- implementation prior to institutional activities governed by policy content such as services
- dissemination throughout the organization and to partners, and so on, as appropriate
- design with common language that includes:

  ○ standardized formatting
  ○ coding or a standard identification for order and categorization, such as human resources and employment practices; general conduct of employees and institutional workers and partners (as appropriate); general conduct for users, customers, and constituents; access to facilities, resources, and services; use and misuse of facilities, resources, and services by all users and constituents; business practices in general; business practices specific to acquisitions of materials; business practices related to users and constituents; professional infrastructure content; other applicable guidelines, and polices that govern behaviors, services and resources, and professional conduct
  ○ consistent terminology within a specific policy as well as among policies
  ○ referrals to other relevant policies
  ○ a focus on clear intent, organized with answers to who, what, when, where, why, and how

- ○ authorship by teams and groups (more than one person), and vetting by groups for excellence as well as to create "buy in" and assist with dissemination
- design with common language that excludes:
  - ○ specific numbers (e.g., transitory) considered short term rather than long term
  - ○ dates or date ranges (except for vetting, approval, and/or review dates)

This content, more typically identified as "policy," is the cornerstone of management document infrastructure. All managers in organizations must have in-depth knowledge of these statements; the role they play in identifying, explaining, and managing all aspects of the organization; and the role they play in the "life" of the manager.

How policies are managed in today's organizations, however, may vary. This variance may be due to how big the organization is, whether or not it is centralized or decentralized, the type and variety of partnerships, the number and type of employees, and the number and type of managers. One person in the organization may have ultimate policy responsibility, while an organization with a variety of middle managers might have managers as process holders or stewards of certain areas of policies given their position functions or expertise and/or a permanent or ad hoc team might be named to track and vet policies. In addition, a policy database or other online mechanism with automatic reminders/triggers for policy assessment can be established. The more the policy process is technology driven, the more opportunities for diverse input, systematic dissemination of information, and systematic vetting of information as well as increased access to content. Whoever is responsible must identify situations that dictate the need for discontinuance, review, revision, and/or creation of a new and/or specific policy. Examples of reasons to review a need for new policies as well as review specific policies for range, coverage, and currency include:

- a new and/or discontinued service
- grant monies for projects, programs, and/or services
- new, revised, or now older or subsumed legal mandates
- identified best practices
- changes in partnerships and/or collaborations
- vendor contracts
- a new population
- a new access point
- new or changing technology

PROCEDURE DOCUMENTS

All policies must have, at the very least, one procedure that outlines how that policy might be carried out or handled in the institution. As such, procedures are a series of interrelated steps that are taken to implement a policy. Procedures are written as emanating from a policy but not as part of policy. Although institutions have created and operated based on procedures for decades, in today's institutions these statements are:

- more readily accessible (e.g., online) and thus need to be more easily understood
- broader to support broader policies in areas that include institutional partners and stakeholders
- reviewed more often, as policies are reviewed more often given broader audiences and diverse coverage
- reviewed more often based on the policy review driven by critical incidents that warrant institutional or partner and/or stakeholder changes
- reviewed, as policies are driven by the need for review and revision of legal compliance issues

Today's institutional procedure content is organized in a series of statements that are identified in diverse ways such as methods, intentions, and/or actions, or with the word *procedure* with the descriptors *standard* and *operating*. Procedures should answer the question "How do you do this?" or "How do you carry out this activity (or activities)?" Procedures:

- flow from policies
- support policies
- provide direction for implementing policies
- must be continuously reviewed and updated
- must be documented for vetting, revision, and new content
- should reflect standard practice—as appropriate
- must be designed and implemented fairly
- must not be punitive when dealing with infractions
- must have referrals to other relevant policies and/or procedures

Just as with policies, procedures must:

- have approval by—when applicable—legal counsel
- have approval at the senior levels of the entity and/or the governing bodies

- provide institutional direction in support of policies, but not be long-lived or for the foreseeable future as policies are
- provide for the implementation of legally imposed mandates
- define—for policies—directives with clear-cut expectations, performance, and behaviors by job function, by title, and/or by process owner
- outline implementation of fair, nondiscriminatory application and consequences, if applicable

Specific design and focus common elements of procedures include:

- review when their umbrella policies are reviewed
- systematic and continuous review for currency and timeliness
- review when critical incident events and activities force policy changes
- implementation simultaneously with policy implementation—prior to institutional activities governed by policy content such as services
- dissemination throughout the organization and to partners, and so on, in tandem with policy dissemination
- design with common language that includes:
  - standardized formatting
  - coding or a standard identification for order and categorization based on policy coding and/or identification
  - consistent terminology within a specific procedure as well as among procedures
  - a focus on clear intent organized with answers to who, what, when, where, why, and—most importantly—how
  - authorship by teams and groups (more than one person) and vetting by groups with recommendations for creating or vetting in partnership with those who are and/or will be using the procedures
- design with common language that includes:
  - specific numbers (e.g., transitory)
  - dates or date ranges (including vetting, approval, and/or review dates)

Just as with policies, all managers in organizations must have in-depth knowledge of these procedural statements, the role they play in supporting policies, and the role they play in the "life" of the manager.

Procedures are managed in today's organizations in the same process chosen by the organization to manage policies. In addition, it is typical and recommended that managers who have oversight or are process holders or stewards of certain areas of policies track and vet procedures. If a policy

database or other online mechanism is employed to maintain policies, procedures must be managed in the same way as well. The more the policy process
and thus the procedural process is technology driven, the more opportunities
for diverse input, systematic dissemination of information, and systematic
vetting of information as well as increased access to content. Examples of
reasons to review content to identify procedural changes include:

- a new and/or discontinued service
- grant monies for projects, programs, and/or services (and often grants have
  required procedures of their own)
- new, revised, or now older or subsumed legal mandates
- identified best practices
- changes in partnerships and/or collaborations
- vendor contracts
- a new population
- a new access point
- new or changing technology

Just as institutions must have policies for some functions (mandates, access,
etc.), there are "must have" procedures about certain actions or services.
These include procedures involving:

- actions on the part of users or constituents that incur penalties or are punitive
- activities where any money changes hands between constituents and the
  institution
- services that include mediated access
- any other organization or institution that requires its own processes such as
  a granting entity, an umbrella department or organization, or a governing
  body, as well as any laws and legislation
- actions and activities involving employees or institutional workers

Just as policies have categories with the institution, procedures follow policies; therefore, the same categories apply. Examples of procedures in general,
however, are:

- checking out materials
- obtaining identification to and processes for issuing library cards
- application and use of facilities (meeting rooms, study rooms, etc.)
- assessing fines and fees
- access to and use of computers at the library

  There are selected times when policies and procedures might remain in the
same document. While this is not widely recommended due to the need to be

PROCEDURAL LANGUAGE

"Dos"

- Use technical writing.
- Maintain consistency (among and within procedures) and with those using procedures.
- Employ specificity (exactly what steps are to be taken and exactly—for example—who is supposed to do what and when).
- Design with an orientation and training focus.
- Vet against specific benchmark and/or best practices that are selected for policies.
- Compare and contrast with neighboring and relevant institutions and with institutional partners.
- Review with same or similar procedures from other libraries.

"Don'ts"

- Create without an overarching policy.
- Put in place without approval within the context of the policy.
- Distribute in a limited fashion or not at all.
- Create in a vacuum.
- Use employee names.

able to update details without having to update entire policies, it does occur. Examples of situations where this might occur are:

- when the overarching institution, partner, or granting agency requires that both policy and procedure be in the same document
- when—given the nature or importance of the issue or activity—all elements of both the policy and procedure need to be approved by governing bodies at the same time and/or with specific content
- when the governing body needs/suggests/requires it for others/peers
- when the area/situation/service is new/unknown/cutting edge (at that time documents might be brought forward together but not necessarily kept together)
- when the area/situation/service or resource is controversial (e.g., fees, fines, intellectual freedom, access, etc.)

HUMAN RESOURCES DOCUMENTS

Human resources management documents are the cornerstone of the manager's bookshelf. Filing or categorizing this content should not be by employee name, but instead by job titles or job functions. Additional ways to categorize human resources content could be by department, location, or project. General categories can include the overall list of responsibilities for managing and supervising and include:

advertising, hiring, and selecting—job ads, job descriptions, institutional/ area marketing packets, interview schedule, EEO guidelines, performance/ rating sheets for hiring, job evaluation/performance plans, contracts/employment agreements, benefits statements

training, staff development—training plan with "market" analysis; match of continuing education or staff development to needs; curriculum; learning style assessment; first-day, first-week, first-month checklists; and workplace calendar

performance expectations—job description, job evaluation, employee goals to match institutional goals, a manager's list of expectations

communication—outline of how communication in the organization works, statement relating to what the management style is, e-mails, memos, internal communication, external communication

productivity—clear assignment of tasks, good calendars and schedules, employee goals, managers' goals, plan for assessing and maintaining morale

a match of learning styles—learning-style assessment matched to employee needs and a manager's teaching and learning styles

a match of management styles—statement on how manager leads and what his or her management style is

a safe workplace environment—ADA/ADAAA, occupational safety information, ergonomics statements/commitments

Although all management documents are critical to successful human resources management, job or position descriptions are the primary document that drives all organizational performance. Descriptions can vary dramatically from institution to institution and, depending on a number of factors including compensation plans, organizational structures, and management styles, descriptions can be individualized per employee, individualized to a specific group of employees, generalized to a specific group of employees, or even made specific or general based on constituents, department, or physical location. In addition, job descriptions can be seen as primarily duties-oriented (objectives or task list) or results-oriented descriptions that combine what is to be achieved, completed, or done along with why it is to be achieved, completed, or done.

Library workers comprise a category that includes volunteers. Volunteers—although not technically employees—should be part of the human resources "equation." Specifically volunteers:

- should have job descriptions
- should be described in terminology that matches other documents such as evaluations
- should be evaluated in the same timeline and within the same process identified for employees

Job descriptions should be assessed by employees vacating a position; revised, if needed; and used as a tool for recruitment and hiring (including writing the job ad), for determining compensation in the human resources process of the umbrella organization and/or the library, and for performance reviews/evaluation.

Management documents are among the most important tools in a manager's toolkit in today's new library environment. It might just as easily be said that management documents create and explain the infrastructure of contemporary organizations and provide the required documentation for successful operations. Given new in-person and digital environments, multiple partnerships, diverse staff, diverse constituents, the demands of governing and advisory boards as well as umbrella institutions and the need for accountability for all activities within organizations, managers must take great care in:

- creating and selecting relevant content

  - With the plethora of online information that is not only commercially produced but also self-published and possibly *not* carefully maintained for accuracy and currency, managers must take care to validate appropriateness, accuracy, and currency. Of the content chosen (benchmarking, best practice, etc.), managers must note appropriate credentials and authorship—if content is used as is—and cite content reviewed if that content is used as a basis for creating new organizational content.

- establishing processes for maintaining content

  - Given the rapidly changing nature of organizations today, managers must establish processes for systematically vetting content as well as seek automatic updating processes that alert the organization to local, state, and federal changes in required and mandated content. In addition, more content today should be reviewed by legal representation, or—at the very least—content should be carefully benchmarked against content identified as vetted by legal representation. In increasing numbers, lawyer-librarians are providing resources and services specific to the profession and provide avenues to good management content.

- implementing use and orientation and training of content

  - Although in today's new library environments a great deal of orientation and training material is delivered online, managers must take great care to identify content that should be introduced to new employees or employees assuming new responsibilities through face-to-face modes rather than in online and/or self-directed mode. Face-to-face content should include all content governed by law/legislation and/or local ordinance, all human resources issues for which the employee is responsible, as well as content that refers to them and health, safety, and security content. All content, including other online or self-directed content, should include an assessment of learner awareness and knowledge levels as well as written confirmation that learners—specifically managers—can apply information as required.

- educating primary and secondary target audiences

  ○ The breadth of secondary individuals such as library workers (not employees), partnerships, Friends, foundation members, and any other umbrella institution groups, governing and advisory board members, and vendors—as appropriate—is expanding in new organizations. These individuals and parties that need to be educated as to the existence, application, and use of these documents grows annually, and the decision to include the wider audience rests with managers. The education process, however, needs the same care and attention found in the process to educate, orient, and train employees. Critical to integrating content processes into secondary audiences is the need for education, including orientation and training as well as identification of awareness and knowledge levels, verification of receipt of information, and—as appropriate—validating awareness and understanding of application of content in writing. Because content and audiences vary, managers should identify what content needs might include, such as more and/or explanatory information such as context, additional glossary; specific application to target audience, entity, and activities content; and insertion of institutional timelines either unknown by secondary audiences or timelines unique to them.

- standardizing vetting, review, and revision

  ○ Following education including orientation and training, secondary audiences need to be integrated into ongoing vetting, review, and revision of content. These individuals need to be "at the table" either in person or electronically for vetting, review, and revision for—at the very least—all content that includes them or relates to them. In addition, dissemination to their audiences might include health, safety, and security issues as well as issues relating to products, projects, and events. As with education, managers should decide on levels of involvement, the need for verification of involvement, and—as appropriate—a receipt of information validating awareness of and understanding of application of content revisions in writing. Also, because content and audiences vary, managers should identify what content needs might include, such as: more and/or explanatory information such as context, additional glossary; specific application to target audience, entity, and activities content; insertion of institutional timelines either unknown by secondary audiences or timelines unique to them; and specific interpretation of impact of revisions on secondary participants and their secondary audiences.

Although library and umbrella organizational documents are the cornerstone of the manager's bookshelf, online resources provide best-practices content as well as updated information for maintaining document and content currency.

INDISPENSABLE RESOURCES FOR LIBRARY MANAGERS REGARDING INFRASTRUCTURE DOCUMENTS

Locating contemporary best practices for documents for library managers is best done by a review of what content can be used with few changes (e.g., tech training materials, nonprofit board training, customer service protocols, laws and legislation for nonprofit human resources issues) and then an identification of similar or related content (e.g., budget accountability, outcomes). A combination of use "as is" and application offers managers a solid foundation for updating and creating new management documents.

"American Library Association (ALA)." Accessed September 23, 2013. www.ala.org.
"Free Management Library." Accessed October 24, 2013. www.freemanage mentlibrary.org.
"OCLC." Accessed October 27, 2013. www.oclc.org.
"Resources for School Librarians." Accessed October 27, 2013. www.sl directory.com.
"State Libraries." Accessed October 27, 2013. www.publiclibraries.com/ state_library.htm.
"State and Regional Chapters." Accessed October 27, 2013. www.ala.org/ groups/affiliates/chapters/state/stateregional.
"Stephen's Lighthouse." Accessed October 22, 2013." http://stephenslight house.com.
"WebJunction." Accessed October 21, 2013. www.webjunction.org.

DISCUSSION QUESTIONS FOR CHAPTER 6

1. If a new manager doesn't find the management documents he or she needs to be successful, what should he or she do first?
2. Does one type or size of library need more policies and procedures than another type or size of library?
3. Are benchmark-management documents from organizations helpful in designing management infrastructure in other organizations; that is, what are the plusses of using benchmark documents, and what are the pitfalls of using benchmark documents?
4. If library managers use benchmark documents from other organizations, can they be documents from profit organizations, or should they only use nonprofit benchmarks? Why?
5. Are old or outdated handbooks and manuals useless in the design of new handbooks and manuals?

Readers are reminded that a case method is intended to be used in conjunction with this chapter. The case designed to be used with this chapter is case 6, "Manuals, Handbooks, Policies, Procedures, Budgets, Minutes, and Plans, Oh My!," located in part II, p. 271.

Chapter Seven

Managing New Services and Resources

- New services and resources
- Marketing new vs. classic services and resources (e.g., traditional, social media, etc.)

A case method is intended to be used in conjunction with this chapter. The case designed to be used with this chapter is case 7, "What's Old Is New—If the Money Is There," located in part II, p. 276. The case can be read and discussed before and/or after reading the chapter content.

NEW SERVICES AND RESOURCES

Although libraries have always been described as quiet and slow-to-change environments, many, if not most, of today's libraries change a great deal *and* at much faster paces and in greater numbers of ways. These changes are due to, for example, technological advances and laws and legislation relating to both technology and information, but *many* changes in libraries are also due to differences and changes in services and resources. Resources or collection differences include new and diverse formats of collections, varieties of delivering or making resources accessible, and types of costs associated with making resources accessible. Service differences include accessibility issues based on changing, diverse resources; new as well as different types of equipment/hardware needed/used to access collections; new services for education and instruction related to technology; and expanded services such as hardware/equipment offered for both in-library use and check out, which dictate changing policies and procedures, instruction in the basics of use, and instruction in basic care.

Libraries have publicized their resources and services for decades. *Marketing* newer resources and services, however, is paramount to the success of the library to identify, match, and disseminate information about services and resources to target audiences. Marketing is critical to allow the library not only to provide and document value of services and resources but also to provide constituents with what they need and want. Libraries should use existing, traditional, or classic marketing techniques including branding, but should also use more contemporary techniques using social networking and a variety of communication opportunities.

New services and resources as well as *marketing* new services and resources prove challenging for managers. With a focus on *managing* new services and resources, managers must deal with:

- changing external management documents and content
- changing legislation, standards, guidelines for services, and resources policies and procedures
- increasingly complex budgets and financial models for providing "new" services and resources
- changing internal management documents and content
- a need to change nomenclature for planning and budgeting as standard codes, policies, and processes change with oversight, formats, and delivery
- required changes in human resources areas such as position descriptions
- required changes in support of employees such as orientation, training, and professional or staff development
- balancing new and "classic" materials
- space issues driven by "more" needed with less space (e.g., remote storage?)
- access decisions such as integration of collections or separate housing (e.g., integrating all media and print into open-access shelving)

Contemporary libraries—immersed in an environment of "new" and "different" at the very least and, at the most, innovation and transformation—deal with the impact of change almost daily. And while this change affects all aspects of libraries, the most basic of aspects—library resources, services, and connecting constituents (or marketing) to these resources and services—continues to be a major area for managing change.

In fact, almost every aspect of managing the contemporary mix of classic and new resources and services is changing continuously including the resources themselves; the services themselves; service delivery; constituent interactions regarding resources and services; usage and usage data on resources and services; policy design and implementation concerning resources and services; facility design for resources and delivering services; and the role that librarians and all employees play in acquiring, organizing, maintaining, and, ultimately, putting resources and services in the hands of constituents in general as well as target populations.

What are the new resources and services issues and what are the management questions for contemporary resources and services discussions? Although it isn't possible to identify *all* of the new services and resources, there are primary areas and issues that drive "new" or contemporary management decisions.

One-Stop Services

Streamlining library reference and research services into "one-stop" arrangements can include:

- combined reference and tech-support service desks
- combined access, such as all authentication or tech sign in occurs at one library location instead of constituents moving among departments/service points
- contiguous library/information settings with key services and/or resource areas abutting or contiguous to each other, such as a joint-use public and school (or academic) library with two centrally located circulation desks
- two types of libraries or a library and a related department co-locating in the same space, such as a library and a community center or an academic library that also houses the tutoring center
- co-branding, such as a public and a school library advertising or choosing a brand that combines two services, for example, "public and school children's library services available at . . ."

Finally, if departments can't be combined, managers can choose to reeducate or orient staff to serve multiple locations through, for example, cross-training or joined professional development opportunities.

Distance Learners/Distributed Learning

All types of libraries are experiencing constituents using resources and services to support distance learning for not only higher education but also K–12 homeschooling in public libraries and after-hours school libraries as well as remote teaching and learning opportunities for decentralized corporate users. While shouldering access to curriculum support materials should be the primary responsibility of the academic library, a variety of services and resources are supporting this activity and other related activities. Managers must choose from among a variety of service models, such as:

- the library serves all users as defined by service and resource contracts
- the library has user fees imposed on constituents from other environments accessing resources and services
- the library has user fees for the host or sponsoring environment, such as a public library charges a college or contracts with a college to provide reference and research support for the college's constituents who use the public library
- homeschoolers use the library's resources and services to support K–12 studies
- homeschoolers buy user cards for public, academic, and/or school libraries

Constituent-Driven Technology

Constituent-driven resource and service activities can include:

- multiple uses of e-resources that trigger purchases
- constituents designing their own custom user interfaces to the library
- constituents enhancing the design of the library's web environment through customizing portals or adding to library blogs or wikis
- constituents creating products in, for example. innovation centers in the library and the library choosing to "host" or serve digital content

The following five Paradigm Shifts cover changes in how services and resources previously were managed any how they are now managed—generally, and in academic, school, public, and special libraries.

PARADIGM SHIFT 7.1.
Managing Services and Resources—Classic vs. Contemporary Libraries

Although some might say that basic services of libraries have not changed over the years, technological support for services and resources, and especially the delivery of services and resources, has significantly changed.

Classic Services and Resources	New/Contemporary Services and Resources
• Managers maintain services and resources such as reference departments (in person, phone, and e-mail assistance with research and reference) and materials collections.	• Managers/middle managers maintain services and resources such as reference departments (in person, phone, and e-mail assistance with research and reference) and materials

Classic Services and Resources	New/Contemporary Services and Resources
These services and resources are managed by (typically) middle managers.	collections. In addition, managers must manage multiple points of access for in-person and remote synchronous and asynchronous access. Print, media, and web collections support reference services and many offer 24/7/365 access to professionals to assist them in meeting needs.
• Managers offer library instruction to educate constituents for understanding and applying critical thinking to information-seeking behaviors.	• Managers offer information literacy services both in person and delivered online (also called information fluency, bibliographic instruction, user education, library instruction) to educate constituents for applying critical thinking to all formats of materials. These services are offered in all modes and methods of design and delivery, and librarians and library professionals assist in designing content.
• Many managers/libraries provide and maintain areas for programming related to instruction, academic life, research, and books and in support of the higher education community	• Many managers/libraries provide and maintain areas for programming related to instruction, research, and books and in support of the higher education community. Additional uses for spaces in contemporary libraries include special collections, alumni events, and student, parent, or family events. Managers must establish relationships with others to design and deliver requisite library and related library services and support.

PARADIGM SHIFT 7.2.
Managing Services and Resources—Classic vs. Contemporary Academic Libraries

Academic library services and resources have changed for all sizes and types of libraries. In addition to dramatic changes in publishing, research, and access, academic library environments (e.g., commons, active learning, etc.) and outreach (e.g., P–16 initiatives, etc.) have redefined how constituents use the library.

Classic Services and Resource	Contemporary Services and Resources
• Many managers organize and maintain guest access to extend the use of higher education environments and collections to the community.	• Managers organize and maintain guest access to extend the use of higher education environments to the community. Some libraries provide events and instruction for guests,

(continued)

PARADIGM SHIFT 7.2.
(*continued*)

Classic Services and Resource	Contemporary Services and Resources
	high school classes, and community groups as well as support for P–16 and community initiatives.
• Libraries support the higher education environment in the support of students, faculty, and staff for ancillary or secondary campus services including providing passwords, identification cards, teaming with tutoring and study skills, faculty and staff relaxation and recreation, or constituent "commons" environments.	• Libraries support the higher education environment in the support of students, faculty, and staff for ancillary or secondary campus services including providing passwords, identification cards, teaming with tutoring and study skills, faculty and staff and high-tech relaxation and recreation, or constituent "commons" environments. Managers maintain partnerships with peers and related areas in the academy to support unique areas for constituents.
• Library managers establish and maintain special collections of faculty, staff, and some student research.	• Library managers establish and maintain special collections in general and specifically collections of faculty, staff, and student research and often create—through commercial or internal or institutional software design—institutional repositories. Libraries provide opportunities for self-publishing including general online and print publishing of research, journal articles, and monographs.

PARADIGM SHIFT 7.3.
Managing Services and Resources—Classic vs. Contemporary School Libraries

School library services and resources have changed for elementary, middle, and high school libraries of all types and sizes. In addition to dramatic changes in curriculum, testing, information literacy, and production of content, school libraries strive to provide seamless transitions of constituents throughout the P–16 educational system.

Classic Services and Resources	New Services and Resources
• Librarians maintain collections and provide assistance in research and reference—typically in a smaller and sometimes one-room setting—to students, faculty, and staff, and often parents and family.	• Librarians maintain assistance for in-person and online research and reference and provide this service— typically in a one-person/one-librarian setting—to students, faculty, staff, parents, and family, and often the

Classic Services and Resources	New Services and Resources
	community. They maintain multiple access points for synchronous and asynchronous assignment assistance. Print and web resources support reference services and most databases offer 24/7/365 access. School librarians may also maintain access to information beyond firewalls.
• Managers offer information literacy services that include supporting curriculum through the design of activities for standardized testing and teaming with classroom faculty to design assignments to educate students for applying critical thinking.	• Managers offer information literacy services that include teaming with classroom faculty to design assignments in support of local, state, and national standardized testing and for information literacy and homework assignment completion.
• Managers organize and maintain public service technology workstations (hardware and software) to assist in accessing content and opportunities for active learning.	• Managers organize and maintain public service technology workstations (hardware and software) to assist in accessing content and active learning in hardwired and wireless modes.
• Many managers/libraries provide and maintain areas for programming related to instruction and books (and book fairs), and in support of the school community.	• Many managers/libraries provide and maintain areas for programming related to instruction and books (and sometimes book fairs) and in support of the school community. Additional uses for these spaces in contemporary libraries include hosting and delivering parent/teacher events or PTA or Friends events, and so on.

PARADIGM SHIFT 7.4.
Managing Services and Resources—Classic vs. Contemporary Public Libraries

Public library services and resources have changed for all sizes and types of libraries. In addition to dramatic changes in availability and access to resources, public library environments strive to identify and meet constituent needs and integrate instruction into services.

Classic Services and Resources	New Services and Resources
• Managers in larger public libraries maintain reference departments managed by (typically) middle managers where assistance in research and reference is provided to library constituents. In smaller to medium-sized public libraries, the highest-level manager coordinates the reference desk schedule and in many smaller	• Managers in larger public libraries maintain reference departments managed by (typically) middle managers where assistance in research and reference is provided to library constituents. In smaller to medium-sized public libraries, the highest-level manager can coordinate the reference desk schedule and in many smaller

(*continued*)

PARADIGM SHIFT 7.4.
(*continued*)

Classic Services and Resources	New Services and Resources
one-librarian libraries, the librarian manages the reference and information service and the circulation desk staff.	one-librarian libraries, the librarian manages all reference and information service and the circulation desk staff. Public library managers must maintain multiple points of access for synchronous and asynchronous access.
• Managers offer user education, which includes instruction (signage, handouts, small-group and one-on-one training, and point-of-use instruction) to constituents for understanding and applying critical thinking.	• Managers offer user education to library constituents, through computer classrooms and online content, and it includes instruction, signage, handouts, small-group and one-on-one training, and point-of-use instruction to constituents for applying critical thinking.
• Managers maintain public service technology workstations (hardware and software) to assist in accessing content and office productivity.	• Managers maintain public service technology workstations (hardware and software) to assist in accessing content and office productivity in both hardwired and wireless modes. Libraries check out technology for use in the library and for home.
• Libraries assist their communities for related as well as ancillary or secondary services, including providing community support services such as income taxes, food stamps, voter registration, tutoring, non-English-speaking classes, and instruction for literacy initiatives.	• Libraries assist their communities for related and ancillary or secondary services (to libraries) including providing community support services such as special collections, tool-lending programs, income tax support, food stamps, voter registration, tutoring, non-English-speaking classes, and instruction for literacy initiatives, maker spaces, and proctoring tests for P–16 entities for in person and online.
• Library managers design both formal and informal opportunities for input by constituents.	• Library managers design and maintain formal opportunities for input by constituents and maintain advisory boards, foundations, and Friends groups. In addition, many specific services have their own advisory groups such as those representing older Americans, youth, new immigrants, and so on.
• Managers offer user education or library-use services, which include instruction (signage, handouts, small-group and one-on-one training, and point-of-use instruction) to constituents for understanding and applying critical thinking.	• Managers offer user education or library-use services in the library, through computer classrooms and online content for library websites, and it includes instruction, signage, handouts, small-group and one-on-one training, and point-of-use instruction

Classic Services and Resources	New Services and Resources
	for understanding and applying critical thinking.
• Managers are committed to designing spaces to provide a variety of spaces for public library constituents.	• Managers are committed to designing spaces to maintain a variety of spaces and in today's contemporary libraries one might find—if space permits— individual reading and study space for constituents throughout library and information environments for study.

PARADIGM SHIFT 7.5.
Managing Services and Resources—Classic vs. Contemporary Special Libraries

Special library services and resources have changed as have their nonprofit and for-profit umbrella organizations. Special libraries—almost more than any other type of library— have significant challenges in proving value in mediated reference services in a world where constituents think they have access to everything and in balancing proprietary information with open access.

Classic Services and Resources	New Services and Resources
• The majority of special libraries are smaller environments and research and reference assistance is provided by the library manager. In addition, library managers offer unique services to integrate resources including "table of contents" dissemination based on corporate or constituent profiles as well as a more in-depth service of selective dissemination of information with profiles directing more narrowly defined and vetted content lists that are placed in pre-defined orders such as the most recent, the most relevant, the most similar to the environment, and/or the most related to organizational research.	• The majority of special libraries are smaller environments and research and reference assistance is provided by the librarians and often the library manager. In addition, special librarians offer unique services to integrate resources including "table of contents" dissemination based on corporate or constituent profiles as well as a more in-depth service of selective dissemination of information with profiles directing more narrowly defined and vetted content lists that are placed in pre-defined orders such as the most recent, the most relevant, the most similar to the environment, and/or the most related to organizational research.
	• Managers must maintain multiple points of access for in-person and remote synchronous and asynchronous access. Print and web resources support reference services and many offer 24/7/365 access.

PARADIGM SHIFT 7.5.
(continued)

Classic Services and Resources	New Services and Resources
• Managers offer user education, which includes instruction (signage, handouts, small-group training in offices and departments, and one-on-one, point-of-use instruction) to constituents for understanding and applying critical thinking.	• Managers offer user education services to constituents in the library, in offices and in departments, through computer classrooms, and through online content for library websites, and it includes instruction, signage, handouts, small-group and one-on-one (in-person and online) training, and in-person and online point-of-use instruction to constituents for understanding and applying critical thinking to resources.

MARKETING NEW VS. CLASSIC RESOURCES AND SERVICES

Library marketing is the practice of identifying and matching resources and services to general and specific constituents and/or target populations. Steps include:

- identifying constituents
- identifying constituent needs
- targeting constituents and their needs
- promoting resources and services
- matching resources and services
- getting resources into the hands of constituents
- assessing use and value of resources and services to constituents and constituent groups

For many years, library managers integrated marketing tools such as publicity and advertising into their business practices as well as marketing practices overall, including data identification and data analysis. In recent decades, library managers have expanded into branding the library and the library's resources and services as well as expanding into reaching and meeting the needs of constituents by providing resources and services through alternative venues such as partnerships, co-location, joint use, and so on.

In more recent years, library managers have expanded their own expertise but also reached out to specialists to "brand" resources and services, which includes design, packaging, message, color, personality, and media used by a company, product, or service to create its image or public perception.

Branding is designed to create an image or combined set of impressions and expectations that a constituent has based on interactions with the library, its resources, and services. Additional more contemporary marketing activities include:

- using social media to serve constituents and/or offer resources at their point-of-interest and use
- using social media to market special collections
- teaching constituents how to use customization and social media to reach out to other like-minded constituents for recommending resources, gathering opinions, and collaborative planning for services

Finally, library managers seek benchmark resources to identify trends, validate choices, and design services and resources.

INDISPENSABLE RESOURCES FOR LIBRARY MANAGERS REGARDING MANAGING NEW SERVICES AND RESOURCES

Managers can locate changing services and resources content through association and state agency content as well as from new facilities content. Societal research that identifies trends and changing expectations of users as well as "new" technologies also offers content on not only the new resources themselves but also how to integrate new resources into operations.

"American Library Association (ALA)." Accessed September 23, 2013. www.ala.org.
"Designing Libraries." Accessed October 27, 2013. www.designinglibraries .org.uk.
"The Future of Libraries." Accessed September 12, 2013. www.davinciinsti tute.com.
"OCLC." Accessed October 27, 2013. www.oclc.org.
"The Pew Charitable Trusts." Accessed October 27, 2013. www.pewtrusts.org.
"RUSA." ALA. Accessed December 1, 2013. www.ala.org/RUSA.
"Stephen's Lighthouse." Accessed October 22, 2013." http://stephenslight house.com.
"Steven Bell's Resource Center." Accessed October 27, 2013. http://steven bell.info.
"Top Technology Trends." Accessed September 21, 2013. http://litablog.org/ category/top-technology-trends.
"WebJunction." Accessed October 21, 2013. www.webjunction.org.

DISCUSSION QUESTIONS FOR CHAPTER 7

1. Do traditional services "need" new management styles?
2. People need managing, but why do services need "managing"?
3. People need managing, but why do resources need "managing"?
4. Very few libraries are large enough to have their own marketing department, but does a library manager *have* to add marketing to the set of competencies they must possess?
5. Should library managers in all types and sizes of libraries concern themselves with marketing their resources and services?

Readers are reminded that a case method is intended to be used in conjunction with this chapter. The case designed to be used with this chapter is case 7, "What's Old Is New—If the Money Is There," located in part II, p. 276.

Chapter Eight

Managing Those Outside the "Sphere"

- Coordinating/serving as team members on organizational or internal projects
- Coordinating/serving as team members on external projects
- Managing nonemployee activities internally (IT, construction, buildings and facilities, etc.)
- Managing nonemployee activities externally

A case method is intended to be used in conjunction with this chapter. The case designed to be used with this chapter is case 8, "But Enough about Me—What Do *You* Think about Me?," located in part II, p. 281. The case can be read and discussed before and/or after reading the chapter content.

MANAGING THOSE OUTSIDE THE LIBRARY

Why become and stay involved in managing those outside the sphere?

While one would think that the most important and time-consuming roles and responsibilities, projects, individuals, and groups that managers need to work with should be *primarily* internal—working *only* with library employees—often the most important role and responsibilities can be those existing *outside* internal areas and activities. These individuals and groups—considered external outside the primary sphere of importance—can be as important and sometimes more important than internal work, individuals, and groups.

In fact, managers should reach out—both in-person and digitally—to those outside their sphere as part of their roles and responsibilities to educate external groups, form networks with critical entities, and establish both formal and informal partnerships that will enrich services and resources for constituents. When managers identify appropriate management styles, preferences, and techniques as well as more specific communication processes for their internal roles and responsibilities, styles, techniques, and preferences chosen for external groups are equally as important.

In addition, these secondary areas are diverse and vary significantly by types and sizes of libraries and often change as projects, budgets, and operating and strategic plans change. Specifically, library managers should reach out and establish connections with:

- partners/departments in support of library activities such as institutional technology, buildings, and facilities
- peers and colleagues within umbrella organizations for relationships
- peers and colleagues within umbrella organizations for related library projects/library involvement
- peers and colleagues within the institution for projects designed for primarily external entities such as commercial entities and other related and nonrelated nonprofits
- partners and relationships for external nonemployee activities such as community events

Paradigm Shift 8.1 presents new ways to work with those outside the library.

PARADIGM SHIFT 8.1.
Managing External Forces—Classic vs. Contemporary Libraries

Contemporary managers need to "pay as much attention" to external forces or those "outside the sphere" as they do internal forces. This attention can include: building advocacy, establishing partnerships, and maximizing functions for constituents through, for example, expanding resources and services.

Outside the Sphere—Classic	Outside the Sphere—Contemporary
• Library managers do not serve or only serve as team members with peers in umbrella institutions or other organizations.	• Library managers lead in-person and/ or digital or virtual ad hoc or ongoing projects in umbrella institutions or other organizations; assign employees to serve as members of ad hoc or ongoing teams; and originate ideas for projects/teams, such as emergency management teams (ongoing), United Way (ad hoc/annual), and so on.
• Library managers serve as team members in external projects.	• Library managers are leaders in external environments and originate and lead projects such as events (historic, seasonal, geographic focus for communities; accreditation visits).

Outside the Sphere—Classic	Outside the Sphere—Contemporary
• Library managers work with/serve on teams with projects (ad hoc, ongoing, and as needed) in support of library and organizational activities.	• Library managers manage in-person and digital/virtual teams, team members, and work roles and responsibilities of nonlibrary employees and workers for internal library and library-related support ongoing, ad hoc, and as needed, such as institutional technology, buildings and facilities, maintenance, and so on.
• Library managers and employees and workers assist in nonemployee activities externally such as representing the library at library, library-related, and nonlibrary-related organization or community functions.	• Library managers and employees manage, lead, assist in, and—as appropriate—originate nonemployee activities externally such as representing the library at library, library-related, and nonlibrary-related organization or community functions such as advocacy events and negotiations for support in budget discussions.

REASONS TO BE INVOLVED OUTSIDE THE LIBRARY

Why become and stay involved in reaching out to those beyond the sphere?

Often special or at least different competencies are critical for managers to achieve success in the coordination of institutional (library with other areas/departments) projects; in the coordination of external projects; in membership and activity in both internal and external workgroups; in both managing and coordinating nonemployee activities internally such as institutional technology, new construction, and/or renovation and remodeling of buildings and facilities; and in managing nonemployee activities externally such as advocating for the city's library budget by Friends, foundation, board, and/or community members or classroom faculty supporting the library's request for more space or for migration to a new online system.

Just as library managers need the competencies and skill sets, they need to be considered professionals as well as expert in their field and they also need visibility for themselves and their own operations to communicate value and worth of the organization, its outcomes, and roles and responsibilities. This visibility for themselves and their operations (including employees and stakeholders) comes from systematic, clear, timely, and appropriate reactive and proactive written and verbal communication as well as from role-modeling and opportunities for positive observation of not only activities but also successful ventures.

Not all communication avenues, however, position the library or the library manager as they need to be positioned, and managers often need to and should seek other areas for involvement to project competency attainment, management and leadership strengths, as well as professionalism and unique levels of expertise.

Strengths realized by managing outside the sphere include both management and leadership competencies as well as professional competencies and attributes and include:

- a high degree of generalized, systematic knowledge with a theoretical base
- application of theoretical knowledge to practice
- a primary orientation to institutional, public, and/or community interest
- possessing and exhibiting the principles of service orientation
- enthusiasm and commitment for service to constituents
- exemplification of the establishment of special relationship with constituents
- publicizing what the profession "does" and "is" and specifically value of the profession in general and specifically the value of the library
- possessing the capacity to solve problems other than library and library-related problems
- conducting and using research and data to make data-driven decisions
- commitment to and ensuring the success of the vision or mission of the overall entity in addition to the success of the library
- the ability to plan operationally as well as strategically
- the knowledge and skills for organizing large-scale projects
- the ability to both manage and lead others (in addition to employees)
- the ability to communicate successfully to those within and external to the profession including written and oral communication to individuals and small and large groups (both presentation and public speaking)
- the knowledge and skills needed for money including managing budgets and seeking funding
- the ability to cope with pressures in general, specifically deadline pressure
- all competencies needed to successfully deal with change
- flexibility
- as appropriate, the ability to advocate as well as strengths in political activity
- knowledge of the differences between management and leadership
- the ability to motivate individuals (other than but in addition to employees)

Examples of projects for managing outside the sphere include:

- managing change from one technological system to another such as the organizations MIS or the higher education CMS

- providing leadership in fundraising campaigns including complex, multi-year development campaigns as well as annual events such as United Way campaigns
- coordinating data-gathering such as surveys for issues such as constituent satisfaction, needs, and wants
- coordinating creative endeavors and projects such as designing holiday and community events as well as designing and redesigning web content environments
- managing buildings and facilities/operations issues such as "going green" or integrating commitment to sustainable environments, renovation and/or remodeling, and new building projects
- leading and managing preventive or responsive activities for emergency management
- leading and managing critical incidents
- managing the design of integrating continuous learning in general and specific to employee and partner needs

While managers have limited time for their *own* specific work, the importance of other work and how that work is related—both generally and specifically—to not only the library and the value of the library, but also the library manager and employees, cannot be minimized. Many opportunities through external management and leadership exist. A manager's bookshelf—when reviewing resources for external forces—has a number of resources considered external as well. These resources may include content from other professional associations as well as content from other professions and related agencies.

INDISPENSABLE RESOURCES FOR LIBRARY MANAGERS REGARDING MANAGING THOSE OUTSIDE THE SPHERE

While it is logical for managers to find content about those outside the sphere from "outside the sphere," a significant number of library associations and state agencies offer content on how to work with/best practices on these new relationships. In addition, library research environments (e.g., OCLC) offer extensive data on roles and responsibilities of these individuals in the "life of libraries."

"EDUCAUSE." Accessed September 15, 2013. www.educause.edu.
"Free Management Library." Accessed October 24, 2013. www.freemanage mentlibrary.org.
"OCLC." Accessed October 27, 2013. www.oclc.org.

"State and Regional Chapters." Accessed October 27, 2013. www.ala.org/
    groups/affiliates/chapters/state/stateregional.
"WebJunction." Accessed October 21, 2013. www.webjunction.org.

DISCUSSION QUESTIONS FOR CHAPTER 8

1. Should library managers try to create awareness or educate internal employees who are *not* librarians about libraries in general, such as IT front-
   line workers and managers or buildings and facilities staff members, and
   so on? If so, how should they? If not, why not?
2. Serving as a member of internal and external workgroups is challenging
   and time-consuming. Is it worth a library manager's time to be a member
   of these groups engaged in nonspecific-to-library activities such as United
   Way campaigns, quality service initiatives, or customer service training?
   What are the pitfalls? What are the plusses of serving as a member?
3. Managing nonemployee activities externally requires both management
   and leadership. What are the management activities of special concern for
   external forces?
4. Library managers have a great deal of work to accomplish no matter how
   large or small the organization. Should they concern themselves with
   external management issues of, for example, working with peer managers
   within umbrella organizations? Is it worth the time?
5. Should all types and sizes of libraries reach out to external forces?

Readers are reminded that a case method is intended to be used in conjunction
with this chapter. The case designed to be used with this chapter is case 8, "But
Enough about Me—What Do *You* Think about Me?," located in part II, p. 281.

Chapter Nine

New Management
"in Action" Communication

- In-person, online/remote/virtual communication

A case method is intended to be used in conjunction with this chapter. The case designed to be used with this chapter is case 9, "Suffering from Past Mistakes," located in part II, p. 286. The case can be read and discussed before and/or after reading the chapter content.

TODAY'S SUCCESSFUL MANAGER

Contemporary research has identified reasons why individuals leave organizations after short periods of employment as well as why they leave organizations in general. While data typically show that employees do *not* leave as much for "low salaries" or "lack of money" or other more typical reasons such as "few opportunities for promotion"—data show that exiting employees indicate they leave because they have problems with how the organization has been managed and, specifically, problems with managers. Paradigm Shift 9.1 shows how new methods of communication will improve employee relations.

PARADIGM SHIFT 9.1.
Managing Classic vs. Contemporary Communication for Libraries

When employees are asked what they want to change within their organization, a common answers is "communication." Although different employees need different approaches or levels of communication in order to be satisfied with managers and

(continued)

103

PARADIGM SHIFT 9.1.
(*continued*)

management of the workplace, common issues regarding communication include there isn't enough communication; communication is uneven; communication doesn't occur in a timely fashion; and communication is confusing, including two many messages in one communiqué, and response to communication isn't clear as to who has to do what, post-communiqué.

Classic Communication	New/Contemporary Communication
• Some processes are in place to standardize communication in organizations.	• Many communication processes are in place in organizations (no matter the size or type), and a specific communication structure as well as a communication plan should be in place.
• In-person, print, and e-mail communication are standard communication modes and methods in organizations. After e-mail has been integrated into the workplace, more e-mail communication takes place than in-person or print communication.	• In-person, print, e-mail, chat, text, wiki, blog communication are all standard modes and methods. Managers and employees should design communication plans to identify what mode and/or method should be used for what type of communication.
• Most employees can be reached by communication within the library system even though buildings may be in disparate locations and employees may have diverse schedules.	• Most employees can be reached by online, virtual, and digital communication processes within the library system even though buildings may be in disparate locations and employees may have diverse schedules. In addition, because many individuals work remotely from home in increasing numbers *and* because many branch libraries are in far-flung locations, communication techniques include reaching employees as well as umbrella institution management in remote locations.
• Communication modes such as e-mails, memos, and so on have random subject headings, although print files have standardized subject headings; however, print file subjects are typically not standardized across employees, employee groups, or departments.	• Managers and employees should work together to create—for the communication plan—standardized subject headings for all e-mails, and standard subject headings for all print and digital or online files within departments (all circulation, all reference, and so on) and within employee groups.
• Information from managers is often unique to each manager as per their writing or communication style; however, all communication is	• Information from managers is often unique to each manager as per their writing or communication style. In addition, all communication should be

Classic Communication	New/Contemporary Communication
typically divided into management vs. leadership.	designed to be specific to the situation, such as the decision on whether or not a memo should be a management or a leadership memo.

The foundation of almost every discussion of what makes a manager successful is the manager's management style. A manager's management style and techniques employed are critical for that manager to be a successful communicator. This critical need for the manager to be a successful communicator in new libraries does not, however, include a requirement for the manager to be an exemplary public speaker, nor does it require him or her to possess outstanding writing skills. Instead, the successful manager must identify his or her management style, determine a preferred communication style, and identify what the organization "needs" in terms of communication, as well as what the employees prefer. In addition and especially in today's libraries, managers must explore and adopt—as appropriate—recommended modes and methods for print and oral/verbal communication as well as techniques for in-person and distance communication.

Today's successful managers must realize that—no matter the management or communication style—in all sizes of organizations and in both centralized and decentralized environments, their success in communicating to both internal and external audiences is enhanced by a communication plan that should include consistent, standardized policies, procedures, and practices for communicating up, down, and across work groups.

Today's successful managers should:

- know what communication styles work in general in management, and in specific organizations, and specifically in their organization
- value the identification of communication styles by assessment and be familiar with the varieties of communication styles and assessment opportunities in communication
- determine what type of communicator they are as a manager and determine what type of communicators (in person, remote/virtual) their employees are
- identify who the audiences are for communication including employees, stakeholders, partners, vendors, and—most importantly—governing bodies and advisory bodies
- match the most effective communication techniques and methods with the most successful delivery (in person, online/remote/virtual) of information, content, and data internal and external to the organization

- design and implement the communication plan for the internal and external audiences including styles, techniques, modes and methods, requirements and expectations, and outcomes for success in communication

COMMUNICATION BEST PRACTICES

There are dozens of definitions of what communication is as well as dozens of explanations of communication processes in all types of organizations. In its simplest form, however, communication is a process and the process typically includes content, data, or information being disseminated or distributed from one person to another or from a source to a recipient or from one person to a source. The content, data, or information that is moved or transmitted can include facts, ideas, opinions, and/or feelings—to name just a few things—from one to another. Other definitions of communication focus on the specific act of transmitting the content, data, or information; the way the transmitting takes place; and/or the message being communicated. More expanded descriptions of the process focus on:

- those communicating with a sender's level or depth of knowledge, a sender's skill set or level, a sender's experience or background, a sender's attitude, the environment of the sender, and the sender's style
- the message being communicated or the content, data, and/or information, including the context of the message, the presentation of message content, issues related to the content, data or information, any examples used in the message, the variety of delivery methods possible for the message as well as the need for repetition of content, data, or information to make a point
- the method chosen to communicate, such as specific modes (e-mail, print, online, texting, etc.), the timing needed or required, and any channel issues such as breadth of distribution to recipients
- the receiver of the content, data, or information, such as the receiver's attitude, his or her experience or background, the environment, context, possible interpretation issues
- any feedback from the process, such as nonverbal signals, verbal discussion, or written follow up, and, in addition, any feedback perceived by the sender given signals sent out after the communication is received

While most organizations would like to think that they have specific communication processes in place, most organizations have patterns of communication—not necessarily articulated and standardized processes. In addition, today's organizations currently have so much communication *and* so many communication opportunities, if a defined process isn't in place with expectations, what they have for communication may be ill defined and unsuccessful to all or part of the employees, stakeholders, partners, governing entities, vendors, and constituents. Good managers will:

- value the identification of communication styles by assessment and be familiar with the varieties of communication styles and assessment opportunities in communication. Managers should support the identification of communication styles throughout the organization and should establish the importance of communication by integrating the process of communication into the creation of institutional and management documents such as planning documents (and consider the design of a communications plan); articulating expectations for successful communications; building communication into position descriptions and evaluations of all employees; ensuring successful communication goals are identified for all levels of employees; and identifying ways to maintain successful communication by integrating language of communication into job advertisements and the interview and hiring process.
- determine what type of communicator they are as managers and determine what type of communicators employees are. Although it isn't reasonable to expect managers to identify and then match each communication to each employee, much less constituents, governing entities, partners, vendors, and so on, it is reasonable to expect managers to identify their own style as well as their preferences for communication. In addition, once their own style is identified, managers should attempt to identify employee preferences for receiving communiqués and, if possible, identify preferences on how they might communicate to their employees as well as how they might communicate with their peers and then upward within the organization. Awareness and/or knowledge of both styles and preferences provides managers with the information to select from among a variety of modes and methods to deliver content, data, and information for the greatest measure of success.
- identify who the audiences are for communication including employees, stakeholders, partners, vendors, and—most importantly—governing bodies and critical advisory bodies. Managers should identify all individuals who will be part of the communication process in the organization. A preferred approach to this identification would be to design a communication plan for the organization; however, in the absence of a plan, at the very least each group or individual, both internal and external to the organization, should be identified as to their communication needs, preferences, the best modes or methods for reaching each group or individual, and expectations for each individual and group.

- match the most effective communication techniques and modes and methods for the most successful delivery (in person, online/remote/virtual) of information, content, and data, internal and external to the organization. Managers should audit the variety of types, modes, and methods of communication available to them and others, as well as audit the general and unique communiqués necessary for business operations. Audit results should then be matched to the variety of audiences both internal and external to the organization. Although it isn't possible or necessary to match each communiqué to each audience group or member, in general, managers should match those messages to appropriate audiences for the greatest success.
- design and implement the communication plan for the internal and external audiences, including styles, techniques, modes and methods, requirements and expectations, and outcomes for success in communication. Communication plans—along with styles, techniques, modes and methods, requirements and expectations, and outcomes for success in communication— should include unique issues within the organization. These unique issues take into consideration management and employees aspects such as the culture of individuals and groups as well as the culture of the organization; ethnicity issues; gender issues; audience's ages; geographic differences; locations, including one location vs. multiple locations; possible problems identified for audiences, such as propensities for passive aggressiveness and/or negativity as well as audiences sharing rumors; communicating in person vs. in digital and virtual processes; and performance problems related to employees.

Some recommendations for successful communications are shown in the textbox on the following page.

COMMUNICATION AUDIT

Communication audit content includes answers to both general and specific questions such as:

- What communication should be consistent internal and external to the organization?
- What communication modes and methods have worked and what haven't worked in the past?
- What won't be tolerated in terms of performance related to communication in the organization?

SUCCESSFUL COMMUNICATION

1. Choose consistent terminology for identifying subjects of memos, e-mails, and so on, and create a consistent terminology list with employees.
2. Practice "kiss" or "keep it simple, stupid" and communicate no more than three ideas per communiqué—keeping in mind the most successful communiqués are those where all ideas included are related ideas.
3. Use standardized forms or templates for communiqués, for example, "reports," "newsletters," "minutes," "chats," and "texts."
4. Assess audiences receiving communication and choose the best match of communication (in person, online/remote/virtual) to audience.
5. Require standardized timelines for communicating specific content.
6. Lessen the amount of e-content (in person, online/remote/virtual) reaching employees by structuring forwarding, replying, and aggregating data by balancing commenting, new information, and so on.
7. Structure processes for preparing for meetings, holding meetings, and meeting follow-up.
8. Design "storage," "filing," "archiving," and retention policies and procedures for communication content.
9. Explore best practices for integrating communication content into job advertisements, job descriptions, roles, responsibilities and outcomes, and ultimately, the organization chart as well as all evaluation documents.
10. Choose standardized verbal and nonverbal protocols to signal clarity in reception of communication (in person, online/remote/virtual) to increase organizational and individual and group performance.
11. Identify unique communication issues including delivering bad news, correcting behavior, handling conflict between/among others, as well as dealing with constituent issues. As needed, consider creating scripts or establish specific needed and critical words/issues and language.
12. Establish communication training and education opportunities and provide opportunities for practice.

- What communication training content is available in the organization?
- What communication scripts are available in the organization?

In addition to general audit questions, as part of communication plans, in larger organizations top-level management and in smaller organizations every manager should identify and define the different elements and levels of communication—up, down, and across the organization—such as what is:

1. important . . . is communicated to everyone and when
2. important . . . is communicated to some and who and when
3. important . . . is communicated to employees on a "need-to-know" basis
4. important . . . stays within management level . . . communicated to very few or to no one

5. not important . . . use as needed
6. other (or other categories)

These categories should be discussed and established at least once a year and labeled on agendas; then, meeting notes should reflect those categories. New employees should be introduced to the categories upon hire, and the list should be reviewed annually. Specifically, managers should match formats of communication with levels by deciding:

- What are the ways that the organization currently communicates (in person, online/remote/virtual)?
- What are definitions of A, B, C, and so on (see the previous list), as well as formal and informal channels of communication?
- How should content, data, and/or information be distributed, such as via e-mails (e-list, designated groups, threaded discussions), memos, bulletin board, "in person," electronic, blogs, wikis, virtual worlds/spaces, social venues (e.g., Twitter, Facebook, instant messaging), charts, graphs, and/or illustrative visuals such as mind maps, and so on?
- Who should content, data, and/or information come from?
- What constitutes effective communication in the organization?
- What is appropriate language in communiqués, such as what are appropriate and consistent tag or subject lines?
- How many issues are included in standard communiqués?
- What communication should be in print and what should be in electronic form?
- What specific actions should team leaders and managers do in order to match appropriate communication to employees or team members?

EASY VS. DIFFICULT, GOOD NEWS VS. BAD NEWS

One of the more difficult aspects of a manager's roles and responsibilities is delivering negative information and/or bad news including delivering negative information to the entire organization as well as, for example, correcting an individual's performance or behavior and/or communicating to a constituent that the library's hours have changed and their needs can't be met.

Typically, managers have to deliver negative or bad news often, and an important part of the organization's communication process and plan is the process for delivering not only positive or good information but also all other forms of communication. Although general principles apply for handling these more difficult roles and responsibilities, some specific aspects of delivering this unique communication include:

- don't avoid or delay negative information. Avoidance increases the chances of misinformation as well as rumors being spread. Other timing issues include when in the work day and work week is the best time to deliver information. In general, managers should not deliver negative information at the close of a business day or business week. Doing so contributes to lack of opportunities to ask follow-up questions from internal sources as well as seek help from external sources.
- be clear and brief in delivering bad information. Be specific about what is being communicated and don't bury the "headline" or negative information in other information.
- don't speculate on the situation; just share facts. If there is information you don't know, let the audience know you will find out what the answers are.
- be specific with employee position descriptions and include cause and effect rather than general information to employees as a whole, rather than mentioning vague but possibly more sweeping effects
- identify ways for employees to share or alert their managers if the message is particularly of concern to them
- identify ways employees can cope if the difficult information affects them individually, in teams, or other work groups
- use direct information and avoid softer language that obscures the truth
- avoid the use of any humor
- repeat the message several times—three if possible—in different but clarifying language
- after the message has been delivered, address specific changes and how— if appropriate—employees' roles and responsibilities will change/might change
- choose the appropriate mode and/or method. Note that although general recommendations include not to deliver bad news electronically, it is not uncommon and is becoming more common each day. If there is no other way to deliver the bad or difficult news other than electronically, then address the fact that the method is not ideal but is necessary.
- decide whether to deliver the information in small or large groups. Although breaking a large group into smaller groups to deliver unpopular information may be recommended, the reality is that delivering to a large group contributes to audiences hearing the same issues in the same manner. To avoid members of larger groups feeling uncomfortable in a Q&A session, however, managers should consider techniques for gathering

questions confidentially for audience members. Obviously, delivering performance information that is negative is a one-on-one situation; however, difficult human resources information can include the addition of employee representatives for maintaining fairness for both employees and managers.
• use language that is specific and promotes the feeling of "we're in this together"

UNIQUE COMMUNICATION ASPECTS
IN NEW ORGANIZATIONS

Although there are many unique aspects to communication (in person, online/remote/virtual) in new organizations, there are a number of specific issues in twenty-first-century libraries. These issues include the growing problem of delivering timely, accurate communication in organizations where electronic communication is the primary method of communication; the need to sort out and articulate management communication from leadership communication; the difficulty and unique aspects of delivering difficult and/or bad news to constituents and other audiences; and the unique aspects of emergency and critical communication.

INDISPENSABLE RESOURCES FOR LIBRARY MANAGERS
REGARDING COMMUNICATION

Management content abounds on "communication" in general and specifically communication in nonprofits and libraries. This rich material is due to the fact that technology has driven changing modes and methods of communication. Managers can locate best practices as well as content on training employees. While less information is available on, for example, in-person vs. virtual management and the role of communication, the literature in general is growing and best practices for "virtual communication" and "leading remotely" can be identified and applied.

"Alison." Accessed September 10, 2013. http://alison.com.
"American Society for Training & Development." Accessed August 10, 2013. www.astd.org/Search?q=management.
"Big Dog's & Little Dog's Performance, Learning, Leadership and Knowledge." Accessed October 27, 2013. http://nwlink.com/~donclark.

"Free Management Library." Accessed October 24, 2013. www.freemanage
mentlibrary.org.

"Libguides Community." Accessed September 21, 2013. www.libguides
.com.

"WebJunction." Accessed October 21, 2013. www.webjunction.org.

"Workforce." Accessed October 27, 2013. www.workforce.com.

DISCUSSION QUESTIONS FOR CHAPTER 9

1. Library management communication—as with other professions—has much language unique to the field. Should library managers provide glossaries or not use library terms at all?
2. Should library managers change the language of the profession or have different sets of terms used for actual or print vs. digital or virtual communications?
3. Is it possible to teach others how to write a management memo or communication?
4. Matching communication to individuals (employees, administrators, peer managers, partners, vendors, board members, etc.) as well as matching style and techniques to the issues is time consuming. Is it necessary?
5. What happens if library managers don't match or vary communication styles and use the same communication style with everyone?

Readers are reminded that a case method is intended to be used in conjunction with this chapter. The case designed to be used with this chapter is case 9, "Suffering from Past Mistakes," located in part II, p. 286.

Chapter Ten

New Managers within Classic and New Organizations

- Working with classic and new ancillary groups (advisory boards, Friends, foundations, etc.)
- Reporting to classic and new managers, boards, commissions, and so on/ reporting "up"
- Working with classic and new peers/colleagues

A case method is intended to be used in conjunction with this chapter. The case designed to be used with this chapter is case 10, "What You Don't Know *Can* Hurt You," located in part II, p. 291. The case can be read and discussed before and/or after reading the chapter content.

NEW ORGANIZATIONS

Not only have libraries and library settings changed in the past few decades, but internal individuals and groups such as boards (advisory and governing), Friends, foundations, commissions and commissioners, councils and council members, advisory committees (academic, curriculum), administrators (city managers, principals, vice presidents, associate vice presidents) have changed as well. These changes have altered how library managers report, recruit, organize, coordinate, assign, communicate (up, across, down, in person, online/ remote/virtual), and operate as well as evaluate these individuals and groups and work products.

In general, although libraries have had far more attention and specifically positive attention in the past two decades, most individuals *not* in the profession don't know what libraries, librarians, and library employees "do." This means that library managers must:

- continue to educate these individuals and groups, but with new content as to what libraries, librarians, and employees do
- aggressively recruit (as before), but with different descriptions of what these individuals and groups do for libraries
- seek involvement based on varied skill sets to include technologically ready individuals and group members
- identify new ways of communicating with individuals and groups/group members
- broaden roles and responsibilities to keep those involved up to date, advocating and being proactive in support of the vision and mission of the institution

Some of these new working relationships are listed in Paradigm Shift 10.1.

PARADIGM SHIFT 10.1.
Managing Internal Operations—Classic vs. Contemporary Libraries

Although library managers have always worked with boards, groups, and other supporting entities, contemporary settings call for greater outreach; more orientation, education, and training; and continuous relationship-building for expanded advocacy by library supporters.

Classic Groups in Organizations	Contemporary Groups in Organizations
• Organizations have some interactions between and among peers, departments/groups, and so on; however, beyond standardized meetings, reportage, training, and planning activities, most departments operate as silos or independently of each other unless grant funding or administration requests or requires collective and cooperative behaviors.	• Organizations require integrated operations including strategic planning, communication, marketing, measurement and assessment, and sometimes budget design and decision-making. Other situations that drive or require cooperation include grant opportunities that require entities to work together to submit funding requests, federal issues such as legislative initiatives, local and state law and ordinance, building and facilities issues, need for standardizing technological infrastructure, emergency management and risk issues, and training and education in general and specific to the organization.

(continued)

PARADIGM SHIFT 10.1.
(continued)

Classic Groups in Organizations	Contemporary Groups in Organizations
• Friends, advisory boards, and foundations are active organizations, and members are participants in the "lives" of all types and sizes of libraries specifically for fundraising and development and support for the values and vision of the organization. Additional support is provided for advocating for support from umbrella organizations at the local, state, and national level. Many libraries, however, have governing boards (appointed, elected) who govern the library overall and hire the library manager).	• Friends, advisory boards, and foundations are active in some library settings; however, given the plethora of nonprofits and social service agencies that need assistance, it is becoming increasingly harder to find people to serve in board and organization group support roles. In addition, where financial support is required such as on foundation boards (seen as "giving" boards), individuals are less likely to serve given tougher economic times. • Service issues for governing boards are present as well with fewer people having time to serve as elected or appointed officials, as they are taking second jobs or are returning to work post retirement. • As technology becomes the mainstay for communication and involvement, one additional issue is that individuals available to serve on these groups who are *not* technologically astute or interested become problematic for service since managers find they must maintain two tracks of communication to keep everyone fully informed and active participants.
• Umbrella organizations have a wide variety of types of managers with a variety of management styles and skills. Some have experience and education in nonprofit and not-for-profit environments; some don't. • Many organizations have "revolving doors" for managers given the political nature of the profession. • Library managers are not necessarily seen as cutting-edge managers.	• Umbrella organizations have a wide variety of types of managers with a variety of management styles and skills. Given the greater number of educational and training opportunities with management of nonprofit and not-for-profit curricula, more managers have both experience and education in these areas. • Many organizations have "revolving doors" for managers given the political nature of the profession. • Library managers are viewed as working in areas that are increasingly more technologically driven and thus library managers are viewed as being more cutting-edge managers.

MANAGEMENT WITHIN THE ORGANIZATION

Many managers discover—either upon new employment or assessing exist-ing employment—that while their management of the library is up to date or meets contemporary standards of excellence, management elements (e.g., styles, activities, preferences, etc.) that surround them are not up to date. This realization is often daunting for accepting new employment as well as discouraging for library managers attempting to alter their existing environ-ments. It is also discouraging for library managers attempting to maintain the library's standard of excellence for management. The questions become:

- How long can an organization run efficiently and effectively within an outdated or outmoded management structure?
- Can a library manager stay effective if the umbrella organization within which the library operates is ineffective?
- Can a manager survive if the person to whom they report is an ineffective manager?
- How can a library manager manage "up" when their manager is ineffective?

The easy answers are "I don't know," "I'm not sure," and "Probably not." The longer answers are complicated. Essentially, however, managers must manage across their umbrella organizations, out to their ancillary, support-ing groups, and up to those within umbrella organizations with as much attention to detail and care taken as when they manage "down" within their organization.

WORKING WITH CLASSIC AND NEW ANCILLARY GROUPS (ADVISORY BOARDS, FRIENDS, FOUNDATIONS, ETC.)

Advisory boards; Friends; foundations; external partnership teams, boards, groups; PTAs; and so on are all vital members of the team that assists and supports libraries and library managers in the success of the library's vision and mission. Whether or not leadership and members of these groups is plentiful, functional, or even available, these individuals and groups play an important role in the support of decision-making in the library. A mainstay in the nonprofit world, advisory and membership groups support the library manager by:

- providing avenues for raising and managing funds not legally allowed within the nonprofit and/or not-for-profit financial structure

- ○ establishing networks for financial and volunteer support of the library
- ○ offering leadership, advice, and support for library managers
- ○ providing advocacy for legislative bodies regarding the library vision and mission

• providing expertise for library management such as legal assistance from attorneys, real estate expertise for buildings and facilities, fundraising advice from development officers, human resources advice from personnel or human resources officers, and so on. Library managers—often alone in organizations given their unique expertise, roles, and responsibilities—should continuously cultivate individuals and groups to assist in carrying out the vision and mission of the library. Although organizations might not have ongoing, successful support groups, managers should "grow" individuals by creating a management infrastructure designed to identify, train, and maintain these people and processes. This infrastructure and process should include:

- ○ maintenance of a list of individuals who can assist library managers in identifying community, institution, and organization individuals who can be potential members and/or leaders of groups
- ○ maintenance of a list of individuals in the community, institution, organization, and so on, who are potential members and/or leaders of groups
- ○ creation, adoption, or revision of a manual to serve as a management document outlining group membership, group roles and responsibilities, structure, budget, and operating guidelines
- ○ the integration of support group meetings and activities within the library's timeline/calendar
- ○ identification—as appropriate—of library employees who can assist group leaders and members in their supporting activities
- ○ integration of leaders and members into the library's planning processes
- ○ integration of group goals and strategies into the library's goals and strategies
- ○ design of orientation and training for group leaders and members
- ○ design of marketing brochures advertising products and services of groups
- ○ design of marketing brochures for recruiting group membership
- ○ design of an evaluation mechanism for leadership, member, and overall group success beyond the "achievement of group goals and strategies"

Finally, in the absence of a structure for managing supporting groups, library managers are destined to spend unnecessary time managing the advisory or support group structure and are also at risk—in the absence of control over the process—of group leaders or members creating issues through overstepping, for example, organizational and/or operational guidelines and/or incorrect handling of public money.

REPORTING TO CLASSIC AND NEW MANAGERS, BOARDS, COMMISSIONS, AND SO ON/REPORTING "UP"

Governing boards, commissions, and administrators and managers within umbrella organizations are among the most important elements of library management. Keeping upper-level administrators and managers educated and informed is critical to the success of the library manager. Whether or not these individuals are successful within their own environment, it is imperative that library managers establish modes and methods of working with their supervisors and upper-level decision-makers. Although identifying the importance of successful work with upper-level administrators includes a number of obvious statements, it is important to identify activities to assist library managers in this endeavor. Managers should:

- identify upper-level management's management style and preference for managing others
- identify upper-level management's communication styles and preferences for communicating with others
- review past reports, meeting minutes, and upper-level management's goals and strategies
- identify leadership competencies among upper-level management's structure
- query upper-level management as to how the library manager should work with upper-level management
- create a process for dealing with upper-level management issues that take into account possible expanded work for the library manager (e.g., documentation of needs not met, data on consequences of needs not met, etc.)

Library managers must work within their structure and should decide on a specific approach for dealing with upper-level management. Although organizations might not have ongoing, successful upper-level management or even peer or departmental management processes in place, library managers should create a management infrastructure that maximizes what *can* be done to carry out the vision and mission. This infrastructure and process should include:

- maintenance of a list of individuals who can assist library managers in carrying out the vision and mission of the library. For example, if upper-level management doesn't respond to library management requests, are there others who can "carry the water" for the library management so that the library's business receives the attention it requires?

- creation of a communication plan that is designed for upper-level management and could include, for example, more written content if upper-level management isn't available for meetings and discussions. Other examples for communication geared to the upper level include: more executive summaries of longer content is not desired or read by upper levels; or more content presented in numbers and data rather than narrative if upper-level management only operates with numbers and data. In addition, managers might have someone who can assist them in presenting information with a context the upper-level management might better understand if upper management is not familiar with library context.
- identification—as appropriate—of library staff who can assist the manager in preparing content suitable to the upper-level administration
- design of orientation and training for upper-level administration or integration of library information into existing umbrella institution orientation and training in general (e.g., if the upper-level administration has a strategic planning workshop, briefing, or training, the library manager could present library content within that forum)

Finally, in the absence of a supportive or successful upper-level administration structure, library managers are destined to spend unnecessary time managing and, in general, communicating "up" just as they do with ancillary groups who are not meeting their needs. Clearly when the library manager's surrounding structure isn't doing what it should be doing, the library manager is at risk of looking ineffective as well. Because of this, library managers *must* define a "new" structure for managing "up" to provide the requisite documentation needed to support the effort and contribute to the body of knowledge as to why the library is or isn't having the success it needs.

WORKING WITH CLASSIC AND NEW PEERS/COLLEAGUES

Some of the most important individuals in a library manager's "work life" include individuals who support the infrastructure of the organization (for external peer and collegial and supporting relationships, see chapter 8). Other important individuals include those who operate peer departments within organizations. Library managers work with a wide variety of peers and colleagues "outside" the library but within the organizational or umbrella structure. In most types and sizes of libraries, these individuals vary in roles and responsibilities within their institutions and also within the peer or collegial structure relating to the library.

In contemporary work environments, *everyone's* roles and responsibilities have changed and not at the same speed or in the same way. While some peers or collegial relationships are more important than others, in general, they can be sorted into categories that include individuals who:

- support the library's infrastructure operations, such as the technology maintenance or repair person
- serve as an infrastructure decision-maker, such as the head of institutional technology for the umbrella institution
- serve as a peer in projects, such as the organization's development officer
- serve as support for enhancements for library operations, such as the grants coordinator
- support daily operations, such as the human resources manager
- provide (internal to the organization either by employment or contract) ongoing building and facilities support for new, repair, and renovation construction as well as maintenance
- provide (internal to the organization either by employment or contract) ongoing building and facilities upkeep and maintenance

Although these peers, colleagues, and relationships represent a wide variety of individuals and roles and responsibilities, library managers can provide a management structure for maximizing new elements and activities that characterize these newer relationships. A library manager can:

- design "job" or relationship descriptions for roles and responsibilities to guide both library employee interactions as well as support, peer, and/or colleague interactions
- include these individuals in overarching library communication plans and actions
- determine the best way to work with (e.g., requests, documentation, etc.) these individuals by requesting desired communication paths, preferred and required forms, and modes and methods of communication and reportage
- build these roles and responsibilities into the library's policies and procedures
- build these roles and responsibilities into library management documents including strategic plans, budgets, and so on.
- build individuals into the library processes for gathering data and providing feedback for decision-making
- integrate these individuals and departments into the library's celebratory moments

- integrate these individuals into critical, basic training and educational opportunities

Although the variety of individuals who managers must work with is challenging, a library manager *can* manage the relationships by:

- requesting feedback from all groups and individuals as to how they wish to manage the library work
- building these groups and individuals into the library's work life, management documents in general, and specifically into policies and procedures
- practicing systematic inclusion in data-gathering, feedback, and discussion on what works best for all parties in the library's operations

INDISPENSABLE RESOURCES FOR MANAGERS REGARDING ORGANIZATIONS AND CHANGE

While much library management content for changes within library organizations is available as best practices and examples from existing "in-practice" content, a growing number of resources are being created for all sizes and types of libraries, especially by state agencies and associations. In addition, online communication tools are growing in number as they are being adapted to use with groups (e.g., Libguides or Libguide-like products used for advisory board content in public libraries).

"American Library Association (ALA)." Accessed September 23, 2013. www.ala.org.
"Free Management Library." Accessed October 24, 2013. www.freemanage mentlibrary.org.
"Libguides Community." Accessed September 21, 2013. www.libguides .com.
"State Libraries." Accessed October 27, 2013. www.publiclibraries.com/ state_library.htm.
"State and Regional Chapters." Accessed October 27, 2013. www.ala.org/ groups/affiliates/chapters/state/stateregional.
"WebJunction." Accessed October 21, 2013. www.webjunction.org.

DISCUSSION QUESTIONS FOR CHAPTER 10

1. Should library managers work with advisory boards and governing boards in the same way regarding communication, orientation, and training?
2. Should all types of library boards, and so on (school, public, academic, and special), support the library in the same way, such as having the same management style or using the same management techniques?
3. Who should be the liaison to the ancillary groups such as Friends groups or foundations: the primary library manager, an associate or assistant manager, or another professional in the library?
4. Do library managers report "up" and report "out" to umbrella organizations in the same way? If yes, why? If not, why not?
5. What are the differences between/among professionals working with/managing Friends groups vs. foundations?

Readers are reminded that a case method is intended to be used in conjunction with this chapter. The case designed to be used with this chapter is case 10, "What You Don't Know *Can* Hurt You," located in part II, p. 291.

Chapter Eleven

New Managers in Classic and New Facilities and Environments

- Maintaining, renovating, designing, and building
- Sustainability and/or green in classic/traditional and new environments

---

A case method is intended to be used in conjunction with this chapter. The case designed to be used with this chapter is case 11, "A Fixer Upper," located in part II, p. 298. The case can be read and discussed before and/or after reading the chapter content.

NEWER AND UPDATED LIBRARY SPACES

Although many would argue that libraries need not only different spaces but also *less* space due to increasing digital resources, remote access, and the changing nature of information and information-gathering in general, libraries are still seen as "in-person" destinations for constituents. Library services are still delivered through a wide variety of old and new physical facilities. In fact, libraries continue to "reside" in and operate from antique or historic environments; in joint use and contiguous settings with and within umbrella institution environments; within and contiguous to profit environments; in a variety of retrofitted buildings; and in kiosk, portable, and/or mobile vehicles.

Historically, however, and in today's profession as well, library education programs and continuing education have provided library managers with little to no education or training in maintaining, renovating, and/or designing new construction. While many organizations provide facilities assistance through their own facilities/buildings departments, library managers should consider seeking out opportunities for learning about this critical role and responsibility. Even if managers are not in environments where new or even renovated facilities may be possible, basic roles and responsibilities for managers will include maintenance as well as updating facilities for ever-changing technology in support of library and constituent needs.

Besides newer and constantly changing technology needs, library managers must seek opportunities to become aware of and knowledgeable about sustainable and green business environments. Not only are sustainable facilities responsible to the environment, but also many green or sustainable values and elements contribute to the efficiency and effectiveness of library business operations. While many sustainable issues typically focus on new construction, there are a wide variety of substantive changes that can be made to existing library buildings and to library practices to illustrate efficiency and effectiveness.

In addition, although there is a great deal of information in the profession on a wide variety of building and facilities issues, this chapter is not designed to provide a "guide to building" or a "guide to renovation," and so on. Instead, this chapter is designed to provide information on managing buildings and facilities aspects of general operations along with the range of buildings and facilities issues in today's environments. In the library profession, perhaps more than others, services and resources drive design of the "box" or the building, the internal operations for constituents, and the internal operations for employees.

Managers should also realize that just because a building is old and even historic, it doesn't mean that the library (services, resources, and employees) cannot be cutting edge. Because new buildings or new library spaces are not always possible or even appropriate, many library buildings are widely diverse environments that can include historic, older environments with completely new furniture and equipment; old buildings with old furniture and new technology (very common); as well as combinations of historic and/or older buildings with new additions, or new floors with combinations of older— even antique—furniture with the newest furniture and the newest technology.

Besides basic and advanced changes in buildings, décor, design, and use (many tech-related in nature), there are significant differences in not only user (or constituent) expectations, but also the expectations and ideas from facilities professionals including architects, contractors, space planners, ergonomics specialists, and interior designers. Changes today include the following.

- Architectural and building trends for today's libraries include more contemporary architecture, and diverse styles are integrated with "heroic" elements for public buildings; concern for sustainability; technologically driven design, space, and furniture to accommodate a combination of constituent work and leisure; diverse lighting; and a focus on flexible furniture to provide constituents (working alone or together/in small groups) both public and private spaces as well as options for self-directed access to resources and services, and space for design and creation.

- Managers who redecorate, renovate, or build new facilities experience increased costs, required and often new e-infrastructure, as well as employee challenges for supporting sizes and types of spaces and newer designs for delivering and supporting tech and private/small group spaces, and so on.
- Constituents and/or users want the latest cutting-edge technology as well as support for their personal tech devices (older, existing, and cutting edge); accessible collections; public and private spaces; small-group spaces for active learning; comfortable furniture seating/spaces; food and beverage; meeting spaces for groups; tech resources to use externally and equipment for innovation and production for use by constituents, as well as training and education on using the resources—both hardware and software.
- Specific or special constituent populations want dedicated spaces, hardware, and software—retrofitted as needed for specific populations, public and private work and meeting spaces for special needs, specific materials in diverse formats in dedicated spaces, and unique furniture for special population needs.
- Employees want (for their own environment) their own office space and, if possible, their own offices, their own computers (networked or nonnetworked), and specific software for general and specific productivity, flexible workspaces and furniture, and leisure and/or recreational spaces in work environments.
- Administrators want lower-end square footage costs, shared spaces for libraries and partners, vetted choices in space and furniture or best/effective practices, collaborative and typically nonindividual/shared office spaces, and longer timelines for replacing technology/technology trade-out costs.
- Architects and designers want to please administrators as well as constituents and employees, opportunities to create award-winning designs, heroic spaces, high-level green/sustainable credentials, and opportunities to experiment.
- Librarians want—for their constituents—public spaces with differentiation of services, professionals, and functions; a mix of public and private space, but not hidden/unsafe environments; teaching/instruction spaces with computers for hands-on instruction; space for one-on-one reference assistance; and production/innovation spaces.

FACILITIES DOCUMENTS/AREAS OF FACILITIES CONTENT

To meet expectations of constituents, employees, administrators, and so on, managers must approach all buildings and facilities issues in a consistent and orderly manner. One of the most important areas of this management role and responsibility is the set of management documents that managers must identify, locate, revise, and/or create and maintain for their spaces.

Significant documents and content are delivered in a variety of ways including online forums (with contributions by managers, employees, library supporters, *and* constituents) for finding and posting images (photos, floor plans, products, etc.) and should be used as forums for expression of need (including "wish lists") and ways to communicate with facilities experts both internal and external to the organization. Managers must not only maintain significant documents/content for managing existing resources, but also maintain significant documents/content on "new" approaches to existing areas at the basic "new furniture and look" levels, ideas for remodels and renovations, including ideas for minor renovations of existing spaces or some add-on construction, as well as ideas for new buildings.

The following sections identify the critical management content, files, and documents (including policies and procedures) managers must be aware of, familiar with, and/or knowledgeable about.

Unique Resources

Unique resources such as rare materials, historic structures, and/or furniture, architectural elements, and designations require specific and specialized documentation. Documents include articulated (print, e-content) floor plans, infrastructure plans, utilities information, building assessments, standards, guidelines, checklists, and information about vendor content, decision-making bodies and outlines of how they weigh in, expert assistance, and constituent partners.

Many libraries have unique facilities elements, resources, and/or materials with some designations of historical significance, rare designations of space, as well as areas that house unique resources or are designated as needing special care. While historic buildings and/or rare architectural elements are clearly facilities in nature, rare and unique resources can dictate unique HVAC, lighting, furniture, and/or architecturally driven terms for access and/or use such as "blackout blinds must be drawn" or "door to remain closed" or "only use table lights when viewing resources."

Obviously the most restrictive facilities issues exist with historic or unique building designations, and these can both allow and prohibit activities and certainly drive unique care, budgeting, and decision-making. Additionally, restrictive and permissive content and directions in management content must be maintained for furniture and architectural elements, and—if these items were gifts and donations—donor restrictions must be articulated/in place.

Deal Breakers/*Don't* and *Do* Lists

Documents include articulated (print, e-content) annotated lists with justification of issues and ranking of issues, specific location and/or other specific issues, floor plans, infrastructure plans, utilities information, building assessments, contact people, any timing or date issues, required and/or requested vendors (e.g., sole source, etc.), funding issues, governing issues (e.g., institutional policies, legislation, contracts, grant guidelines), and approvals and/or permissions needed.

While most management lists, activities, presentations, and/or encounters typically don't (and probably shouldn't) begin with "no" or "don't do," managers must communicate roles and responsibilities of employees for facilities issues. Managers, employees, and other stakeholders (e.g., decision-makers, community first responders, etc.) identify what must happen and what must be changed regarding facilities. Specific issues include maintenance activities such as timing, cleaning (products and timing), safety and security needs, and notifications as well as what policies and procedures govern buildings and facilities such as ADA/ADAAA requirements, special populations needs, and the impact of buildings and facilities issues on resources and services such as programming (summer, beginning of school years, peak usage times, etc.).

Prevention and Avoidance

Documents include articulated (print, e-content) lists with annotations ("Deal breakers," "Don't dos") and explanations as needed, built into management expectation documents, and roles and responsibilities for employees regarding good stewardship of resources, commitment to sustainability, and so on. Additional content includes floor plans, infrastructure plans, utilities information, and building assessments.

Managers must communicate roles and responsibilities of employees for safeguarding institutional resources regarding prevention and avoidance as they relate to facilities. Preventing or avoiding issues related to facilities requires identification of specific areas for employees to avoid including timelines, the institutional dos and don'ts content as it relates to prevention, as well as areas such as decisions on a project to avoid expanded costs (e.g., facilities change orders during remodeling/construction). These behaviors should be accompanied by directives such as "avoid high costs by researching choices first before interviewing vendors" or "avoid change order costs by careful vendor interviews, note-taking, and recordkeeping as well as during-project reviews of work stages and products." Additional areas include "avoid paying high costs for special needs materials by aggregating orders among branches." In addition to funding, categories of prevention should include safety, such as "avoid user problems by minimizing and scheduling pest control for non-peak times and building closures" and/or "minimize staff health concerns and focus on employee safety by identifying—within HIPAA guidelines—special needs of employees regarding cleaning, painting, and pest control."

Although prevention is similar to avoidance, prevention in many institutions is more closely aligned with good practices to have to place rather than the combination of "don't do" and "avoid." Specific effective practices for prevention include, for example, having signs for maintenance workers as well as remodel, renovation, and new construction workers. Signs in multiple languages will prevent misunderstanding and should adhere to safe workplace and safety practices guidelines. While this activity illustrates ways to "avoid" mistakes, prevention is a recognized area of emergency management.

People, Places, and Things

Documents include articulated (print, e-content) lists with organized content that includes an identification and retrieval system with justification of content, contact people, specific dates, required and/or requested vendors, and approvals and/or permissions needed.

Managers should maintain a historical, current issues, and future needs facilities record regarding specific files on all buildings and facilities aspects such as repairs, replacements, and new elements (divided by building location as well as facilities areas such as rooms, areas, lighting, flooring, etc.), and vendors used and required, including, when appropriate, sole sources in place based on guidelines, requirements, procedures, and so on. If processes or decision-making is unique, this content should be identified, flagged, and maintained as well. This uniqueness can include but not be limited to cost, selection, and/or designations such as historic issues, unique technology needs, and/or ADA/ADAAA identified spaces.

Cost Issues

Documentation includes articulated (print, e-content) lists with floor plans, infrastructure plans, utilities information, building assessments, justification of content, contact people, specific dates, required and/or requested vendors, approvals and/or permissions needed with content integrated into budget categories, types and codes, as well as accountability with budget forms and/or spreadsheets and links to budget software and purchasing information. Additional critical content includes information built into management expectation statements, and roles and responsibilities for employees regarding good stewardship of resources as in other areas but especially legal issues regarding misuse of monies in organizations.

In consultation with upper-level administration, managers should identify buildings and facilities departments, risk-management officers, local authorities and first responders (e.g., fire, police, etc.), and purchasing departments as well as any vendors (such as sole source vendors), budget rules for expenditures related to buildings and facilities, such as required and/or legal issues for federal, state, and local costs, caps, or ceilings for parts or all of projects, cost issues that trigger multiple bidding, permissions for expenditures, deadlines for costs expended vs. encumbrances, and so on.

Constituents

Documentation includes articulated (print, e-content) information on checklists; signage, internal, umbrella, and/or related internal business communiqués; and press releases, publicity, and marketing information.

Managers are responsible for and must focus on maintaining business continuity during building and facilities issues specifically in the areas of safety and security as well as accessibility to resources and services, accessibility to ongoing and special events, and changes to accessibility, with special concerns for safety and security.

Employees, Internal Groups, and Partners

Documents include articulated (print, e-content) needs on checklists; signage, internal, and umbrella internal business communiqués; and announcements/discussions at employee meetings and meetings with internal groups as well as external including but not limited to worker (or volunteer meetings) board meetings, Friends meetings, and partner meetings.

Just as managers are responsible for and must focus on maintaining business continuity for constituents, they are also responsible for outlining business continuity and management expectations for required and requested behaviors. This content is equally important for the safety and security not only of people but also of institutional resources.

A Plague Upon Your House

Documents include articulated (print, e-content) contracts for pest/rodent care; standards and guidelines for managing and cleaning the library; checklists, vendor content, employee guides for safety, expert assistance, constituent partners, and timelines; and the trail of constituent (if involved) correspondence, public relations, and marketing content to inform and manage what is potentially a difficult situation for the constituents immediately involved.

Whether or not libraries carefully maintain their own facilities to prevent, manage, and minimize the presence of pests and pestilence, the reality is that library facilities have resources coming and going in many if not all areas; incoming items are infected, and resources and materials may be infected, often with little initial visible effects. Managers must maintain careful, specific records of managing these situations due to potential safety, HIPAA, and public relations issues.

Green and Sustainability

Documents include articulated (print, e-content) contracts for maintaining green building and operations credentials; other contracts, standards, and guidelines in general; as well as those unique to green and sustainability, checklists, vendor content, employee roles and responsibilities, and expert assistance.

Library buildings age—as do their furniture and resources—and combinations of old and new elements "clash," such as older buildings and retrofitting for technology. Positive stewardship in today's buildings, however, includes both a commitment to and a budget for green and sustainable buildings, along with careful management of levels of green and sustainable processes and policies. While this commitment often causes more dollars to be spent (not only for supplies but also for remodel, renovation, and new building), the return is great not only for the environment, but also for exemplary management of the library building and its resources.

Unique Facility and/or Space Issues

These issues include but are not limited to remote storage; shared spaces; libraries and the "out of doors"; and outdoor elements brought indoors. Documents include articulated (print, e-content) plans, including floor plans, infrastructure plans, utilities information, building assessments, standards and guidelines for managing and cleaning, checklists, vendor content (insurance adjustors), employee guides for safety, expert assistance, constituent partners, security needs for multiple locations, timelines, and external facility issues such as walks, parking lots, and greenery. Shared spaces with profits dictate additional content such as banking issues, alternate insurance, and cash-handling guides.

Library facilities are more than just designated library locations. Although libraries have always had a variety of spaces, today's libraries include an even wider range of environments as well as unusual library environments. Examples of these unique spaces that dictate management issues include:

- offsite storage for library supplies, and so on
- remote storage for library materials and resources
- partnership space to support Friends, foundation, partnership initiatives
- external library space for constituents such as gardens, courtyards, seating, performance, play spaces
- external library space for design and decoration purposes such as statuary, garden design, donor recognition, and water treatments
- shared for-profit library-related storefronts such as Friends book sales or boutique fundraising spaces
- shared for-profit nonlibrary-related storefronts such as grocery stores
- shared not-for-profit and nonprofit library-related storefronts such as meeting rooms
- shared not-for-profit and nonprofit nonlibrary-related storefronts and/or businesses such as child care, and so on

Additional unique spaces for managers include within the library, water treatments, playscapes, performance spaces, business centers, and productivity and/or innovation and production spaces.

Unique Facility Business

These issues include, but are not limited to assets, risk management, and insurance. Documents include articulated (print, e-content) asset identification with budget figures for business and any legislative guidelines for assets. Other management documents include contracts for facility care, standards and guidelines for managing and cleaning, checklists, vendor content (insurance adjustors), employee guides for safety, expert assistance, constituent partners, and timelines as well as inventories of facilities, equipment, and furniture, insurance information, and guidelines for risk management.

As businesses or sub-businesses of umbrella organizations, libraries must adhere to all local, regional, state, and federal content (e.g., rules, guidelines, legislation) concerning insurance, managing risk (prevention, post-event activities, etc.), as well as managing library resources as assets.

Business Continuity/Continuity of Operations

Documents include business continuity plans for the library, continuity plans for umbrella organizations, and—as appropriate—continuity and/or related plans for partners and shared spaces.

Business continuity isn't a new term, but as libraries expand their own vision of themselves as a business *and* as emergency management and facilities management consume more of operations planning, library managers must expand their knowledge of and skills in designing plans to accommodate general operations as well as interrupted operations due to commonplace facilities issues (e.g., remodel, renovation, repairs) and unique or emergency situations (e.g., treatments, floods, fires).

Parameters

Documents include articulated (print, e-content) behaviors, procedures and processes with documented support for commitments, budgets and actions from standards, guidelines, checklists, vendor content, employee guides for safety, expert assistance, constituent partners, and timelines, as well as stated breadth and depth of impact and application to outline flexibility.

Although parameters of behavior, application, and enforcement should be integrated into individual sections for identification of management depth and breadth of decision-making, the realization of the need for parameters is critical. That is, many library policies, procedures, and processes are absolute in their direction; however, a number of them are *not*. It is important for managers to identify absolute processes, policies, and procedures; however, it is just as important for managers to identify those elements that have flexibility in their interpretations for a clear design and application of employee roles and responsibilities.

MAINTAINING, RENOVATING, DESIGNING, AND BUILDING

As mentioned earlier, few librarians have specific education or training in the management of facilities; however, today's library managers spend a great deal of time maintaining library space, including preventive practices. Managers also spend a great deal of time retrofitting space for comfort and technology, including use of constituent tech devices as well as access to and delivery of content on library devices. This retrofitting for comfort or tech can include remodeling, renovating, restoring, redecorating, relocating, or repairing, to name just a few areas. In fact, whether the space is owned or rented by the umbrella organization or the library itself, managing space is a multifaceted issue and can include maintaining; renovating, and remodeling; and designing and building environments, as well as relocating and sometimes restoring library spaces and other related spaces such as remote storage. While a variety of management issues underpin facilities management, terminology issues are significant when requesting, identifying, or labeling and ultimately delivering new spaces. For example, funding from the library budget, the umbrella institution, a grant, a bond, and/or donors may be tied to how a constituent activity is identified. That is, there may be grant money for a restoration or a remodel, when there is not money for new construction; or occupancy/seating limits in "stack spaces" according to municipal codes may be limited, while "computer-use" spaces may be calculated differently.

Because very few libraries are large enough to have their own facilities manager or facilities department, the majority of library managers have significant facilities roles and responsibilities and because facilities management is its own profession, there is significant content in the discipline to provide structure for outlining these roles and responsibilities. Categories of facility responsibilities for library managers can include a wide variety of areas.

Health and Safety, Risk, and Security

The terminology in these areas is diverse and inconsistent. That is, some entities have an overarching "safety and security" office that incorporates "health" and/or "risk," while other organizations incorporate "safety and health" under "risk." Still other organizations have security issues managed in a separate area, and these locations may change given the organization's officers; that is, an organization can have its own safety and security staff in a security force or in a police department.

No matter the organization of these functions within the library or umbrella organization, these areas include safety-related issues for public and/or constituent areas; general health or prevention issues and occupational safety for employees; risk management and insurance; and protection functions such as security gates, cameras, mirrors, and fire safety. These areas address requirements and the importance of and need for thoughtful design of space, signage, and labeling; hardware, software, and other infrastructure elements such as wiring and wireless; as well as compliance with standards, required documentation, and the awareness and in-depth training, permits, and required/recommended certification. A related area to safety, health, risk, and security is business continuity or the design of the maintenance of operations to minimize or prevent the loss of constituent services or business operations before, during, and following events and activities.

An additional security area for managers is security of institutional and/or constituent data, which can be within this set of library management roles and responsibilities but more likely is within the processes and activities identified as institutional technology for library operations as well as infrastructure and institutional partnerships.

Building Operations

General building/facilities management roles and responsibilities include planning for and supervising the duties of library or umbrella institution employees or outsourced employees related to or involved in building operations. As with any employees, internal or outsourced employee performance oversight includes organization, recordkeeping, and documentation, as well as communication regarding on-demand, routine, and daily as well as scheduled and sporadic building roles and responsibilities.

For all types and sizes of libraries, roles and responsibilities for managers regarding buildings include maintenance. While the overarching concern for building maintenance is 24/7 upkeep or cleaning and simple repair, there are many aspects of upkeep, such as basic, daily, weekly, and in-depth attention, that could include deep cleaning of not only facilities but also heavy use, public service elements including furniture and shelving. Other aspects of cleaning include maintaining facility areas for requisite "wear and tear" and the basics of attention to areas that must be consistently cleaned, such as (constituent, employee) bathrooms, kitchens, as well as employee personal, recreation, or break spaces. In addition to internal or building maintenance, maintenance might also include upkeep for lawns, gardens, walkways, parking lots, and/or contiguous or common-use spaces, given location and—if a rental—applicable contracts.

Additional issues with maintenance and general upkeep include procuring items for maintenance and upkeep; contracts for service for cleaning; contracts for other facilities elements such as internal/indoor plant maintenance; external lawn and garden upkeep; maintenance of infrastructures for constituents, including external lighting, parking lot surface issues, external repairs, painting, roofing, sidewalks, and other library space responsibilities; as well as any building partner responsibilities.

Commercial Property/Rental or Alternate-Use Operations

Specific attention should be paid to library "living" in a rented space or space not operated by the library or umbrella organization. Any number of permutations of issues can exist related to the facility/building. They include contracts; use of the library by primary, secondary, and unrelated constituents; relationships with external vendors; and safety and security issues that might arise from commercial property issues, such as clientele issues and/or problems caused by other renters or owners. Obviously renters in spaces have fewer responsibilities for facilities than owners do; however, it can be more time-consuming to facilitate external workers, contracts, and the repairs process, as well as general maintenance.

Ergonomics/Space Allocation

Identifying and designing successful ergonomic environments and general space allocation for constituents as well as employee nonpublic space, including private/office space, is a primary management responsibility when building or renovating facilities. Ergonomic issues include comfort, logical design, and contiguous and shared space and service issues for constituents and employees. Space management issues include legal issues (e.g., ADA/ADAAA) and recommended spaces for employees, fire safety, lighting, signage air quality, and temperature/HVAC. In addition, comfort levels for constituents and employees now also include food and beverage issues (e.g., library-provided and constituent-provided food and beverage). Additional ergonomic and space allocation issues include:

- ratio of public to private space for constituents
- ratio of public to "behind the scenes" employee space
- dedicated space for ancillary or related workers (Friends, foundation, etc.)
- flexible furniture spaces for constituents to design/redesign
- production space for clients (print, media, and maker space)
- collaborative workspace for clients
- storage space for the library, ancillary groups, and facilities services
- dedicated quiet space

Sustainability and/or Green in Classic/Traditional and New Environments

There is a growing body of knowledge on sustainable and green building and services initiatives. Although much of this content is applicable to libraries, library managers should seek library-centric content by experts with both library and sustainable/green credentials to determine the best approach to integrating a commitment to sustainability into the management of libraries. The need for a multifaceted expert with library experience is even more important for a number of reasons, including:

- standards in green/sustainable areas (new editions every three or so years)
- requirements by some organizations to operate (build, remodel, renovate, etc.) under a certain green/sustainable standard (e.g., LEED certified, silver, gold, or platinum; Green Globes, etc.)
- green decision-making for a library within another building
- green decision-making for historical or unique designations (e.g., state, national historic designations, etc.)

- green decision-making as it drives assignment of space (e.g., public printers in enclosed spaces, etc.)

In general, green/sustainable issues for library managers include:

- commitment to green/sustainable issues in general, including the importance of going green/sustainability to communities, institutions, and constituents
- green/sustainable fundamentals for building activities (e.g., new terminology, costs including impact on operating supplies, space, utilities, etc.)
- integration of green/sustainable changes into the intellectual infrastructure of library management content, including vision, mission, strategies, goals, objectives, outcomes, and both short-term and strategic plans, and so on
- planning for integration of green/sustainable focus into operating budgets
- planning for green/sustainability changes for building infrastructure, including energy; lighting; materials for buildings, furniture, fixtures, and equipment, as well as operating guidelines for building, furniture, fixtures, and equipment; quality of air and HVAC equipment and processes; quality of water and any infrastructure and processes for employee water availability and overall conservation practices
- planning for construction for new and existing spaces
- planning for operations for new and existing spaces

As with other areas of concern for library managers, "who" is involved with going green/sustainability is a critical part of the commitment. These concerns include:

- who is involved in the commitment of the organization to the initiative, including administration of any umbrella and library organizations, public officials, governing and advisory boards, employees, institutional departments such as purchasing and the business office, internal and external partners, affiliated groups including foundations, Friends groups, parent/ teacher groups, vendors, contractors, and constituents, and—as appropriate—groups such as donors and consultants hired, for example, to assist with planning, construction, development, and so on
- who is involved in the strategic and operational planning of the organization
- who is involved in the management of library operations including budgeting
- who delivers services in these "new" environments that focus on green and sustainability

A paradigm shift of nongreen to green environments includes a number of activities and elements.

PARADIGM SHIFT 11.1.
Managing Classic "Non-green" Environments
vs. Contemporary "Green" Environments

Areas/Items	Older/Non-green/Sustainable	Newer/Green/Sustainable
Library Needs New, Existing	• Managers maintain files and processes as well as wish lists for building needs, constituent needs/issues for future renovations, remodels, relocations, and new building.	• Managers maintain files, processes, and wish lists for building needs, constituent needs/issues for future renovations, remodels, relocations, and new building. In addition, managers should maintain lists of identified, related best practices and projects as well as required standards and certification requirements.
Operations	• Managers maintain organizations based on general building standards as well as individually identified issues of e-infrastructure, equipment, space, and operations issues.	• Managers maintain organizations based on general building standards, individually identified issues of e-infrastructure, equipment, space, and operations issues with an overarching commitment to and concern for green sustainability standards and guidelines and maintaining any levels of certification deemed required or recommended by the administration and/or board.
Design—Existing	• Managers bring their ideas to work with architects and designers on spaces.	• Managers' pre-project work includes a review of previous projects and best practices, their wish lists, and identified needs as well as extensive reviews of prior projects of architects, construction companies, and designers.
Equipment	• Files for library equipment are maintained with maintenance contract data, warranty information, special materials, and supply needs, as well as replacement and retirement timelines.	• Files for library equipment are maintained with maintenance contract data, warranty information, special materials, and supply needs, as well as replacement and retirement timelines. Additional recordkeeping is critical to

Areas/Items	Older/Non-green/Sustainable	Newer/Green/Sustainable
		ensure standards compliance and that levels of certifications are maintained.
Supplies	• Lists and purchasing information for library supplies—typically divided into public vs. office supplies—are maintained.	• Lists and purchasing information for library supplies—typically divided into public vs. office supplies—are maintained along with required and recommended supplies needed to maintain certification levels and standards compliance.
Environ	• Environ issues for air, water, power, and—in general—HVAC practices and processes are maintained.	• Environ issues for air, water, and HVAC practices and processes are maintained as well as environ additions needed to maintain certification levels and standards compliance in general, but specifically for power.
Budgeting	• Budget lines are maintained and tracked using general budget codes.	• Budget lines are maintained and tracked using general budget codes as well as new budget lines for green/sustainable required and recommended dollars to be expended and along what timeline.
Communication	• General communication (including signage) is maintained in public and support services spaces and to employees.	• General communication (including signage) is maintained in public and support services spaces and to employees. In addition, signage is posted as needed for green/sustainability information; directions are posted for equipment, services and resources, and education and marketing.

Finally, when the wide variety of library management roles and responsibilities are reviewed for twenty-first-century emphasis and change, the areas of buildings and facilities management are among the most unique. Along with technology, managing space is time-consuming and requires significantly different information and unique, initial ongoing education, as well as extensive and in-depth training and continuing education.

INDISPENSABLE RESOURCES FOR LIBRARY MANAGERS REGARDING FACILITIES

Rich content is available for library managers on facilities including content from architecture and content from a public or library building focus. In addition, there is a growing body of literature on multiuse environments as well as renovation of facilities for technology retrofitting. Online resources that allow self-posting are the cornerstone of extensive visual content to generate ideas as well as communicate needs and wants to architects, designers, and funders. In addition, there are a significant number of revisions of guidelines and standards for facilities practices; these typically emanate from the industry as well as from state agencies and associations.

"American Library Association (ALA)." Accessed September 23, 2013. www.ala.org.

"Designing Libraries." Accessed October 27, 2013. www.designinglibraries.org.uk.

"The Future of Libraries." Accessed September 12, 2013. www.davinciinstitute.com.

"Library Technology Guides." Accessed October 27, 2013. www.librarytechnology.org/LibraryTechnologyReports.pl.

"State Libraries." Accessed October 27, 2013. www.publiclibraries.com/state_library.htm.

"State and Regional Chapters." Accessed October 27, 2013. www.ala.org/groups/affiliates/chapters/state/stateregional.

"Top Technology Trends." Accessed September 21, 2013. http://litablog.org/category/top-technology-trends.

"WebJunction." Accessed October 21, 2013. www.webjunction.org.

"The Whole Building Design Guide." Accessed October 27, 2013. www.wbdg.org.

DISCUSSION QUESTIONS FOR CHAPTER 11

1. How do library managers find out how to manage a facility? What do they read to determine best practices for building and facilities management?

2. Where should library managers "go" to create or expand a skill set in library buildings and facilities for maintaining, renovating, designing, and/or building?
3. Older library buildings fall short in many areas. Should library managers forgo new construction discussions for new building discussions, or are most/all libraries able to be renovated for twenty-first-century services? What should library managers focus on for designing twenty-first-century libraries?
4. Do library managers find green buildings easier to manage?
5. Are green library buildings a thing of the future? Or are they critical to meet contemporary needs?

Readers are reminded that a case method is intended to be used in conjunction with this chapter. The case designed to be used with this chapter is case 11, "A Fixer Upper," located in part II, p. 298.

Chapter Twelve

New "Landscapes" for Library and Information Settings

- New environments (communities, higher education, P–16, etc.)
- Contracts, partnerships, collaborations, and cooperative relationships
- Societal issues—economy, politics

A case method is intended to be used in conjunction with this chapter. The case designed to be used with this chapter is case 12, "Penny's Partners Proliferate due to Punctual, Prioritized, and Positive Planning," located in part II, p. 303. The case can be read and discussed before and/or after reading the chapter content.

THE CHANGING WORLD

Just as libraries, librarians, employees, organizations, and umbrella structures have changed, the "world" around them has also changed. Cities, counties, institutions of higher education, and elementary, middle, and high schools are different and do business differently. Vendors, partners, nonprofits and not-for-profits, for-profits, and commercial environments are involved in the world of libraries; other groups actively involved with libraries include constituent populations such as homeschooler families as well as organizations, associations, and small businesses. Finally, the changes brought about by technology are pervasive in the new landscape of libraries, as all entities not only are now in the "in-person" landscape but also have a presence and are doing business in a digital landscape.

In addition, libraries now have competitors, including businesses with competing resources such as media and print materials (bookstores, rental unit/vending machines); online resource environments (media outlets such as Amazon.com); and private, charter, and proprietary educational environments with and without library support. Finally, some of the biggest changes in the library landscape can be economical and/or political changes that drive:

- changing laws and legislation for typical elements such as facilities and human resources, and for providing and controlling the technology infrastructure throughout the landscape
- costs of technology as well as costs of the frequently upgraded tech environment as systems and processes previously "working" for three or so years now are upgraded at the very least annually and often throughout an annual budget year
- a brave new world of social media revolutionizing communication, marketing, and public relations
- decreased and/or different funding models and budgets for umbrella organizations and libraries
- voluntary and mandated collaborations and partners
- rising costs from vendors
- political powers shifting to downgrade or upgrade the library's image
- community dollars driving fewer new construction projects, and therefore more frequent renovation and remodels

Paradigm Shift 12.1 shows some of these changes.

PARADIGM SHIFT 12.1.
Managing Classic vs. Contemporary Library Communities

The major issue in all landscapes should be change in and of itself, as well as the rapid nature of change not only for libraries but also for all entities in the new landscape. While products such as software and hardware used to change once every two years, then once every year, libraries now see products changing multiple times during the annual budget cycle. Just as libraries struggle with this focus on change, so do all other related environments. Library managers must therefore not only keep up with their specific changes but also keep up with changes in all primary and secondary groups, as well as with ancillary groups and formal and informal relationships and partnerships.

Classic Library and Information Landscapes	Contemporary Library and Information Landscapes
• Communities are defined as the immediate and only environment in which libraries are located.	• Communities are defined as the broad environment, which includes the immediate environment but also more local and state communities, as well as global communities present with the advent of technology.
• Relationships are primarily in-person usage and access opportunities between and among institutions.	• Relationships are technology driven and focus on expanding resources and services and increased access.

(continued)

PARADIGM SHIFT 12.1.
(continued)

Classic Library and Information Landscapes	Contemporary Library and Information Landscapes
• Contracts to identify relationships are entered into by a "short list" of individuals legally designated as representatives of funding areas.	• Contracts to identify relationships are entered into by a broader list of individuals—typically separated out by size of contract.
• Agreements other than contracts are possible for relationships (MOUs, etc.)	• Agreements other than contracts are possible for relationships (MOUs, etc.) and often accompany contracts to identify specific outcomes for all constituents.
• More traditional partnerships with other nonlibrary groups are available and include other libraries, social service agencies, and local businesses.	• The number and type of partnerships have expanded to include the broadest definition of involvement including sponsorships, ad hoc naming opportunities, target constituent support, and so on.

NEW ENVIRONMENTS (COMMUNITIES, HIGHER EDUCATION, P–16, ETC.)

All environments evolve. Organizations, entities, and institutions evolve, and if they don't evolve quickly enough *or* if they don't evolve at all, *or* in today's world if they don't transform more traditional resources and services into tech-driven resources and services as well as integrate technology into "new" environments, changes in the surrounding environment will more than likely leave them behind. These surrounding environment changes represent different entities, altered entities, new entities, and certainly a variety of managers. These new environments include new communities and new educational environments.

"Communities" in the broadest sense of the word change in size, status, and governing entities. In today's world, communities may maintain or increase support for libraries while others might dramatically reduce funding, require funding from outside sources, or require libraries to partner to find additional outside funding. Just as existing communities may change, the reality is new communities are being formed and those communities may exist either digitally or remotely given the reach of technology.

Educational environments today include the P–16 or the life cycle of education from primary through university; K–12 (only); higher education or past high school; and those schooled at home. Today, libraries serve students both in person and in a digital environment. In addition, educational settings now include public and private, elementary, middle, and high schools; homeschooler organizations; the four-year liberal arts educational setting; the classic halls of Ivy League schools; the research ivory tower academy; the thirty-thousand-seat-filled public university institution; the bustling urban high-rise four-year diploma environment; the private alternative educational four-year retreat; and the wide variety of community college environments that house over 60 percent (and growing) of the country's freshman and sophomore population. Serving the spectrum is daunting, and among the biggest challenges are those related to seamless delivery of educational support opportunities to match those in in-person environments.

What do all of these diverse environments have in common in contemporary society and political issues?

- Communities are seeking alternate ways of funding traditional infrastructure, including tech infrastructure and entities such as libraries (e.g., taxing districts, soft money, etc.).
- Student numbers are growing to surpass the capacity of traditional infrastructures (e.g., home schooling and community colleges) at a higher rate.
- Clients and potential clients are shopping for education among all types of educational settings, including K–12 and higher education.
- Program costs, workload, compensation, and instructional issues deter some from shifting from more traditional instructional programs to twenty-first-century instructional and technological models.
- The Internet and info tech and e-reader devices are becoming more widespread.
- Performance expectations for constituents include proficiency in computer literacy, and now computer literacy is accompanied by proficiency expectations for technological awareness and technological fluency.
- Many education structures are changing to focus on design and implementation of programs and processes of "academic accountability, competency-based outcomes, outsourcing, content standardizing, and adaptation to learner-consumer demands" while having to shift data-gathering and assessment to match technologically driven software and service.
- Funding challenges are increasing with critical, ongoing expensive investments needed and fewer resources to meet demands; these challenges force many libraries to move to commercial products and/or consortial programs or offerings rather than investing in substantive and permanent changes in institutions.
- Although constituent profiles are changing, constituents still need extensive support for technology-driven resources (hardware, software, and courseware).

- Knowledge and information are growing rapidly, and some data say that information doubles every four years.
- For-profit educational institutions are the fastest-growing sector in higher education.
- K–16 education is becoming more seamless between/among high school, college, and further studies. Higher educational environments are blurring . . . specifically two- to four-year environments.
- K–12 environments are experiencing shrinking budgets.
- Successful identification and marketing of value is required for all types and sizes of organizations, especially libraries.
- Higher education is looking outside standard operating procedures and processes for outsourcing opportunities and partnerships with other colleges, universities, companies, and other kinds of institutions to share technology and to produce and deliver courses.
- Political environments are requiring extensive accountability for tracking and spending funding, including goals, strategies, and outcomes.
- Political environments have long required elements be present prior to funding availability, including matching dollars and multitype goals. Additional credentials for contemporary entities include new areas, some of which are geared to political party content, such as "an organization must be family friendly before it receives funding" and/or "institutions must pledge levels of sustainability prior to eligibility." More than before, contemporary libraries must show evidence of partnerships prior to eligibility for funding.

CONTRACTS, PARTNERSHIPS, COLLABORATIONS, AND COOPERATIVE RELATIONSHIPS

Relationships such as partnerships, collaborations, cooperatives, and contractual arrangements are prevalent in many professions such as social work, adult education literacy education, religious or church work, P–16/educational settings, governing entities, and libraries, to name just a few environments. These relationships are diverse and represent connections between and among entity managers, individuals, groups, organizations, and entities to share interests, share concerns, create visions for the future, and, ultimately, better serve constituents.

Historically, relationships are formed to educate, open discussion, and solve problems among all parties involved. In addition, there are as many different types of relationships as there are names for relationships. They can be both formal and informal and can include outreach, collaborations, cooperative agreements, access statements, arrangements, consortiums, contractual agreements, MOU (memorandum of understanding) relationships, liaisons, facilitators/facilitations, joint-use, contiguous services, and or "just" relationships. Other terms that may be used synonymously for discussing serving or supporting constituents between or among environments include articulation agreements, guidelines for service, constituent support agreements, universal service agreements, affiliation agreements, statements of service, service commitments, cooperative service agreements, and service plans. In addition, other than "contractual agreements," the majority of terms can be found in both formal and informal definitions. No matter how you identify the relationship, entities within relationships can include:

- public libraries
- academic libraries
- special libraries
- school libraries
- constituent groups (homeschoolers)
- workforce environments (federal, state, and locally funded entities)
- employees (as groups)
- employers (as groups)
- corporate/profit sector
- related nonprofits (museums, etc.)
- social service entities (federal, state, local, etc.)
- government/governance (local, state, national, international)
- educational environments (P–16, homeschoolers, etc.)
- social groups (book clubs, literature circles, etc.)
- organizations (Boy Scouts, Girl Scouts, Boys & Girls Clubs, etc.)
- associations
- religious environments
- foundations
- health care environments including profit and nonprofit/not-for-profit
- commercial sectors (corporate sectors, small businesses, etc.)

Trends for relationships by type of library include activities in academic, public, school, and some special libraries. Academic libraries are playing a major role by extending their reach through relationships, mutually beneficial alliances, and creative ventures. These activities update/change library images, share expertise, and promote services. In order to successfully partner with others, many libraries are assessing older mission and goals statements and designing broader vision, mission, goals, and outcomes to match the changing institutional vision and to play a leadership role in partnerships. Higher education libraries are:

- expanding their roles of support for students, faculty, and employees, including expanding partnerships for research, grants, and fundraising
- articulating and marketing their support and partnership expertise as librarians-as-discipline and/or department liaisons (increased embedded librarians, cross-departmental support for curriculum, etc.)
- becoming increasingly involved in campus-wide interdisciplinary programming and cross-departmental partnerships such as college orientation, career counseling, tutoring, alumni outreach, parent programs, family focuses
- increasing marketing for their service and expertise in research support
- creating a role of assistance in institutional enterprise activities (bookstores, publishing, research)
- moving out beyond campus walls to provide and partner with a wide variety of groups and individuals (K–12 community members including work with students and teachers, hospitals—beyond the health sciences workforce curriculum)
- working with community commercial entities with research support for small businesses

The constant twenty-first-century changes in the public political and social arena are forcing public library managers to rethink their vision and mission, strategies, outcomes, and institutional roles; restructure their image or "rebrand" themselves; and reposition themselves within city and county government and community life. Public library managers—longtime supporters of the "whole" community—are now finding they must partner with others in order to offer complete up-to-date services. Public libraries are:

- working with P–16 environments in creating new public librarian teaching roles critical to working with the new info-laden public
- articulating and marketing their expertise as information specialists
- expanding marketing of their role as information specialists to support small businesses and community enterprises with space, research and resources, hardware, and software
- returning to (post-1960s levels) involvement in community workforce relationships such as job placement and career information
- realizing they must create a formal educational support role for distance learning in support of P–16 environments and proprietary educational institutions

The constant twenty-first-century changes in K–12 (P–16) educational environments are forcing school librarians to rethink their vision and mission and school/educational role, reinforcing their teaching role responsibility and image, repositioning themselves within their schools' and districts' technology arena, and educating constituents about their role in providing relevant and available resources in the broader community beyond students and school walls.

School libraries are playing a role in this new collaborative environment by thinking outside the box for strategic partnerships and becoming involved in discussions/collaborative relationships for themselves and their constituents. School libraries are:

- expanding their roles of instructional support for students, faculty, and employees
- articulating and marketing their expertise as discipline/department liaisons within and across districts
- becoming increasingly involved in school interdisciplinary programming and cross-departmental partnerships
- moving out beyond campus walls to provide and partner with a wide variety of groups and individuals

Special libraries are typically not able to form extensive external relationships due to the presence of and concern for proprietary content as well as management practices for client billing for all employees within the environment. These entities also seek assistance in offering digital content, and special libraries in greater numbers are joining consortia and other relationships to meet the needs of their unique constituents. Special libraries are:

- forming relationships for delivery of content in digital formats
- entering into relationships with consortia to expand digital content
- seeking environments to assist in their delivery of professional development and continuing education

No matter the type of entity, however, the same general reasons to form relationships and partner apply and include:

- maximize resources
- economize
- solve a problem
- make money for the umbrella institution
- indicate worth for services within an environment
- give good/better constituent customer service
- information literacy

- meet a need
- change an image
- create a need that should be there
- do a good deed
- provide access to information, resources, buildings, services, and experts
- serve the unserved and the underserved (new and existing service and non-service populations)
- build community with the broadest definition of the term

The specific benefits for relationships with umbrella environments (cities, countries, academic institutions, businesses, P–12, and P–16 environments) include:

- recognition of the variety of roles that libraries play—both traditional and nontraditional—in the life of the organization as a whole
- an opportunity to form internal partnerships and collaborations as well as external roles
- in higher education—increased involvement with enrollment in the institution as families view higher education as more accessible and "possible"
- in K–12 environments—the opportunity for employees to learn about, work with, and bring "in" the parents of children as well as to meet them in other parts of the community and workplace
- forming a base to justify local/statewide funding as others view partnerships as an efficient and effective use of money
- consistent and effective attention and instruction in twenty-first-century learning/skills needed
- opportunity to access unique collections/services and information and individual expertise

The specific benefits for relationships with communities include:

- a more organized/better-prepared/better-educated twenty-first-century citizenry
- a more knowledgeable constituent/potential user who sees opportunities in information environments and maximizes resources
- a more solidly networked and informed community—everyone now knows what the others are doing
- creation of a network of people to "make things happen"

And, no matter the type or size of entity, the specific benefits for all types of libraries are:

- an increase in the network of library supporters for library activities and future needs (bond issues, funding battles, legislation, etc.) as well support for the relationship activities themselves
- an increase in the information network that improves services for constituents
- visibility for library services/activities as well as visibility for partnership and collaborative activities
- library employees energized by new activities, new recognition, new services, and possible new skills
- greater knowledge base of people who know what the library is and what it can do
- increased dollars, for example, to increase access for new partners expand collections for different constituents, and so on
- public relations and marketing opportunities
- opportunity to discover and access new and unique collections, as well as increase collection size and design and create new collections and ways to access
- possible increase in employees to handle new arrangements, temporary or permanent

Library managers must understand that studying both success and failure is critical to new success, and no matter the type or size of entities, relationships fail. Identifying what areas might be within the control of managers to minimize failure is a critical step in data-driven decision-making. Although no one can guarantee control, failures can be a learning experience.

SOCIETAL ISSUES—ECONOMY, POLITICS

No one is sure whether politics drives the economy or whether the economy drives politics. That being said, both the economy and politics—local, state, federal, and international—drive both profit and nonprofit environments. In recent years, however, the rapidly fluctuating economy, as well as major political issues and in some places turmoil, have contributed to libraries and other entities seeking relief from "going it alone." Instead, they have turned to creative ways to work together to function in not only new but also everchanging landscapes.

While *extreme* social and political environments exist throughout the country, post-9/11 issues often dictate restrictions on funding, fewer dollars but a strong need for upgrading, different visions for "doing business," and dramatically different focuses for global and local activities. All library managers must deal with politics of all kinds in all types of institutions on a

REASONS FOR FAILURE

- In evidence but possible to control:
  - beginning activities without documents in place
  - no group discussion of vision
  - no broad education of all stakeholders/users
  - rumors . . . in general and left unattended
  - done to save money/not spend money
  - no early buy-in
  - too long a process

- Less evidence of control possible:
  - administration/management changes
  - out of our control (access to public buildings after 9/11)
  - uneven power
  - forced into it
  - big project designed and not enough money came in

SOCIETAL AND POLITICAL ISSUES

- General societal issues:
  - change and change driven by technology
  - different values among partners and potential partners
  - keeping up with tech funding (maintaining, upgrading, migrating)
  - critical need for win/win successful partnerships when people aren't educated in teamwork and/or partnership relationships
  - critical need to express business results in outcomes and impact terminology not only for libraries but also for library partnerships

- General political issues:
  - bipartisan support for providing overarching funding to upgrade and maintain structures
  - economic downturns driving party platforms or political agendas
  - changing parties in power
  - frequent turnover in political power
  - no turnover in political power
  - political wrongdoing (any party) that causes uncertainty and instability in government
  - local, state, and federal regulations that change "how entities do business"

daily basis. Just as communities (county, municipal, and parish) have political and social leaders, academic institutions have new presidents and boards, and the K–12 arena has new principals and superintendents. Special libraries are not immune to general politics, either. They also must deal with changing management and the ever-changing profit margin, which affects all of the organization's departments. So, although library managers are advised not to declare political or social support or allegiance, they must be versed in all political and social aspects of their environments.

INDISPENSABLE RESOURCES FOR LIBRARY MANAGERS REGARDING NEW LANDSCAPES

Although identifying information about partners and those outside the immediate sphere of libraries isn't difficult, the challenge for library managers is to relate that content to their organization. Considerable information is available on partnerships, cooperatives, and consortial activities, although it is typically not divided up by size of library, nor is there a great deal of content on how different types of libraries partner the same or differently. Content on the future—specifically economic changes, doing business differently, and working with institutional technology—is growing and provides direction for managers. Association content has a growing body of collaboration and similarities and differences (e.g., EDUCAUSE) as well as best-practice recommendations for working with others.

"American Library Association (ALA)." Accessed September 23, 2013. www.ala.org.
"Designing Libraries." Accessed October 27, 2013. www.designinglibraries .org.uk.
"Free Management Library." Accessed October 24, 2013. www.freemanage mentlibrary.org.
"The Future of Libraries." Accessed September 12, 2013. www.davinciinsti tute.com.
"Ken Haycock & Associates Inc. Blog." Accessed June 23, 2013. http:// kenhaycock.com/blog.
"Libguides Community." Accessed September 21, 2013. www.libguides.com.
"Librarylawblog." Accessed September 30, 2013. http://blog.librarylaw.com/ librarylaw.
"Library Networking: Journals, Blogs, Associations and Conferences." Accessed October 27, 2013. www.interleaves.org/~rteeter/libnetwork.html.

"OCLC." Accessed October 27, 2013. www.oclc.org.

"The Pew Charitable Trusts." Accessed October 27, 2013. www.pewtrusts.org.

"Stephen's Lighthouse." Accessed October 22, 2013." http://stephenslight house.com.

"Top Technology Trends." Accessed September 21, 2013. http://litablog.org/category/top-technology-trends.

"WebJunction." Accessed October 21, 2013. www.webjunction.org.

DISCUSSION QUESTIONS FOR CHAPTER 12

1. Libraries used to be considered the "heart of" the institution, the community, the school, and so on. Should library managers consider that same perception to still be in place? If so, how should they nurture that? If not, how should they return to/create that?
2. Should library managers reach out to establish relationships and form partnerships with other libraries in their areas? Or should managers consider all libraries as competition for funding?
3. Do global societal issues affect all types and sizes of libraries? If so, how do library managers plan for and cope with these global issues?
4. Do local societal issues affect all types and sizes of libraries? If so, how do library managers plan for and cope with these local issues?
5. Should library managers assume a political stance or take a political role in the community? If so, what role? If not, why not?

Readers are reminded that a case method is intended to be used in conjunction with this chapter. The case designed to be used with this chapter is case 12, "Penny's Partners Proliferate due to Punctual, Prioritized, and Positive Planning," located in part II, p. 303.

Chapter Thirteen

Managing the Balance to Meet New Constituent/Customer Expectations

- Traditional and new constituents
- Traditional and new expectations

A case method is intended to be used in conjunction with this chapter. The case designed to be used with this chapter is case 13, "Keeping Up with the 'Joneses,'" located in part II, p. 313. The case can be read and discussed before and/or after reading the chapter content.

TRADITIONAL AND NEW CONSTITUENTS

It stands to reason that if society and almost everything else changes regarding libraries, their constituents will be changing as well. These changing constituents bring both old and new expectations with them, and library managers find themselves attempting to please not only existing constituents with possibly more traditional or classic expectations but also those newer constituents with contemporary and cutting-edge technology expectations. Due to the varied constituent populations using all types and sizes of libraries today, library managers find themselves:

- defining and redefining target population needs with greater frequency, including assessing more specific population needs regarding technology, e-resources, and e-services
- challenged by budgets that, for the most part, can't meet all traditional and contemporary constituent needs

- using shorter timelines for strategic planning to allow for the greatest flexibility to meet changing needs
- choosing to shift dollars among accounts and thus services and resources to meet varied needs
- thinking creatively about meeting traditional and contemporary in-person and tech constituent needs through both formal and informal partnerships

Paradigm Shift 13.1 outlines these changing issues.

PARADIGM SHIFT 13.1.
Managing Classic vs. Contemporary Constituent/Customer Identification in Libraries

Reaching out to today's mix of constituents means using marketing and assessment techniques as varied as the target populations they serve. Given the breadth of constituent issues and expectations, managers find providing and matching services and resources to constituents—for maximum use—one of their most important tasks. This important task begins with identifying changes in constituents and their expectations.

Classic Constituents	Contemporary Constituents/ What Does It Mean for Management?
• Constituents have some of their own technology and bring it to the library such as laptops.	• Constituents have *much* technology and their technology is often newer and more diverse than the library's. For example, libraries offer laptops and constituents have laptops, smartphones, iPads, e-readers, and so on. Managers must balance expenditures among different formats, hardware, and software.
• Constituents "use" the library and library resources in person, over the phone, and by fax.	• Constituents "use" the library and library resources in person, over the phone, by fax, and in many if not all digital and virtual methods such as text, tweet, e-mail, blog, chat, and so on. Managers must decide—in consultation with employees—what and how many delivery venues are used for library services and resources.
• Constituents are typically referred to as patrons or users as well as by their specific target populations such as "students." Some variance in identifiers occurs by type of library (e.g., "patrons" is used more by public libraries while "users" is often used by special and academic libraries).	• Constituents are referred to by a wide range of identifiers that vary by both type of library and user profile. Managers must choose how they will identify their users for general operational and strategic planning as well as marketing and public relations.
• General classic use of libraries has always been for information and	• Constituents use libraries—no matter the type or size—to meet their

Classic Constituents	Contemporary Constituents/ What Does It Mean for Management?
research assistance and content such as books and periodicals as well as access to media and unique materials for target populations. This includes, for example, public libraries for lifelong learning/education, culture, recreation, and information; school libraries for recreation and supplemental curriculum information as well as training in research skills; academic libraries for research and information and training in research skills; and special libraries for specialized, in-depth information on narrow topics such as a library in the advertising agency for marketing and branding information.	information, research, recreational, and cultural needs. That includes using all types of libraries for curriculum support for in-person and online academic support, accessing all types of information and research online, using technology (hardware and software), and consulting librarians as experts to assist in information seeking and research. Managers must lead communities and umbrella organizations in the realization that libraries are changing environments and continue to change based on assessment of constituent needs.
• Constituents seek and use information, media, and research from authors, illustrators, researchers, and so on.	• Constituents seek and use information and research from authors and researchers and produce *their own* information, media, and research and participate in the library's web publishing program or publish on their own/in their own web environment. Managers must decide, with employee input, on the provision of newer services for constituent self-publishing.

Traditional Constituents

What we call or name our library constituents varies dramatically by geographic location, and by type and size of library. Identifying constituents can also change by time period. For example: Is it summer reading club time? This fall should we push for freshman or first-year information-literacy classroom integration rather than last year's graduate school focus? Should the middle school teachers be our target for the design of online science/STEM information pathways this spring due to spring testing?

In addition, there are typically a number of backstories in organizations about identifiers chosen such as, "It's always been done that way," or "The community center identifies seniors as such, so we do as well," or "The last principal asked that we work with/identify our testing focus for her middle school teachers but only STEM faculty." Managers should choose library constituent identifiers or monikers for communicating and marketing services and resources appropriately and should establish parameters for identifying needs of library constituents as target populations for assessing outcomes.

The number of identifying terms used in libraries today is surprising and includes (in no particular order of current or suggested use) general terms such as *patron, customer, user/nonuser, borrower, visitor, reader, member, guest, learner, constituent*; specific terms (in no particular order of current or suggested use) including *students, faculty, employees, toddlers, babies, children, youth, young adults, adults, seniors, older adults, alumni, families, high school students, homeschoolers, elementary school students*; or terms by part of town/community/county/township or status; by students in a *particular* institution; where individuals live; or by the living arrangement such as *homeowners, apartment-dwellers*, etc.; by level or type of matriculation (*freshmen, sophomore, distance learners* etc.); by status in family or life (*single parents, parent*, etc.); by general occupation such *businesspeople, executives*; and by special populations, such as *visually impaired, homebound*, and/or *differently "abled."* Identifiers can also be chosen either to reflect an interest, talent, or competency or to market a service or resource, such as "the library has added a computer center/training room for basic and intermediate level computer users," "social media users," or even more specifically "the library has expanded its research workstations to include Macs to accommodate the growing population of Mac users." In general, identifiers can be:

- used temporarily or permanently
- used publicly for general communication such as signage, publicity
- used publicly for identification
- used publicly for tracking if self-selection or sign-in is necessary
- used publicly for marketing
- used internally for management purposes including tracking, recordkeeping
- used internally for reportage
- used internally and externally for fulfilling requirements of groups such as umbrella institutions, communities, partners, and so on
- standardized for measuring library use, such as how much and by whom across constituents groups

The first step in identifying who constituents are includes deciding what constituents should be called or named. Choosing appropriate names or identifiers for constituents historically and in contemporary times continues to be a moving-target process, but the reality is that organizations and communities should choose identifiers through researching a number of elements in the environment that include:

- what contemporary societal practices for identifying people are, in general
- what general contemporary societal practices for identifying people are in the state, region, community, and/or a specific environment
- what specific needs or directives the organization defines or has defined for identifying users and nonusers (e.g., what an umbrella organization might require)
- how constituents prefer or expect to be identified or have self-identified to the institution
- what identifiers need to be in place to ensure any necessary and appropriate tracking, measurement, and overall record-keeping

Specifically, identifying people as *users* or *nonusers* is a popular choice; however, managers should ensure that the library does not place too much emphasis on serving or gathering information only for those who are *using* the library. In addition, contemporary issues of *ways* to use libraries has dictated that users and nonusers be further subdivided into categories such as electronic or in-person users or both—with even further breakdowns possible by types of electronic users such as those accessing e-resources vs. those using e-reference, and so on.

The positive aspects of using *user* and *nonuser* are that the terms can be broadly applied, do not represent only specific or target populations, and can be used for all types of libraries (including situations where partnerships among types of libraries require identifying and counting in the broadest sense).

The negative aspects of these terms include the levels of detail and breakdown of terms needed in some environments, and the lack of specificity needed for some measurements and assessments. In addition, for marketing purposes some managers feel that the term *nonuser* indicates someone that is aware of services and resources and has chosen not to use them rather than someone who is unaware of the services. With the latter, some managers identify these individuals as "potential" users, separating them from nonusers and labeling them as someone they have yet to reach and convince of the value and importance of the library.

While there are more classic terms such as *patron*, *borrower*, or *reader*, many feel that these are limiting terms and, sometimes, *politically* limiting. For example, *reader* might discourage individuals from using the library to learn *how* to read if they assume that only those who *can* read can use services and resources successfully.

Constituent, which has been typically used for voting indicators or levels of responsibility for individuals by appointed or elected officials, *does* imply that these individuals are those for whom the institution has responsibility. If managers and/or administration don't feel that it introduces the aspect of politics too much or in a negative way, the term *constituent* meets a number of needs.

The most important aspect of naming isn't the name or identifier only, but the process put in place for choosing identifiers. These processes vary but should include input from a number of people within and, as appropriate, external to the organization—in some cases with input from the constituents themselves. Within this process, managers should consider:

- seeking input from constituents through surveys, ad hoc committees, or focus groups
- seeking input from governing boards/umbrella institutions
- managing the process or seeking input through advisory boards
- assessing what the environ "calls" individuals or how others identify the people for whom they are responsible
- working with partners to coordinate identifiers to standardize terms and data-gathering
- piloting terms to gather responses and data from target populations

Managers must also maintain lists of terms identified as "politically charged" or "politically incorrect" that should *not* be used, as well as terms once appropriate that should be altered or replaced. Terms such as *residents* and *citizens* are often now considered problematic because, for example, in academic institutions, tuition is based on elements of residency or "membership." Also, individuals in communities, institutions, and/or districts of service may not be residents or considered homeless. An additional example is one where immigration and border issues (legal and illegal) as well as naturalized citizen issues have caused the word *citizen* to be removed from the lexicon of library constituent identifiers. *Not* using these terms isn't because resources, programs, and services aren't designed for them; instead, they aren't used to avoid pejorative identifiers and perceptions of exclusion.

New/Changing Constituents

Most library managers would agree that library constituents have changed dramatically over the past ten years. In almost every category of constituent status or interests, including desires, needs, competency levels with technology, reading and learning levels, and ownership as well as experience with technology, constituents use libraries, resources, and services in classic, new, and cutting-edge ways.

A variety of organizations and associations responsible for and interested in change and the future and in identifying constituents' future preferences, needs, and desires have identified general issues driving behaviors as well as describing or defining today's constituents. These issues include different experiences, education, and attributes. Today's constituents may differ because they:

- view technology as basic to living and a successful lifestyle
  think they know more about hardware and software than they really do
- have experienced rapid change in the past fourteen to fifteen years (dog-year change)
- are more used to change and/or rapidly changing environments
- have (typically) shorter attention spans that match and adapt to more rapidly changing activities and environments
- are attracted to contemporary marketing in general and often more unique marketing techniques designed to attract and keep constituents' attention
- are not aware of or (if they are aware) don't value tradition and traditional ways of research processes and finding information (e.g., everything online is good and new and everything in print is old and out of date)
- are often not culturally literate and appear to know contemporary and current "factoids" and not actual facts, and not historical references
- are more skilled (than previous constituents) in being "self-directed" but are not used to or don't know how to work well with others in small groups or in teams
- desire and often need context or frame of reference, such as, "How does this specifically relate to me/my job/my future?"
- are trying to "multi-task" and balance multiple work environments as well as family responsibilities
- need continuous opportunities to develop their critical-thinking skills and, as such, need problem-based instruction, training, and education

TRADITIONAL AND NEW EXPECTATIONS

Paradigm Shift 13.2 contrasts some differences in older vs. newer constituent expectations for library services.

PARADIGM SHIFT 13.2.
Managing Classic vs. Contemporary Constituent/Customer Expectations for Libraries

Classic Expectations	Contemporary Expectations
• Materials in libraries are placed in specific locations based on age level and subjects using a variety of organizational schemes (LC, Dewey, NLM, and so on). There are limited acquisitions publications; therefore, materials are easier to identify and acquire, and fewer formats mean fewer budget lines; therefore, funding lines are easier to manage.	• Materials are published in a wide variety of formats; material reviews are published in print and online publications, and content is available and accessible in all formats. Because of the diverse content available and the broad reading levels that often vary among formats (e.g., titles published in both adult monograph and young adult graphic novel form), materials are located throughout the library. Given the footprint of the library, funding, constituent needs, and hours of operation, managers must assess how the collection is arranged in both physical and online environments.
• Constituents expect to need help to find what is needed.	• Constituents feel—often incorrectly— that they can find what they need in electronic environments by themselves. Managers must ensure that instruction in both identification and use or application of resources is available through training in information literacy for employees who serve constituents by creating web environments, identifying readily available content, designing content specific to the library's needs such as choice of online links to generic or general instructions, as well as instructions both in print and online specific to the library.
• Constituents understand that libraries do not allow—for the most part— drinking or eating throughout library spaces. This doesn't mean, however, that they *don't* bring in drink or food throughout library environments.	• Constituents are used to having drink and food throughout previously restricted environments such as bookstores, boutiques, academic environments, and around technology. Therefore, given relaxed standards in both public and private environments, constituents not only seek the right to bring in drink and food but also expect many environments to provide access to (for sale, donation) drink and food. Managers must identify the safety, maintenance, commercial/enterprise,

Classic Expectations	Contemporary Expectations
	and legal issues surrounding the allowance and provision of drink and food in library spaces.
• Constituents expect that most library resources, services, and assistance are available for "free" or, more specifically, "pre-paid" from taxes, tuition, and so on. Primary financial interactions emanate from usage issues such as overdue materials and fines and fees. In addition, managers have found ways to raise money as well as provide aspects of constituent support (printing, paper, pencils, etc.) by working through third-party groups such as Friends, and so on.	• Constituents are not surprised at and sometimes expect to pay for some library resources and services. Managers—educated as nonprofit managers—have struggled for years to integrate enterprise aspects into library environments. Library managers have worked with third-party groups such as Friends, foundations, PTA, as well as umbrella institution departments for fundraising, fines and fees, and providing enhanced services for fees (rental "bestsellers," vending machines for office supplies, etc.). Managers design amenity RFPs, negotiate contracts for services and rent, and work with the food-safety industry and with vending and third-party businesses (e.g., cleaning, maintenance, etc.).
• Constituents are used to libraries of all types and sizes being relatively consistent in their environment.	• Constituents are used to both public and private environments changing more often, and some seek and enjoy the logical change that many libraries employ to integrate high use, marketing, a match of resources to services and programming, as well as ease of access into their resources and services. Managers should strive to balance marketing and browsing, for example, to determine areas appropriate for change based on assessment of constituent needs and desires.

Whatever the terms used for library constituents, these individuals have new and diverse expectations for hardware, software, services, resources, and programs in all types and sizes of libraries. These diverse expectations include classic or traditional expectations as well as contemporary and cutting-edge expectations. Examples of today's expectations include:

• access and hardware to provide online information research resources education at not only academic but also public and school libraries, including access to either print or online textbooks

- standardized, articulated infrastructure for constituents accessing hardware and software internal and external to the library, as well as the ability to use their own hardware and software within the infrastructure
  updated computer technology within the library
- technology available to take to class and to take away from the institution/home/other work environments
- 24/7 access
- infrastructure for offsite, remote use of the library's resources
- access to cloud work and storage spaces
- comfortable public spaces
- individual work spaces
- creation or innovation spaces including collaborating spaces and maker spaces
- private spaces for individual and small- and large-group work
- food and beverage available or at least allowed
- free "membership" including access to facilities and resources for all types and sizes of libraries
- "single-service" environments (*not* moving among desks or departments for service)
- a wide variety of partnerships and collaborations to enhance their access/meet their needs
- green/sustainable facilities and resources
- instruction, training, and education in finding and using information resources and research content, and in using hardware and software
- support for homeschooling families
- support for alumni
- printing
- current materials such as bestsellers
- extensive genealogy content
- local materials
- opportunities for secured uses such as testing for educational programs (e.g., in public libraries, in schools other than the one they are enrolled in) "live," synchronous assistance 24/7 or as much as possible
- assistance during traditionally "closed" hours
- opportunities for feedback

In addition to these more general expectations, specific constituent groups will have specific expectations.

Expectations by individuals or groups other than children exist; these specific individuals or groups will include many diverse groups and their expectations will vary dramatically. Management's role is to create processes

---

EXAMPLES OF SPECIFIC CONSTITUENT EXPECTATIONS

- Expectations by children and for children's areas (by children, parents, caregivers, teachers, family members, etc.)

  - Children's area hardware and software are safe for children to use.
  - Children's areas are for play, especially when spaces look like children's/play areas.
  - Circulating all library materials for children outside the library is part of the service (e.g., if they are for me/children to play with, why can't they be removed from the library/taken to classrooms, care centers, home?).
  - Children can be left unattended because there are employees here hired to provide children's library services (e.g., it looks like a safe area, so I can leave my child unattended).
  - Children will play here quietly; therefore, parents and caregivers may leave (e.g., the area, the library, attend library programs elsewhere).
  - Children will pay attention to a storytime performance by themselves so parents and caregivers can leave the area.

- Expectations by many youth, pre-teen, teen, young adults

  - It is likely I won't get good customer service because of my age; that is, adults will always receive service before I do.
  - They aren't going to have the most current materials (e.g., graphic novels, the latest movie, the music I like).
  - My advice or opinion is not likely to be sought after or valued.
  - Using libraries is [not cool, old school, and so on], and I don't want my friends to see me [using the library, with a book, etc.].
  - I probably know more about technology than they do.

---

to identify individuals, groups, and expectations, and to make balanced, data-driven decisions regarding resources, services, and programs. In addition, managers must employ all exemplary customer service techniques, both general and specific to type and size of library, to provide environments that meet identified constituent needs. To this end, managers should design customer service programs, physical environments, and digital environments; employ targeted communication and marketing techniques; and continually assess how libraries, library employees, library spaces, and library resources, services, and programs meet needs.

INDISPENSABLE RESOURCES FOR LIBRARY MANAGERS REGARDING CONSTITUENTS

While general resources provide excellent information on society at large, association and agency content can provide targeted content on existing, potential, and the changing nature of constituents from all types and sizes of libraries. In addition, expert analysis on societal constituent trends provides a solid foundation for managers, and library research content (e.g., OCLC, Urban Libraries Council) offers constituent profiles with needs, wants, and overall expectations.

"American Library Association (ALA)." Accessed September 23, 2013. www.ala.org.
"Designing Libraries." Accessed October 27, 2013. www.designinglibraries .org.uk.
"Ken Haycock & Associates Inc. Blog." Accessed June 23, 2013. http://ken haycock.com/blog.
"Library Networking: Journals, Blogs, Associations and Conferences." Accessed October 27, 2013. www.interleaves.org/~rteeter/libnetwork.html.
"Library Research Service (LRS)." Accessed September 23, 2013. www.lrs .org.
"Library Technology Guides." Accessed October 27, 2013. www.librarytech nology.org/LibraryTechnologyReports.pl.
"OCLC." Accessed October 27, 2013. www.oclc.org.
"The Pew Charitable Trusts." Accessed October 27, 2013. www.pewtrusts.org.
"Resources for School Librarians." Accessed October 27, 2013. www.sl directory.com.
"Stephen's Lighthouse." Accessed October 22, 2013." http://stephenslight house.com.
"Top Technology Trends." Accessed September 21, 2013. http://litablog.org/ category/top-technology-trends.
"Urban Libraries Council." Accessed October 27, 2013. www.urbanlibraries .org.
"WebJunction." Accessed October 21, 2013. www.webjunction.org.

DISCUSSION QUESTIONS FOR CHAPTER 13

1. Should library managers in all types and sizes of libraries strive to meet all of their constituent needs—specifically, all desired technology needs?
2. What should library managers expect from constituents?
3. What factors play a role in library managers trying to achieve balances between constituent expectation and the realities of providing library facilities, services, and resources?

4. Do constituents from all types and sizes of libraries have the same expectations?
5. What two things do contemporary library managers do to balance constituent needs and expectations?

Readers are reminded that a case method is intended to be used in conjunction with this chapter. The case designed to be used with this chapter is case 12, "Keeping Up with the 'Joneses,'" located in part II, p. 313.

Chapter Fourteen

Accountability, Measurement, and Assessment in New Management Organizations

- Seeking input and gathering and tracking for data-driven decision-making

> A case method is intended to be used in conjunction with this chapter. The case designed to be used with this chapter is case 13, "Torture the Data," located in part II, p. 319. The case can be read and discussed before and/or after reading the chapter content.

THE IMPORTANCE OF ACCOUNTABILITY, MEASUREMENT, AND ASSESSMENT

While all libraries have always been required to be responsible for any public and private dollars, today's libraries are now required to be accountable in greater numbers of ways and to greater audiences. This accountability is greater in today's fiscal environments as technology drives diverse numbers of formats; formats—ill defined in many budget codes—are purchased across the budget-code spectrum; technology varies dramatically in cost; and technology costs for maintaining and upgrading occur at multiple times across an organization's budget year. In addition, since partnerships are often focused on technology, partnership costs (through contracts, subscriptions, etc.) also have divergent timelines and varied budget codes.

Funding from umbrella institutions, whether from private funders; voter dollars; federal, state, and local dollars; grant dollars; or any source, must be managed for accountability, income and spending, appropriate and legal application of dollars, the value of the "dollar" as well as where and how the money is spent, and—the hardest accountability of all—outcomes attributed to use of resources, services, and facilities funded. Ensuring accountability for outcomes includes managers having data and rationale to answer the questions:

- Did the money spent reach target audiences or constituents?
- Did the resources and services fulfill outcomes promised?
- Did funding have the promised impact on target audiences or constituents?

Because of the increased need for accountability in today's libraries, library managers must justify expenditures, design outcomes for dollars, track expenditures within accounts by funding agencies and organizations, and illustrate value as well as effectiveness and efficiency.

Accountability, measurement, and assessment in libraries are issues with diverse activities and meanings. Accountability or responsibility in libraries today goes beyond fiscal accountability or accountability for completing or ensuring successful goals, objectives, and strategies. In addition, few can identify "one recommended way" or even just one or two best practices for measuring and assessing resources and services for accountability. In fact, not only do different kinds of libraries measure and assess in different ways, but also accountability, measurement, and assessment can vary from state to state, regionally, from federal to state agency requirements, within or among consortia, within grant guidelines, based on umbrella institutional requirements, and at local levels.

Traditionally, libraries have used a wide variety of methods to identify accountability and measure and assess use of their resources and services. Although the concept of measuring results (e.g., use, costs, customer satisfaction) and/or success of programs and services is not new in the profit and nonprofit business world, a focus on accountability by measuring outcomes or desired and actual impact of programs and services is becoming the norm. In addition, for many umbrella organizations and granting agencies, accountability through outcomes and impact is now required for most library environments.

Because so many environments now require extensive accountability, institutions must acculturate all library managers and employees in the importance and required elements in building measurement and assessment into all processes and activities. Creating this new culture of value and use of measurement and assessment is a critical process and includes:

- expanding accountability elements beyond fiscal and umbrella organization accountability
- defining the value and role of measurement and assessment in the organization overall and in organization documents

- identifying and integrating an overall assessment model not only for the organization, but also one that builds on the umbrella organization's measurement and assessment practice
- identifying (in position descriptions and in orientation and training) library employee roles and responsibilities in the assessment process
- designing opportunities for assessment throughout the organization including ongoing, single-shot, short-term, long-term, and pilot opportunities
- encouraging overall departmental, service, and program assessment as well as one-time event/activity measurement
- identifying and nurturing assessment as an employee expertise/focus
- creating ad hoc and/or ongoing assessment teams and team leaders
- creating incentives for design and support for assessment processes in general, as well as rewards for measuring, assessing, and—as needed—correcting identified problems

Accountability

Since a primary responsibility for managers is accountability, managers must embrace the fact that they are accountable, responsible, or "answerable" for all events, actions, decisions, activities, outcomes, and results, as well as enforcing policies of the organization. Included in the responsibility for all operations, resources, and services (and all rules and policies guiding them) are all fiscal matters of the institution as well as the ethics of institutional "behaviors." Many management philosophies identify multiple areas of accountability and include management, administrative, political, legal, ethical, stakeholder relationships, customer satisfaction, and all financial or fiscal areas. Historically, "moral" accountability is included in the identification of responsibility; however, in most organizations today, ethical responsibility is included, but "moral" responsibility is not.

Managers are not the only individuals accountable or responsible within the organization, however, as all library employees are and should be individually responsible for their own actions, their roles, and responsibilities in work groups or divisions such as departments, projects, teams, or committees, and for their roles in institutional outcomes and results.

Whether or not a manager is in a public or private institution, a nonprofit or not-for-profit environment, or a profit/business environment, they are accountable to their governing entity and to their constituents. Accountability must be:

- of primary importance to the manager, all library employees, and all decision-makers

TYPICAL LIBRARY MEASUREMENTS

Collections/resources (e.g., print, digital/online, hardware, software, etc.):

- number and type of items in the library/available through the library
- number and type of items used in-house/internally
- number and type of cataloged resources (e.g., media, print, etc.)

Constituents/patron/customer/stakeholders—digital, in person:

- number of people who use materials (e.g., check out books, browsing, internal/room use)
- number of people attending programs
- number of people who use a service (e.g., by age, home zip code, etc.)
- levels of customer satisfaction (e.g., by age, by event, activity, etc.)
- usage counts (e.g., e-entry/access/door counts/page counts, etc.)

Programs and services—general:

- number of programs offered (e.g., by age, interest, etc.)
- numbers and types of databases used
- attendance (e.g., in person/virtually) at programs

Programs and services—education/instruction:

- pre- and post-use of library resources with library instruction/information literacy/user education presentations, classes, etc.
- awareness and/or use of resources designed for constituent use (e.g., wikis, blogs in online resources guides), general and pre- and post-presentations, classes, etc.
- awareness and/or use of widgets in general and pre- and post-library instruction/information literacy/user education
- awareness and/or use of web gateways designed by the library
- use of modes and methods of virtual/digital reference
- tutorial use/performance on tutorials (e.g., completion rates, grades, etc.)
- grades on classroom assignments after librarian assistance
- behavior toward library and/or information use of resources
- awareness of library resources and services
- knowledge levels regarding existence and use of library resources
- attitudes toward library resources

Facilities/space:

- square footage including measurement of different library areas, departments, public space vs. private/employee space
- locations (e.g., number of, variety, etc.)
- space needs (e.g., space per constituent, space use per constituent, space per department, resource area, etc.)
- money
- money spent on resources (e.g., capital, operating, bond, grant, etc.)
- money spent on programs and services (e.g., capital, operating, bond, grant, etc.)
- programs and services "cost" per constituent, by use
- organizational income/inputs

- governed by appropriate policies and procedures
- governed by law and/or legislation and ordinances, and so on
- based on policies, guidelines, and rules of the organization and any applicable fiscal oversight such as guidelines
- the "responsibility" of all employees and decision-makers

Accountability is everyone's job and therefore measurement must be everyone's job as well.

Measurement

All types and sizes of libraries have been counting and keeping track of what they have, what they do, their constituents (users and nonusers), and how they are used by constituents for many years.

Newer areas for measurement include more in-depth use of e-resources and relationships (e.g., type of partnerships, consortia, resources available, and use due to relationships). In addition, contemporary measurement seeks to:

- standardize data forms
- standardize data collected
- standardize measurement terminology among resources, vendors, and so on
- standardize measurement—as possible—among types of libraries
- standardize measurement—as possible—among sizes of libraries

Other measurement issues in contemporary libraries include the following.

- Today's commitment to measurement includes a strategic approach to counting and tracking including a commitment to tracking training for all employees of primary organizations and organizations with whom they have a relationship.
- Although counting—both simple and complex—includes filling out templates and forms for activities and events and at public service desks, and identifying and gathering processes for pulling data from vendor and constituent data, all counting and tracking must be integrated into orientation, basic skills, advanced skills, and unique skill sets for specific individuals in the organization. In addition to basic training, managers must define and instill a commitment for measurement and assessment to ensure that employees have awareness, knowledge, and commitment to integrating measurement processes into business operations. This commitment to measurement includes the orientation and training content mentioned above

as well as the design and distribution of measurement commitment statements, expectations integrated into job descriptions, performance measures built into employee evaluations, and the identification of process owners for measurement activities.

- Managers understand and communicate to employees that just because you *can* prove it or count it or measure it doesn't mean you should.
- Because libraries have counted for years, many numbers are archived and available and historically meaningful, but not necessarily required for today's data-gathering profile. Tracking and forms should be consistently evaluated for continued and/or ongoing data-gathering.
- Managers understand and communicate to employees that just counting or measuring does nothing unless it is reported within a framework or for a specific outcome.
- Managers must assess all performance language (goals, objectives, strategies, tasks, outcomes, etc.) to match data gathered to assessment measures. Data gathered that is not matched to performance language should be analyzed and—as appropriate—altered or discontinued.
- Focused or snapshot counting can be as successful as bean or hash-mark counting.
- Contemporary measurement (counting and tracking) includes not only employees recording content (in print and electronically), but also vendor data, software data, and data gathered by equipment. Because data must be specific to performance statements (goals, objectives, strategies, tasks, outcomes, etc.), ongoing data-gathering must be systematic but does not have to be hourly or daily data or to be event- or activity-based. Data that can be gathered systematically but not consistently can be gathered through snapshot or focused tracking that includes defined events, activities, and routine but less frequent counting. For example, the number of hours of computer use—rather than gathered every hour open—could be gathered two specific weeks and two matching weeks in the spring and summer. Comparing and contrasting data between or among years must match the number and choice of weeks.
- Many measurements are required by the umbrella organization: from local entities or guidelines and rules, from state law/legislation and regulatory agency, regional guidelines, federal law/legislation, regulatory agency, and/or partnership tracking, requirements for membership, and so on. Besides library performance measures, other organizations and entities may require that data be gathered and reported, for example, to meet overarching performance needs, to meet membership requirements, or to meet reporting requirements for funding opportunities.

Assessment

Counting and tracking activities is not enough to provide data for account-ability to all who request or require data to illustrate performance of services and resources. Instead, counting and tracking data must include comparing and contrasting data to support or refute performance.

Why do we assess? Libraries need to assess to address the contemporary questions:

- Why isn't the (school district, city, county, umbrella organization, business, company, etc.) funding the library?
- Why don't decision-makers understand what the library provides for its constituents?
- Why doesn't the umbrella organization value what we do?
- How do we prove our worth to our constituents? Our decision-makers?

But libraries need to address the contemporary questions with more than past simple answers, such as:

- because we are the heart of the institution
- because we are the fabric of the community
- because pooling resources to support everyone is good business
- because everyone knows education is important and libraries are education
- because we said so

In fact, to answer questions, libraries have assessed materials, resources, services, employee performance, and constituents, as well as facilities, for decades. Assessment content has been used to identify types and frequency of use of materials and resources, customer satisfaction and preference, successful public relations, and marketing, to name just a few areas.

Although all of these areas of assessment are still of importance for today's organization, contemporary assessment in libraries seeks to integrate the importance of assessment into all employee activities, organizational functions, and organizational decision-making. In addition, contemporary libraries seek to focus assessment results on how libraries identify worth and demonstrate value. To this end, for creating a culture of assessment, organizations should:

- design a statement of commitment to assessment
- use the statement of commitment to assessment as a foundation for a culture of assessment in the organization
- articulate the importance, role, and value of measurement, evaluation, and assessment in all appropriate organizational/institutional documents

- build an assessment model to mirror the governing organization's measurement, evaluation, and assessment
- identify all employees' roles and responsibilities in assessment of the library's functions, programs, and services; reflect roles and responsibilities into job descriptions and performance evaluation
- identify and design opportunities for assessment throughout the organization
- build training and education about assessment into the organization's professional development
- identify and nurture assessment as an organizational expertise
- identify individuals and groups to serve as assessment teams and team leaders
- create incentives and rewards for integrating assessment into organizational activities and functions

Following the creation of a culture of assessment, organizations can focus on why there is a need for accountability and/or a need to assess. While the basic answer might be "demonstrating value and worth in libraries is good business and—in some organizations—is required by governing entities and regulatory agencies, and so on," reasons to assess for value and worth include a critical need to answer the following questions.

- Why should the library exist in the [city, county, college, school, company, community]?
- How does what the library provides matter to and/or make a difference for the constituents for whom they are responsible?
- Why does the library [save clients and/or constituents money, improve interactions with the organization, provide critical products for the company, affect or improve the quality of life]?
- In the midst of cutbacks, why does the library need the same level of funding?
- Why does the library need more funding than last year?
- Why should the library receive more funding than [police, fire, parks, road maintenance, legal, and so on]?

Answering these more in-depth questions is possible with both general information and information by both type and size of library.

GENERAL METHODS FOR LIBRARY ASSESSMENT

There are many long-standing *and* contemporary library assessments that generate data. These general methods for library assessment should include a focus on identifying, gathering, and applying general library data through contrasting, comparing, identification of context, and use of outcomes and outcomes language to provide immediate value, worth content, measurement, and assessment appropriate for all libraries. Specifically, both classic and contemporary general processes for assessment include:

- inputs (what goes into or what is invested in the library, such as funding)
- activities, resources, services, outputs (what the library has created, provided, delivered)
- constituents (characteristics and profiles)
- outcomes (the effect and/or impact of what the library has created, provided, delivered on the constituent)
- interpretation (expanded impact including what it all means, why it all matters)
- historical perspective, such as inserting a historical probe as a cause and effect
- comparing and contrasting, such as comparing support now to support prior to the last bond funding, budget year of significant increase, and so on
- pre- or post-significant evens such as pre-9/11 vs. post-9/11
- case method for problem-solving and decision-making
- scenario method for speculating about and identifying the future and identifying the impact of the future or "what if"
- storytelling from the organization's, employees', or clients' perspective
- futures, such as using the Delphi method of identifying future issues, needs, or predicting needs based on expert knowledge from an identifying expert or a panel of experts; forecasting, including gathering data from models, experts, and basing predictions based on analysis of data, and trend analysis with identification of meaningful and appropriate trends identified to meet needs
- statistical analysis software package or formula analysis of research data gathered
- benchmarking as comparing and contrasting data from similar environments
- best practices as comparing and contrasting data from identified, vetted, recommended environments

General methods for gathering data for assessment work best with outside facilitators, interviewers, and researchers who work with constituents, staff, stakeholders, partners, individuals in governance, and so on, using:

- interviews, using scripted questions for specific or random individuals (interviews gather levels of knowledge, awareness, attitude, and behavior change and assist in increasing levels of awareness of individuals)

- focus groups, using scripted questions for general or invited individuals (focus groups gather awareness, general attitude, behavior change, and assist in raising levels of awareness and educating individuals)
- observation studies (observing individuals allows for gathering information about behaviors, behavior change, and usage patterns and competency levels)
- surveys (surveys gather attitudes, identify levels of importance, satisfaction, and awareness, and provide base knowledge and can also provide self-assessments)
- tests (tests can be conducted pre- and post-events, activities, and instruction and can determine if attitudes were changed and if an individual learned a skill, gained awareness, and/or adopted a practice; in addition, standardized tests can demonstrate knowledge)
- e-analysis (log or data analysis from subscription e-resources or web environment provides content on what was viewed, how often, for how long, as well as pathways to reaching/finding data or "usage patterns")
- self-assessments (self-assessments can take place pre- and/or post-event/ activity and can also include journaling, where individuals write about experiences, skills acquired, attitudes changed, application of skills in specific settings, and grades)

Other specific ways for tracking and counting data include but are not limited to:

- constituent assistance (online: e-mails/chat; in person: in-library, office hours, class, small group, large group, etc.)
- percentage of constituent populations, such as target populations, grades, disciplines/curriculum supported electronically
- percentage of budget spent on "e" vs. print
- percentage of collection available electronically
- number/use of print titles vs./in relation to online subscriptions
- number/use of e-books (reference vs. circulating, e-reserves, fiction vs. nonfiction)
- number/use of/type of "other" including digital collections/repositories, stored materials, and so on
- resource use/assessment such as scholarly vs. popular, and so on
- pre- and post-use of resources in libraries offering instruction/orientation
- awareness and/or use of resources designed for constituent use (wikis, blogs, online pathfinders) in general and both pre- and post-assessment
- awareness and/or use of widgets in general and pre- and post-information literacy

- awareness and/or use of gateways
- use of modes and methods of virtual/digital reference
- identification of resource and service benefits by constituents
- identification of resource and service benefits by constituent usage
- benefits of online content (identified, designed, etc.) to constituent groups
- benefits of online venues vs. in-person venues
- library perception by constituent groups
- attitudes toward library resources
- knowledge(s) regarding existence and use of library resources and basic application
- behavior toward library and/or information use of resources
- use of methods of assessment including quantitative, qualitative, input/output, and outcomes measurement and assessment
- using research methodology including best and effective practices to illustrate value, benefit, and worth

Assessment by Type and Size of Library

Public Libraries (City, County, or 501c3/Nonprofit)

Public libraries use all general types of assessment. Due to the amorphic constituent group and privacy issues, however, public libraries have a more difficult time gathering data longitudinally, data about individual or specific constituent knowledge and skills/abilities, and data from remote users. In addition, given the nature of the reference interview, it is hard to identify constituent needs and measure outcomes by identifying impact and affect.

In some states, public libraries must assess to meet standards and guidelines of umbrella entities. Additional specific types of measurement that gather appropriate data in public libraries include: surveys, general and specific invitation focus groups, e-analysis for aggregated data, and some observation studies. The smaller the public library environment, the harder it is to use labor-intensive assessment modes and methods. With the advent of online and/or web-based resources, smaller libraries with fewer employees can gather data using surveys that include web-delivered content and internal print surveys.

School Libraries

School libraries use all general types of assessment. Additional specific data for student learning is possible and includes longitudinal data (as students progress from grade to grade and as they move among reading levels), data from standardized tests, outcomes data from pre- and post-testing, and data from some observation studies. Other assessment includes counting and tracking data to meet accreditation standards and guidelines from state and regional environments, as well as relevant standards and guidelines from associations at both the state and national level.

Special Libraries

Special libraries use all general types of assessment. Additional assessment is possible—in the aggregate due to privacy and proprietary issues—regarding client use as well as use of resources. Additional assessment in special libraries includes value of information to clients and to the organization, and worth of information and research services.

Academic Libraries/Higher Education

Academic libraries use all general types of assessment. Outcomes assessment, which is the primary assessment used to evaluate student learning, is critical to the success of the library within the academic institution. It includes the design and delivery of information literacy curriculum to match educational outcomes and any state, regional, or national competencies (such as SCANS competencies). Additional specific assessment is required for regional accreditation as well as for accreditation for specific subject disciplines. Other specific accreditation assessment includes, for example, how many social sciences faculty use and assign social sciences print vs. online materials; the depth of the library's philosophy collection in relation to the size and coverage of the curriculum for philosophy master's and doctoral programs; and evidence-based library/health-sciences-specific assignments integrated into core and advanced curricula.

Although most association standards are not required for practice, they provide benchmarks and best practices to guide libraries in designing and delivering resources and services. Standards include ACRL's thirty-plus statements that outline suggested quality and quantity as well as recommended concepts and functions; other association standards, such as guides for delivery and support of distance learning and architectural and design guides; and state regulatory agency mission statements for statewide best practices.

Data-Driven Decision-Making

Managers make decisions based on data that include education, experience, intuitiveness, facts, and supposition, to name just a few elements and activities inherent in the decision-making process. While a combination of one or more of these elements constitutes data-driven decision-making, contemporary governing bodies and funding entities seek more data in general, as well as more specific data.

In meeting the data needs of governing bodies and funding entities, managers must look at data in diverse ways including types of data; the order in which data should be used; enhancing with data; the research on data; and examples of data. The choice of what data to use—if there is flexibility in what content to provide—depends on a variety of factors that include what is required, who is seeking data, what data best illustrates content, what best convinces those requiring or requesting data, and what data is the most accurate. General processes include:

1. identify what the organization needs to report on and/or prove
2. identify any specific data—one- or two-dimensional—that you already gather or count
3. gather general data (local, regional, statewide, national, partnership, etc.) that is specific to your type, size, or assessment
4. compare data against "other" general data by categories, need

Data More Common and Less Common to Libraries

More Common to Libraries

Manager/Librarian Opinion—Although it may depend on the type and/ or size of library, no matter the expertise, unique training, education, or experience of the manager and/or librarian, individual opinion may not be enough to convince decision-makers of large-scale funding and/or need. Managers should always include this data (and present it as data); however, they should use this as indication of agreement, different views, and/or in general part of the rationale for choices or recommendations.

Anecdotal Data—Historically libraries have gathered and used constituent anecdotal data that is requested as well as gathered without specific solicitation and instead through general feedback opportunities. This data can be very meaningful as it can provide specific, real-world examples, tell a story, and serve as a general or target audience endorsement information, and the more unsolicited it is, the more significant it can be. Anecdotal data is powerful alone but shouldn't typically be used alone; rather, it should be coupled with facts or additional data such as substantial and/ or irrefutable data.

Substantial Data—Libraries have gathered substantial data for decades. Typically identified as data from surveys, it can be gathered pre- and post-event, in ongoing surveys (online and in print), and can yield extensive data such as in a large survey or targeted or smaller-scale surveys. Snapshot surveys (intermittent, etc.) can yield accurate, substantial data as well. Although it is considered substantial, it should be—as all data—coupled with additional types of data.

Less Common to Libraries

Irrefutable Data—Libraries of all types and sizes can generate statistically significant, robust data from credible sources; however, given the nature of nonprofits, this is often a difficult type of data to gather. This data might include assessments of standards and practices, specific programs, and so on, and should be in-depth data gathered from vetted data-gathering sources. Although it is considered irrefutable, it should be—as all data—coupled with additional types of data.

Commentary from Experts or Specific Individuals with Unique Aspects—Using experts or individuals can be problematic based on umbrella institutions having different standards for excellence in consulting or commentary, the expense of gathering commentary, and the need for commentary to be time-sensitive. These individuals can include vendors, individuals from best practices or benchmark environments, as well as recognized peers in the field (e.g., benchmark school districts or counties, cities, or colleges and universities). A subset of commentary can include data such as quotes from constituents that might be gathered deliberately from other data sets, such as surveys or focus groups, as well as quotes from anecdotal data gathered from general constituent feedback processes. Both commentary and quotes should be used coupled with other data such as substantial and/or irrefutable data.

Data typically gathered in libraries is one-dimensional data. While this data may be used with other data, additional techniques for using data include dividing justification information into primary and secondary sources, and assessing decision-makers to determine which sources have had recent successes. Examples of library data that supplement the above list of common and less common data-gathering include:

- statistics of the library for relevant years
- percent and dollar increases and decreases in the last x years (e.g., three, four, or five as a sample number or placed in the context of a significant budget year for the library or the budget entity)
- applicable professional standards
- applicable professional formulas
- consumer price index for the area related to library data
- lists of cost from professional agencies and journals

- relevant census or entity "population" data related to library populations
- articles/information that relates, justifies, or explains requests
- portfolio of formal and informal dialogue
- output measures information/outcomes information
- formal/informal constituent requests
- reports—monthly, annual, special
- paper trail of information memos
- outcomes, goals, objectives results
- umbrella organizational data

Presenting Data

Not only should choice of data match the specific need (e.g., convincing management to fund a project), but also data should be meaningful by design and presentation. Convincing data include data presented though a combination of content and visuals. Visuals can assist in convincing with memorable design and unique specificity, layouts specific to the type or size of environment, use of color, use of symbols or pictures, use of streaming media/video, and use of images of individuals or product from testimonials or commentary. Additional meaningful data can include: unusual or newer data such as social networking information/data gathered; data gathered through contrast and comparison; compelling data such as length of time, depth of information; data that illustrates pathos (specific constituents, etc.); a unique approach to gathering data presented, such as from unique remote or nonlibrary locations; and establishing contexts specific to the decision-makers, such as a council member or commission in real estate would understand usage data presented through a neighborhood or zip code context. Other interesting data presentations include aggregated opinion such as numbers illustrating the "will of the people" with overwhelming numbers and/or significant data from target constituent populations; data that support meeting mandates; and data that illustrate that umbrella institution visions, missions, or goals are met.

Traditional Data vs. Contemporary Data

The profession of library and information science is like any other profession in that types of data, use of data, and application of data go in and out of style, and are valued at different times by different individuals. Examples of this include the following.

- One-dimensional or "flat" data is no longer enough to convince decision-makers. It is still critical for decision-making and convincing decision-makers; however, this type of data such as aggregated number of materials that circulate, or the number of children who signed up for summer reading club, or the number of faculty who receive content offering information-literacy presentations should be—in contemporary libraries—coupled with other data such as "the number of children who signed up and completed the summer reading club with a reading score of 75 books or more."

- Inputs and outputs of libraries such as dollars, materials purchased, and so on, no longer are the only or even the best data to use for data-driven decision-making. While such information should continue to be tracked and retained, the focus in contemporary environments should be to use data in support of showing impact and evidence of impact specific to organization goals, outcomes, and so on.
- Gathering data on use and levels of use of online resources has greatly changed from past data-gathering and varies from vendor to vendor and product to product. Contemporary libraries strive to standardize how this content is presented and many third-party entities, such as consortia, are designing rubrics to illustrate and deliver standardized usage data.
- Although often considered hard to identify, produce, and use, contemporary libraries are being asked to produce data that prove value, worth, perception of value, perception of worth, impact on constituents overall, ability to change constituent lives, impact on quality of life, return on investment, and cost/benefit analysis of entities overall as well as for organizational elements such as automation, delivering resources, and services. Most value and impact studies use a survey-based approach where the organization and user constituents talk about the impact the information/service has had on interactions, behaviors, and results such business being conducted differently based on library service/information, or if/how a user's life was impacted by the library service/information.

Assessing Employees

Although there is extensive information on evaluating performance of employees in a variety of chapters and in case studies throughout this book, at the heart of performance evaluation is the need to hold employees accountable for the roles and responsibilities for which they were hired. In order to maintain a fair and equitable performance-evaluation process, managers must design and maintain foundation documents for the process. These foundation documents must have consistent terminology with other organizational foundation documents and must "match" each other; that is—human resource compensation information with employee categories must serve as content for both general categories of job descriptions (e.g., all reference librarians, all circulation desk library assistants) and specific job descriptions (e.g., the head of reference vs. reference librarians, advanced or senior library assistants vs. lower-level library assistants such as library assistant 1 vs. library assistant 2). In addition, organizations should have job descriptions with roles and responsibilities for workers not identified as employees, such as volunteers, Friends, interns, field study students, and community service workers.

Additional foundation documents that flow from general and specific job descriptions include: organizational outcomes and employee roles and responsibilities in outcomes; individual employee annual goals and/or objectives; project, team, or workgroup plans, goals, and/or objectives; department, location, service goals, and/or objectives; and both performance evaluations for library employees and evaluation forms for workers (e.g., volunteers, Friends, interns, field study students, community service workers).

Using foundation documents as reference documents, managers then identify ways to track and count (or gather, document) employee individual goals and/or objectives completion or shortfalls, as well as success or shortfalls in project, team, or workgroup activities, and department, location, or service area. Ways to track and count (or gather, document) for accountability and assessment for performance include:

- tracking individual employee products, data generated by outcomes, goals, and so on
- tracking department, location, service products, data from outcomes, goals, and so on
- peer reviews of individuals
- peer reviews of projects, teams, and so on
- benchmark comparisons (internal such as previous years, department to department; external such as other institutions)
- constituent feedback, such as specific data from individuals, surveys
- constituent feedback, such as general customer/constituent feedback forms
- gathering and assessing data such as numbers using services or attending events and activities
- constituent feedback on point-of-use satisfaction with services and/or resources
- constituent feedback on point-of-use satisfaction with assistance by employees
- observation—general manager observation of employee performance
- observation—specific manager observation of employee performance against a standard performance rubric

Maintaining successful performance and improving performance are goals of any evaluation process of employees. While many managers do not enjoy the evaluation process, it is easier if managers articulate specific performance expectations and require articulated roles and responsibilities from employees. The more forms or standardization of this articulation, the easier it is to track and "count" performance. It is not unusual and is very appropriate for library managers to have a variety of evaluation forms to cover the diverse performance opportunities and individuals, as well as different forms for different stages of performance, such as midyear performance evaluation for general review of roles and responsibilities and midyear or point-of-problem, specific-issue-based performance evaluations for specific review to correct performance and/or behaviors.

Other issues that drive performance in organizations include the presence of unions in the organization for some or all employee groups, the presence or a variety of management or organizational internal structures (such as employees located at multiple locations), and/or the variety of managers one employee might have (such as job-sharing, split roles, and responsibilities).

Evaluation processes and forms are hard to keep current, just as job descriptions are hard to keep current. In addition, many performance forms need to be tailored to specific issues for employee performance. Specific performance and evaluation elements may differ depending on the status/level of the employee being evaluated.

Librarians

Librarian evaluations can be general evaluations based on the umbrella organization and thus reflect fewer elements of librarian job functions with more professional performance measures, or they can be specific to library functions or be a hybrid or combination. The more specific the performance assessment documents are to roles and responsibilities, the easier it is for managers to track and document and—if needed—illustrate outstanding or improved performance.

In some settings, such as academic or school environments, performance must include specific status of employees within the organization, such as academic librarians identified as instructional (more K–12 environments) or faculty, or having faculty or academic status (more higher education).

Professional and/or Technical

There are a growing number of library employees in libraries who are considered professional or exempt employees but are not librarians. Given the expertise needed in libraries in the past, these employees are often in human resources, development, and facilities areas. Contemporary libraries need professionals with expertise in those areas identified as necessary in past years as well as in technology, partnerships, and, for example, community groups such as nonprofits. These individuals need significantly different performance evaluations as their roles and responsibilities are not librarian in nature, nor are they classified employee in nature.

Classified/Clerical

Employees considered classified and/or clerical have a diverse set of job descriptions and roles and responsibilities, and thus, a diverse set of job performance documents. Not only are their positions support in nature, but they are also more technologically driven, customer service oriented, and "front line" oriented.

Other areas of unique performance assessment include some positions in technical services (also technology in nature), administrators, hourly employees, work study workers, or community service workers.

Assessing Facilities

Although there is expanded information throughout the monograph and through case studies and paradigm shifts on facilities, library and information facilities must be assessed consistently, whether the library owns or rents the space. This assessment must track and gather data so that:

- public and private space meets local ordinance, regional, state, and national law and legislation
- association guidelines and standards are met
- credentials such as certifications, and so on, are maintained (e.g., green, sustainability)

Additional facilities assessment includes remodeling and renovation for areas including information commons for tech use integrated into research and leisure practices; small-group productivity space, teaching and learning space, as well as a more contemporary focus on flexible furniture; recreational spaces; expanded personal/constituent tech support with wireless/flexibility; and, in general, multiple use and shared uses.

Assessing Services

Some libraries are combing old and new data-gathering as well as purchasing commercial products for assessment designed specifically for libraries such as customer service assessment products. Other service data-gathering in contemporary libraries includes virtual reference, assessment of website portals, database usage, and services with social networking integrated.

Assessing Organizational Design and Structure

Although there is expanded information throughout this book and through case studies and Paradigm Shifts on organizations and organizational design, contemporary structures are assessed for their appropriateness to providing services and resources, multiple management functions, shared employees, and the management of remote employees.

It is important, especially in such critical areas, for managers to envision and document how they are accountable, how they gather data, and how they measure input and outcomes, and general as well as specific usage of services and resources. The following two Paradigm Shifts provide the vision of those activities.

PARADIGM SHIFT 14.1.
Managing Classic vs. Contemporary Accountability, Measurement, and Assessment in Libraries

Library managers manage and thus are held accountable for public and private dollars. Increasing pressures for articulation of value and affordability of library facilities, resources, and services have increased the need for managers to assess how *they* are held accountable not only for expenditures but also for use and condition of environment and resources.

Classic Accountability, Measurement, and Assessment	Contemporary Accountability, Measurement, and Assessment
• The primary responsibility for the library's resources, services, actions, employees, and facilities resides with the governing body (board, council, commission, etc.) of the organization and the designated top-level manager. Groups assuming responsibility are *accountable* to the constituents or stakeholders as well as to other governing entities or groups as well as advisory groups. This accountability includes responsible expenditure of any and all dollars (no matter the source); existence, appropriateness, and condition of resources and services; management and employee actions; and condition, appropriateness, and	• The primary responsibility for the library's resources, services, employees, facilities, and critical infrastructure such as technology connections, hardware, software, wired, and wireless resides with the governing body (e.g., board, council, commission) of the organization and the designated top-level manager. Groups assuming responsibility are *accountable* to the constituents or stakeholders as well as to governing entities or advisory groups. This accountability includes responsible expenditure of public dollars; existence, appropriateness, and condition of resources and services; management and employee actions;

(continued)

PARADIGM SHIFT 14.1.
(continued)

Classic Accountability, Measurement, and Assessment	Contemporary Accountability, Measurement, and Assessment
use of facilities and organizational goals, objectives, and strategies.	and condition, appropriateness, and use of facilities.
	• In contemporary libraries, entities and governing (and other) groups are accountable for goals, objectives, strategies, and so on, but also outcomes, as well as a specific impact of some resources and services and funding sources, partners, and contractual and memorandum of understanding relationships.
• Foundation documents for libraries are designed to outline roles and responsibilities as well as all elements of accountability. This content includes mission statements for multiyear/long-term and "big picture" direction as well as more specific annual goals and objectives.	• Contemporary/new libraries have a broad, simple, overarching vision of what the library means to the community, the institution, and so on, as well as a mission statement, and annual goals and objectives. Objectives may also be identified as strategies, although some libraries identify strategies as more specific than objectives and thus activities and tasks. In addition, outcomes and impact are now required in many environments and articulate a focus on impact and outcomes of resources and services on constituents.
• Services are measured by usage in the aggregate and by constituent profiles. Levels of satisfaction with services are measured.	• Services are assessed by attendance and use for in-person and digital and/or virtual modes and methods of delivery. In addition, services can be reviewed for reaching constituents considered target audiences and compared and contrasted to benchmark services. Customer satisfaction with services in general and—depending on the organization—unique services to targeted, diverse constituent groups are measured.
• Duplicating/copying and printing have been services that in most circumstances require charges/fees. Counting printing when there is no print-management system can be labor intensive, and often, charging for printing is more trouble than it is worth since print solutions are expensive.	• Contemporary print solutions require authentication/sign in and, while costly, are needed for accountability for sustainable activities. Printing solution software can provide data-gathering in the aggregate and, when authentication is present, by target audience profile elements.

Classic Accountability, Measurement, and Assessment	Contemporary Accountability, Measurement, and Assessment
• Managers are accountable to administration and management for decisions and activities regarding all aspects of the library. • Managers are responsible for their own and employee ethical behaviors.	• Managers are accountable to administration and management for decisions and activities regarding all aspects of the library. • Managers are responsible for their own and employee ethical behaviors. Managers are held accountable not only to the umbrella organization or governing body but also to constituents for the organization's outcomes and impact as well as the vision, mission, goals, and objectives.

PARADIGM SHIFT 14.2.
Managing Classic vs. Contemporary Data-Gathering
Infrastructures for Library Environments

The majority of contemporary library managers are responsible for strategic data collection and analysis to ensure data-driven decisions. Managers today must be able to identify, design, gather, assess, and apply information gathered from data on usage and nonusage for all services and resources. Although all libraries and librarians have gathered data, contemporary assessment (e.g., digital uses, outcomes, etc.) has changed the nature of gathering and analyzing.

Classic Accountability, Measurement, and Assessment—Data-Gathering	Contemporary Accountability, Measurement, and Assessment—Data-Gathering
• Historically, libraries have gathered and reported input and output data or more one-dimensional or "flat" data. Examples include "how much spent on books last year" and "how many people came through the library doors last month." Two-dimensional data includes data that combines two or more flat data such as "30 percent of the book budget is spent on the children's collection but 70 percent of the circulation statistics are from the children's collection." The more relationships are established between and among data, the more libraries have been able to identify levels or types and kinds of impact.	• Historically, libraries have gathered and reported input and output data or more one-dimensional or "flat" data. Examples include "how much spent on books last year" and "how many people came through the library doors last month." Two-dimensional data includes data that combines two or more flat data such as "30 percent of the book budget is spent on the children's collection but 70 percent of the circulation statistics are from the children's collection." The more relationships are established between and among data, the more libraries have been able to identify levels or types and kinds of impact.

(continued)

PARADIGM SHIFT 14.2.
(continued)

Classic Accountability, Measurement, and Assessment—Data-Gathering	Contemporary Accountability, Measurement, and Assessment—Data-Gathering
• Data-gathering is the responsibility of those in public service and managers who track and assess data.	• In today's organizations, managers must build a culture of assessment to ensure that all employees are committed to designing, tracking, and assessing events and activities for maximum accountability.
• Data gathered includes tracking and measurement of events and activities, typically on an annual basis.	• Data-gathering includes tracking and measuring events and activities on an annual basis but also snapshot data-gathering for events, activities, use of online resources, and services for two to three years as well as longitudinal data.
• Some decisions are made using data and these guide directions for the library.	• Organizations and umbrella organizations want the majority of decisions to be data driven—using data that provide accountability, justification, and evidence.
• Measuring use of print materials is standard and includes specific LC and Dewey acquisitions inputs and outputs as well as all external circulation and often in-house use. There is aggregated counting of online (primarily citation-only resources.)	• There is extensive depth and breadth collection analysis for all formats. Counting issues exist specific to standardized counts across vendors and tech platforms. Additional counting issues exist for nonstandardized terminology for online resources including differences in counting pages, hits vs. downloads, and so on.
• Data is gathered, counted, assessed, and analyzed.	• Data is gathered, counted, assessed, and analyzed, and data about data or metadata is gathered, counted, assessed, and analyzed.
• Institutions present data and data analysis in annual reports for umbrella institutions and some external agencies.	• Institutions present data and data analysis for internal decision-making; internal and external entities in annual reports; local, regional, state, and federal reportage; ancillary groups; granting entities; consortia; and so on.
• Public relations materials use institutional data to illustrate use of resources and services.	• Institutional marketing, public relations, and branding processes and activities use data for informing, persuading, and representing institutional value, usage, and need and how decisions are data driven.

Classic Accountability, Measurement, and Assessment—Data-Gathering	Contemporary Accountability, Measurement, and Assessment—Data-Gathering
• Reporting data is consistent, systematic, and based on specific annual timelines.	• Reporting data is consistent, systematic, and based on specific timelines throughout the year as well as on multiyear timelines. Timeline grids are maintained to illustrate what is due and when it is due.
• Print and online collections are measured and assessed and/or "counted" in the aggregate as well as in subdivided or discrete collection areas such as purchase and/or usage by constituent group, age level, discipline, and format. • While most data gathered focuses on circulation, checkout, and use, other data gathered includes browsing and in-room use of materials.	• Print and online collections are assessed by circulation and/or usage for checkout and viewing as well as browsing and in-room use. In addition, collections today are compared and contrasted to benchmark collections and bibliographic network assessment services are purchased to assess collection depth and breadth. Customer satisfaction with collections is also measured and, depending on the organization, collections can be matched to (in academic and school libraries) curriculum and (in public libraries) to constituent groups.
• Libraries have vacillated between not keeping much data to keeping lots of data every minute of every day to measure use of services and resources. In addition, many libraries who have gathered data have not reported or used the data other than to report basic inputs, outputs, and usage. • Data-gathering forms require a classic hash-mark approach for counting in person as well as virtual/digital interactions and support for constituents. Nuance to hash marks has included a cross or plus on hash marks to indicate expanded time spent with a constituent and a "p" to indicate a phone interaction and some letter designed to indicate a count for e-mail interactions.	• Libraries are systematically gathering data and identifying data-gathering tools and techniques from purchased products and subscriptions or third-party "generated-data" from software and are choosing a variety of ways to gather data including gathering through snapshots. • Data-gathering for "new" results such as outcomes and impact necessitate a thoughtful decision on the tools and techniques needed as well as decisions on identifying constituent interactions and levels of success in interactions and customer satisfaction with the interaction.

INDISPENSABLE RESOURCES FOR
MANAGERS REGARDING ACCOUNTABILITY

While general content is available on assessment and accountability, there is a growing body of library research on assessment, outcomes, and accountability. Some of this content is specific to types and sizes of libraries. Associations and agencies provide specific content as well as specific interpretations of content as well as best practices (e.g., Urban Libraries Council).

"Free Management Library." Accessed October 24, 2013. www.freemanage
     mentlibrary.org.
"Library Research Service (LRS)." Accessed September 23, 2013. www.lrs.
     org.
"OCLC." Accessed October 27, 2013. www.oclc.org.
"State Libraries." Accessed October 27, 2013. www.publiclibraries.com/state
     _library.htm.
"State and Regional Chapters." Accessed October 27, 2013. www.ala.org/
     groups/affiliates/chapters/state/stateregional.
"Urban Libraries Council." Accessed October 27, 2013. www.urbanlibraries
     .org.
"WebJunction." Accessed October 21, 2013. www.webjunction.org.

DISCUSSION QUESTIONS FOR CHAPTER 14

1. Are library managers in all types and sizes of libraries held accountable for their actions? If yes, by whom? If no, why not?
2. How do library managers seek to standardize measurement and assessment of library resources and services?
3. How do library managers use data from tracking, measurement, and assessment in their decision-making?
4. Should library managers seek to differentiate between and among actual, in-person, in-print, virtual, digital data, and so on? If yes, why? If no, why not?
5. What use can library managers make of older data—for example, anecdotal data of constituent use of resources and services?

Readers are reminded that a case method is intended to be used in conjunction with this chapter. The case designed to be used with this chapter is case 14, "Torture the Data," located in part II, p. 319.

Chapter Fifteen

New Budgeting with (Mostly) Classic Budgeting Issues

- Fiscal management (organizing, tracking, spending)
- Money issues (justification, accountability)

A case method is intended to be used in conjunction with this chapter. The case designed to be used with this chapter is case 15, "Matching Data to Data Requests," located in part II, p. 324. The case can be read and discussed before and/or after reading the chapter content.

BUDGETING AND TODAY'S LIBRARY MANAGERS

Fiscal management or—as most managers identify it—"budgeting" is a complex process. In today's libraries, budgeting includes the process of understanding the laws and business practices that govern financial management in general, as well as nonprofit financial management, identifying needs, categorizing areas of expenditures, designing financial support for resources and services, justifying monetary assignments, organizing budgeting timelines for employees responsible for spending, designing tracking mechanisms, maintaining tracking mechanisms, reconciling expenditures, communicating accountability, and evaluating outcomes including conducting audits of expenditures.

Libraries have a variety of mechanisms provided to them from umbrella organizations to support the budgeting process, policies, and procedures. Library managers must monitor their own dollars as well as organizational spending and expenditures from secondary or ancillary groups, and, at the very least, they must use the budget formats required of governing bodies.

   Since libraries acquire resources and design services, as well as deal with multiple budgets, policies, and procedures, today's managers easily find themselves juggling large numbers of budget categories and accounts. In addition, with accountability requirements for public money (as well as private money), reconciling dollars must happen more frequently, and reporting on expenditures may be required for multiple funders. It's often surprising for nonprofit managers to find out that budgeting is one of their primary roles and responsibilities and that it is often the most complex process they must master in the workplace. Paradigm Shift 15.1 shows changes in financial management for today's managers.

PARADIGM SHIFT 15.1.
Classic vs. Contemporary Financial Management in Libraries

Library managers are responsible and accountable for public money. In the process of accountability, they must use the organization's budgeting processes and add, as appropriate, reporting unique to the library, requests for money with justifications, use of money, and value of dollars spent. Although basic processes for budgeting have not changed significantly, there are many aspects of budgeting that are contemporary including budget complexity, timelines, justification, and usage of dollars as well as articulations of value of dollars expended. Contemporary formats including issues of print vs. digital expenditures as well as local, state, and federal guidelines have changed due to the varieties of definitions of resources (e.g., digital resource subscriptions vs. digital resource purchases or journals vs. e-books).

Classic	Contemporary
• Library managers have a variety of budget categories to manage.	• Library managers have a large number of budget categories to manage given varieties of external funding, required accountability, increased dollars for consortial services, expanded partnerships, and unique fiscal issues such as diverse location and co-location of libraries.
• Libraries seek expanded budgets and provide justification and documentation for requests.	• Libraries provide justification for expanded budgets; however, today's libraries need in-depth outcomes documentation to participate in the umbrella organization's competitive budgeting process.
• Library budgets are organized and maintained on the organization's spreadsheets—typically simple spreadsheets.	• Umbrella organizations, libraries, and other nonprofit organizations use a wide variety of budgeting software packages as well as organizational management-information systems for budgeting processes.
• Laws and business practices of an organization govern budgeting policies and processes.	• Laws and business practices of a variety of organizations (many of which are not local, but state, regional,

Classic	Contemporary
	federal, and a variety of other funding groups) must be adhered to given contemporary issues of ownership, access, subscriptions, and partnerships governing budgeting policies and processes.
• Resources are acquired within guidelines of local, state, and federal as well as business and tax law guidelines.	• Resources are acquired within guidelines of local, state, and federal as well as business and tax law guidelines; however, as formats change, guidelines change.

FISCAL MANAGEMENT
(ORGANIZING, TRACKING, SPENDING)

Today's managers' general roles and responsibilities are varied, and most primary roles and responsibilities relate to financial management. Those that relate specifically to budgeting and financial management include research, planning, organizing, elements of staffing, communicating, and the primary, specific role identified as controlling/budgeting.

Organizing

The *easiest* budgeting and financial management areas to learn are those general areas of financial management such as the organization's budget recordkeeping processes; the procedures for tracking budget dollars using the organization's forms; the organization's terminology for budgeting and recordkeeping; and the timelines for asking for, receiving, tracking, and expending organizational dollars. Additional areas include any general financial policies and procedures; overarching state, grant (agency, organization), regional, consortial, or partnership budget guidelines and timelines; as well as any unique reporting out of budget information required for internal or external auditing procedures. What's *hard* about budgeting lies in:

- the complex nature of the processes where multiple funding sources exist
- identifying available dollars
- balancing timelines
- the presence of multiple budget categories within and among funding sources
- requesting and receiving additional operational/annual dollars

- receiving permission to move dollars among operations (services, resources, etc.)
- increasing the organization's capital dollars
- identifying and learning upgraded budget software packages
- grant writing
- requesting completely new budget lines for—among other areas—employees, new facilities issues, and major facilities issues, as well as for major expenditures such as initial or migration of automation systems
- the simplest process of "balancing the books"

Financial management competencies (knowledge, skills/abilities, and attitudes) for librarians who manage all sizes of libraries include: being knowledgeable about both the library and the umbrella organization; being knowledgeable about how their organization fits into the organization as a whole; having the ability to plan; having the ability to budget/management money in general and specifically money within nonprofit environments; being knowledgeable about persuasion techniques, as well as the ability to persuade; being knowledgeable about the ways others learn and their communication skills—oral, written, nonverbal; and being knowledgeable about and skilled in both leadership and management and the ability to negotiate.

Managers must be conversant in the general types and styles of budgets and in budgeting terminology. The more that is known about the process and the approach, the more competitive one can be when requesting funding. Library managers must be also be conversant about budget issues in other types and sizes of institutions since so many managers are involved with a variety of partnerships and most partnerships include elements of budgeting and financial management.

There are some obvious differences, however, among and between types and sizes of libraries. Some generalizations about differences include the following.

- Many smaller environments don't have detailed budget forms for requesting, justifying, or presenting budget requests.
- Libraries of all types and sizes are finding themselves managing multiple budget categories.
- Many budget systems use primarily only the spreadsheet approach to categorizing and tracking dollars.
- Most organizations do *not* have justification requirements for every budget category and expenditure, but certainly for new dollars as well as moving major dollars around that necessitate a change in services.

Tracking

Some generalizations about yesterday's and today's general budgeting and financial management approaches for tracking include lump-sum, line-item, zero, and program budgeting.

Lump-Sum Budgeting

"Lump-sum" budgeting is an older, general approach to budgeting that includes fewer categories of expenditures with undesignated funds giving managers discretion for spending money. Lump-sum budget funds are harder to track and best used for smaller categories of expenditures. If the organization uses or allows lump-sum budgets and does not provide specific processes for these lump-sum categories, managers should track funds in those accounts separately.

Line-Item Budgeting

"Line-item" budgeting lists categories of expenditures according to specific areas of the organization, such as cost, department, or service. Categories can be easily tracked as they are specific to narrowly defined expenditures, and these specific categories provide opportunities to illustrate change, such as comparing between or among budget years. Line items are used as the underlying budget form for other types of budgets. Line-item budget spreadsheets are maintained annually and some recordkeeping includes more than one year. Spreadsheet "lines" are often umbrella categories, such as "materials"; then categories within the "materials" category can be further subdivided in a variety of ways such as (but not limited to):

- by format (books, journals, databases)
- by constituent/target audience
- by location
- by subject area
- by access (circulating vs. reference)
- by delivery (onsite only, remote access, etc.)

Other examples of line-item categories include: human resources with further subdivision by full time and part time; location, type, or level of service, such as children's and youth materials; building-level librarian vs. district-level or media specialists (school library); categories of material expenditures such as reference materials in print vs. databases vs. e-books; and client billing (special library) broken down, for example, by advertising campaigns.

Zero Budgeting

"Zero" budgeting, in general, represents "zero base" and "zero increase" as well as "zero sum." Considered a different approach to budgeting, as it requires dollars divided into categories or packages that include funding from a variety of accounts, the process requires managers annually to justify their request for each category of expenditure and, in some cases, justify their request for the existence of entire packages. Variations of the "zero" process include departments having to justify all dollars required for existence of an entire service, as well as having to justify additional dollars for change or growth. At the heart of all "zero" packages is the organization's view of packages as competition for dollars available. Zero-budgeting packages for each request outline consequences of no funding, zero increases in funding, and then some funding (e.g., no increase, a 5 percent increase, a 10 percent increase). Managers must provide extensive content and documentation and must have contingencies identified if dollars are not approved at requested levels.

Program Budgeting

Program budgets are older budget styles and were initially used to analyze costs of, for example, areas of the organization as well as services offered and/or departments. Program budgets present data on what it costs to offer the service along with justifications for dollars expended per user and/or potential user and then justification for requests for increases or changes to the program. Additional justification is needed when analysis indicates that the program is expensive (such as an expensive service to a small target population) but is justified given the importance of the service, the unique support the service provides, the critical need of the target population, the mission or vision of the organization, or organizational values. Examples of more classic discussions of program budgeting include cost assessments within program budget processes for converting or migrating manual circulation systems to automated circulation systems, and cost comparisons of establishing temporary or smaller service delivery points such as kiosks rather than full branch or departmental libraries and traveling collection such as a bookmobiles or deposit collections. Additional examples include kiosk library services and/or bookmobiles.

Spending

Great care needs to be taken when spending public or private money. The more structure managers use in financial management, the better, since spending "other people's money" is a public trust.

The primary infrastructure to put in place is the set of steps used to spend the organization's money. These steps include:

1. determine the overall vision/match of a library's vision to funding vision/ umbrella organization
2. determine the directions of expenditures—operating or maintenance, new, diversion, redirection?
3. determine a course of action: How will money be spent? Timing? Tracking to be established? Measures to be integrated?
4. design/select the budget/forms/justification needed by the organization and specific to the project/area of expenditure
5. insure accountability/justification for expenditure
6. develop estimates for courses of action/expenditures
7. review/modify/evaluate estimates of expenditures
8. rank/prioritize as needed (based on need, input, data)
9. prepare documentation
10. prepare presentation as needed based on audience (e.g., who is to be persuaded)
11. presentation to the target audience
12. negotiation for dollars needed
13. approval process
14. dissemination of budget with interpretation of effect or match to requests
15. management of budget including revisiting and revision as necessary as well as tracking of spending

MONEY ISSUES (JUSTIFICATION, ACCOUNTABILITY)

Historically, many libraries received their funding because they were identified as the "heart of the institution" or "the heart of the community" and others were funded based on an organization's funding formulas. As with any other business today, however, libraries must justify their existence and their funding, as well as requests for new money and, in many cases, requests to move money from one area to another. In addition, budget requests are now going head to head with funded and unfunded mandates, student-success initiatives, and first-responder needs, to name just a few competitors for library dollars.

Library managers today must create scenarios, provide paradigms and Paradigm Shifts, create clearinghouses of data, and match justification content to umbrella organization terminology in order to illustrate why the same level of funding is needed as well as why new money is needed. Other areas of justification include why you want to move money, either temporarily or permanently, from one account or area to another. Questions frequently asked include the following.

- Why do you need larger sums of money?
- Why do you need a new library when there is another large library across town?
- Why do you need a new automation system?
- How did you arrive at the budget figures in your request?
- Why did you choose this system over this system?
- Why should we give the library this money for the next five years and not the _____ department?

Although there is no guarantee of funding, no matter how perfect the combination of words and requests might be, there are:

- techniques that work better with some decision-makers than others
- better ways to present ongoing funding requests for existing services
- clever ways to illustrate and justify new or expanded dollars needed for services and materials
- ways to speculate on and build annual or multiyear budget scenarios

At the foundation of justification of techniques, ways to illustrate, and techniques for persuading is the commitment to research and analysis to yield data and metadata about library needs and issues. This primary responsibility of a library manager includes the design, gathering, and application of research to support decision-making for budgets. There are a variety of ways to use research and research methods for the budgeting process, including: presenting budget information through a historical perspective, such as inserting a historical probe as a cause and effect; discussing or profiling by case method; looking ahead by creating and using scenarios; and/or telling a story by providing an accounting of need and use in story form to illustrate context and consequences.

Other more common ways to gather data for use in budget justification include:

- survey research, or gathering data by survey instrument or seeking brainstorming, feedback, and opinion through interviews or focus groups
- Delphi methods for gathering future or predicting opinion based on expert knowledge (a panel of experts)
- forecasting by gathering data from models and experts, and basing predictions on analysis of data

- statistical analysis with software package or formula analysis of research data gathered
- benchmarking through comparison and contrasting data from similar environments

Research and the importance of research as supporting data for budget decision-making and accountability is crucial to managers. Research data provides data to support library managers in their quest for funding approval for requesting more funding, for requesting to move funding, as well as requests to remove/reduce funding. The need for more funding can be illustrated and/or supported by data illustrating:

- increased activity in an area (visiting, attendance, circulation, reference, etc.)
- a need to promote to gather interest
- unsuccessful promotion results
- that an initiative matches a new direction (by umbrella institution, partners, the library)
- that something is mandated by local, state, national, regional, partnerships
- that it is the only area where money is available
- the need to take advantage of alternative funding
- gaps in services/materials
- new materials/services now available
- media hype/event
- new groups in the community

Need to move funding can be illustrated and/or supported by data illustrating:

- that there is no longer a need
- that there are changed priorities, values (by umbrella institution, partners, the library)
- that funding is no longer possible (because of presence of technology, lack of technology, etc.)
- that the current system is no longer cost effective
- superseded possibilities
- that something is outdated
- that change is mandated by local, state, national, regional, partnerships

Need to remove funding can be illustrated and/or supported by data illustrating:

- that there are fewer people in area
- that constituents are no longer there or their location has moved

- that the commitment was met in previous years
- the redirection of goals/objectives/activities/energy
- that talent is no longer available
- that soft money is available
- that materials are available in an alternative, more appropriate/cheaper format
- that gift replaced expenditure
- the need is greater in another area
- that something is no longer relevant

General data to be tracked and gathered to assist library managers with budget documentation includes a large number of areas for recordkeeping. While larger libraries may want to maintain datasets in all areas, it is unrealistic to expect all libraries to gather all data. Instead, managers must scan their environment to assess who needs to be convinced, which data might be best used to convince, and how might data be organized or prioritized to best illustrate need. The following list includes some of the information and data that, when assembled and placed in perspective, might support justifying new money or moving or removing old money.

1. statistics of the library for relevant years
2. percent and dollar amount increases and decreases in the last x years (three, four, or five as a sample number or placed in the context of a significant budget year for the library or the budget entity)
3. applicable professional standards
4. applicable professional formulas
5. vendor/commercial information
6. consumer price index for the area
7. lists of cost from professional agencies and journals
8. relevant census data
9. articles/information that relates, justifies, or explains requests
10. consultant recommendations
11. portfolio of formal and informal dialogue
12. survey data
13. output measures information
14. formal/informal constituent/user requests
15. reports—monthly, annual, special
16. paper trail of information memos
17. working and measurable goals/objectives/strategies of the organization
18. umbrella organization data

Consider, also, dividing this justification information into primary and secondary sources, and assessing management styles to determine which sources carry the most weight. Additional data needed by library managers includes:

- financial trends—local, state, U.S., global
- demographics
- involvement of people in local focus groups
- marketing information
- convincing administration on the library's important role in the institution
- community plans
- institutional plans
- what current library constituents (users and nonusers) need
- history of library successes and failures
- consortia plans
- the effects of technology on employees, constituents, and so on
- what else is available in communities—competition, commercial marketplace
- what other community groups are doing
- minimum/maximum standards and guidelines
- partnerships in communities
- legislation
- mandates
- what the library would buy if it could (wish lists)
- what stories will convince
- how decision-makers learn and process
- what decision-makers value

Library managers must focus on budgeting and budgeting issues throughout the year and *not* just during the design and defense time period, or more specifically March or April though the end of the institution's budget year. Recommendations for library managers to deal with budget issues throughout the year include the following.

1. Begin a budget portfolio.
2. Relate data/information to request.
3. Link all methods of statistics and recordkeeping to functions and activities.
4. Assess current statistics to determine what "proof" they are.
5. Establish relationships with umbrella organization money-management employees.
6. Have statistics reflect internal and external use.
7. Compile peer institution and community benchmarking data.

8. Update/create vision/mission/goals of the library.
9. Maintain approved/measurable goals and objectives, which can be used/evaluated in light of budget requests.
10. Build justification features into your existing budget forms or choose a budget style that allows justification and explanation, or just attach justification/explanation forms to your budget forms.
11. Encourage management styles that allow for participation in choice of expenditure areas.
12. Stress what you are trying to accomplish with expenditures.
13. In line-item budgeting and on all line-item forms, relate items to requests, programs, and services.
14. Avoid (at all costs) padding in requests and justification.
15. Define the "profit" or "impact" of expenditures in your environment.
16. Be careful of adding and be ready to justify "cushions."
17. Be familiar with constituent/client billing for extensive services.
18. Consider use of professional standards in justification.
19. Keep an ongoing folder of information that discusses costs—especially in comparison or in contrast to previous costs or forecasting of expenditures.
20. Keep all constituent dialogue—formal and informal.
21. Consider surveys that determine roles and assess constituent needs and wants.
22. Compile all environmental, cost-of-living, consumer-price-index, and profit information that relates to library resources/services/constituents.
23. Become aware of the basic costs of library functions.
24. Use charts, graphs, and comparison data to illustrate need or use.
25. Emphasize constituent ease of use and need.
26. Separate fixed costs from variable costs.
27. Be aware of political climate and timelines of political issues.
28. Be aware of umbrella organization/administration interests.
29. Know your competition.
30. Have ongoing PR/information campaigns.
31. Develop a specific timeline and plan of action for budget processes.
32. Review the format of existing reportage to see if it lays the foundation for building information/data requests.

Finally, library managers should gather best practices for justification for increasing, moving, and removing money from all types and sizes of libraries. While finding public budgeting examples is typically difficult, given concerns for sharing proprietary content, library managers need to seek varieties of ways to identify and measure budget outcomes—specifically, successful budgeting requests and justification. (Additional information on financial accountability can be found in chapter 14.)

INDISPENSABLE RESOURCES FOR
LIBRARY MANAGERS REGARDING BUDGETING

Library managers will find much content on general budgeting information. There is a growing literature on accountability and significant literature on using content on the value of libraries for preparing and justifying budgets.

"Free Management Library." Accessed October 24, 2013. www.freemanage mentlibrary.org.

"Library Research Service (LRS)." Accessed September 23, 2013. www.lrs .org.

"Library Technology Guides." Accessed October 27, 2013. www.librarytech nology.org/LibraryTechnologyReports.pl.

"OCLC." Accessed October 27, 2013. www.oclc.org.

"Top Technology Trends." Accessed September 21, 2013. http://litablog.org/ category/top-technology-trends.

"WebJunction." Accessed October 21, 2013. www.webjunction.org.

"The Whole Building Design Guide." Accessed October 27, 2013. www .wbdg.org.

DISCUSSION QUESTIONS FOR CHAPTER 15

1. Where can library managers find education and/or training with a focus on nonprofit budgeting?
2. Is there one budget style that works for library managers in any and all types and sizes of libraries?
3. Do classic budget styles of justification (or requests for expenditures) work for managing contemporary/twenty-first-century resources and services?
4. Should library managers delegate budgeting roles and responsibilities to other managers within the library? If yes, why? If no, why not?
5. How should library managers track their funding?

Readers are reminded that a case method is intended to be used in conjunction with this chapter. The case designed to be used with this chapter is case 15, "Matching Data to Data Requests," located in part II, p. 324.

Chapter Sixteen

Emergency Management Roles and Responsibilities of New Managers

- Disasters (prevention, recovery, business continuity)
- Critical issues (prevention, recovery, business continuity)

A case method is intended to be used in conjunction with this chapter. The case designed to be used with this chapter is case 16, "Building Tomorrow's Future on Today's Expertise," located in part II, p. 330. The case can be read and discussed before and/or after reading the chapter content.

EMERGENCY MANAGEMENT IN LIBRARIES

It's not clear to even the most seasoned managers whether or not we simply have *more* large-scale emergencies than in previous decades or if we just hear about more large-scale situations and more individual emergencies. Other thoughts about the number of emergencies we are now aware of and must deal with include: better technology for communication; older buildings; more extreme changes in weather; green and sustainable issues dictating different processes and products for cleaning, repairs, and new construction; and economic downturns with less frequent repairs and delayed upkeep. Whatever the correct answer is, library managers must have some in-depth knowledge about emergency management for their buildings, their employees, their umbrella institutions, and their larger communities and partners.

Related areas library managers must be familiar with include risk management and critical incidents. And all emergency management information must include dealing with facilities, employees, and constituents. Additional issues for today's managers include protection of the organization's data within the building and within remote storage areas, and protection of services and resources or the library's assets. Not only must library managers be knowledgeable about emergency management areas and issues, but also all library employees must be familiar with their own roles and responsibilities for the organization. Paradigm Shift 16.1 discusses some of these changes/issues.

PARADIGM SHIFT 16.1.
Classic vs. Contemporary Emergency Management in Library Environments

Although libraries have always had emergencies and managed emergencies, managers in general today have significantly new and more issues related to preventive measures, managing business continuity during emergencies, as well as recovery and evaluation. Because emergency-management issues—once the purview of first responders only—are now on everyone's list of roles and responsibilities, there are significant changes to identify and manage.

Classic Emergency Management in Yesterday's Libraries or "Pre-9/11"	Contemporary Emergency Management in Today's Libraries
• Historically, "disaster planning" in libraries focuses on materials and saving materials/collections ravaged by fire and water as well as materials/collections affected by dampness, mold, dust, and sunlight.	• "Disaster planning" in libraries is now superseded by "emergency management," which includes disaster planning, critical incidents, preparedness/prevention and mitigation, business continuity, and recovery for all issues with resources and services, facilities, employees, and constituents, as well as events and activities for umbrella institutions, community, partners, and so on.
• Content created focuses on collections.	• Content created focuses on all aspects of emergency management for all aspects of the institution.
• Plans focus on internal activities with outside and vendor activities related to collection.	• Plans focus on internal and external activities as well as activities within the bigger community or umbrella organization and partners.
• Libraries are not viewed as primary supporters for others in disaster situations.	• Library managers and employees are viewed as first responders in some areas for their "during" and "post" event support for their primary and broader community including shelter-in-place activities and delivery of resources for recovery.

Most library managers *never* thought that their roles and responsibilities would include handling the type or number of critical incidents and disasters that need managing in libraries today. So, although critical incidents and disasters *have* been a reality for decades, current and future environments have expanded issues due to:

- aging environments
- changing weather
- more general infrastructure to manage
- more situations where public facilities such as libraries are co-located with other city and/or county services such as city hall, police, fire, and other first responders
- more technology and technological infrastructure available today
- the magnitude of information including diverse terminology
- 24/7 expectations
- rapidly changing environments where "new" becomes out of date quickly
- more complicated facilities issues such as sustainability, green standards, technology, safety and security, HVAC
- more and broader legislation and public policy at the federal, regional/county, and/or local levels that layer organizations with roles and responsibilities to protect employees and constituents
- a more complicated workplace in general with significantly more policies and practices
- constituents "in two places at once" or both in-person *and* digital virtual constituents thus different expectations
- constituent issues for safety and security
- expanding avenues for and a need to balance communication
- leadership issues for organizations and individuals during critical incidents and disasters
- umbrella institution issues regarding responding to unique library needs
- issues with "others" including partners, stakeholders
- general issues vs. issues by size and type of library

With these issues facing many if not most managers, critical incidents and disasters must be identified and categorized. Managers must prevent issues if possible; respond quickly and efficiently; safeguard resources, employees, and constituents; and maintain business continuity as well as assess and evaluate to "close that loop" and increase prevention and preparedness. And, although many critical incidents and disasters can be addressed through standard policies and procedures, two unique issues for library managers are dealing with these issues based on the type and size of library.

Size of Library

Sizes of libraries are typically categorized by small, medium, and large based on a number of reasons, including the size of the physical facility, the size of the constituent population, the number of employees, and/or the number of materials/size of collections. Among the many issues specific to the size of the library are as follows.

- The smaller the library, the more likely management will need to establish policies and processes within umbrella institution parameters.
- Managers of smaller environments must reach out to partners and stakeholders to form critical-incident and disasters teams for design of policies and processes.
- Larger environments extending over expanded geographic areas must employ sophisticated e-communication techniques for all critical-incident and disaster situations.
- The larger the library, the greater the possibility for large numbers of partnerships and the more complex the critical-incident and disaster process.

Type of Library

When libraries are identified as a "type" of library, the type "category" includes academic (or higher education), public (city, county, or 501c3/nonprofit), school (K–12—public, private, charter, and homeschools), and special (profit, business environments, nonprofit, or .org). In addition, for many years, libraries have existed and coexisted in shared and contiguous spaces, as well as partnered with a wide variety of organizations (other types of libraries, other organizations, and businesses) to expand services and resources. Given the myriad of environments libraries exist within, it is not hard to imagine the myriad of issues when managers address emergency management. Examples of issues, organized by type of library, are given below.

Academic Libraries/Higher Education

- While some academic libraries are in one primary location, many academic environments are decentralized (across town, across counties, as well as across states), and designing and implementing critical-incident policies and processes among locations is very challenging.
- In the last decade, higher education environments have had a number of tragic emergency-management situations occur as well as a number of natural disasters. Coordinating prevention, recovery, and business continuity among the many higher education offices is challenging and often

delays the creation and dissemination as well as business continuity and incident management.

- Academic library environments house not only extensive technology infrastructure but also diverse special collections with unique needs for emergency management.
- Umbrella institutions offer their own police or security force. Although coordinating with these forces expands complexity for emergency management, this extra enforcement adds much-needed safety and security in both critical-incident and disaster management.
- Some higher education environments are smaller, and smaller numbers of employees provide fewer team members for emergency-management activities.
- Many academic libraries facilities are older, which increases problems with recovery and business continuity.
- Academic institutions/library managers partnering with other libraries and organizations for library services must expand their already-complicated emergency-management policies and processes to include other management—including library and umbrella organization management.

Public Libraries (city, county, or 501c3/nonprofit)

- Many, if not most, public libraries do not have onsite police or security. This lack of protection onsite increases the importance of library managers creating emergency management policies and procedures that focus on prevention and incident safety as well as alerting and awareness communication between libraries and security or police with oversight.
- Many public library facilities are older, which increases problems with recovery and business continuity.
- Having fewer public library employees at smaller locations is a safety and security issue.
- Most public libraries are not funded for adequate support of emergency preparedness policies and procedures.
- While some public libraries are in one primary location, many city and county environments have main libraries and branches or are decentralized in providing services and resources. Designing and implementing emergency management policies and processes among locations, therefore, is very challenging.
- Public library environments house extensive technology infrastructure and print collections, and recovery from natural disasters is expensive.
- Umbrella institutions offer their own police or security force. Although coordinating with these forces expands complexity for emergency management, this extra enforcement adds much-needed safety and security in both critical-incident and disaster management in public libraries.

- Some public library environments are smaller, and smaller numbers of employees provide fewer team members for emergency management activities.
- Public library institutions/library managers partnering with other libraries and organizations for library services must expand their already-complicated emergency management policies and processes to include other management, including library and umbrella organization management.

School Libraries

- School libraries do not have individual budgets for support of extensive emergency management plans. Library managers should actively pursue leadership in the building-level and/or district-level activities related to critical incidents and/or disasters.
- Library managers should ensure that materials collections are assessed and data related to repair, recovery, and continuity are integrated into emergency management plans.
- Many schools do not have school librarians assigned full or part time to work at campuses. School district library personnel should identify emergency management process owners for individual schools as well as system-wide systems.

Special Libraries

- Umbrella organizations for special libraries offer their own police or security force. Although coordinating with these forces expands complexity for emergency management, this support provides much-needed safety and security for both critical-incident and disaster management.
- Library managers must take the lead in assessing collections and other resources unique to their library and informing emergency management planners about, for example, their proprietary information and the unique issues in recovery and continuity.
- Most special libraries have very few employees. Smaller numbers of employees provide fewer team members for emergency management activities.

EMERGENCY MANAGEMENT—MANAGEMENT CATEGORIES

When managing critical incidents and disasters (or disaster planning), library managers focus on the three stages used in addressing emergency management issues: prevention or mitigation, business continuity, and recovery.

- Prevention—or mitigation—is the process employed to prevent or reduce the likelihood and impact of critical incidents and/or disasters. This process includes the design, implementation, and maintenance of policies and procedures both generally and specifically related to emergency management.

*   Business continuity refers to those practices, planned and implemented in advance of a critical incident or disaster, that are designed to maintain service and general institutional functions (as many as possible) for customers/patrons/constituents. These continuity activities may range from core services to specialized services and include maintaining digital or virtual infrastructure as well as services and resources. These activities are in place prior to an event and take place during an event through recovery.

*   Disaster recovery is considered a smaller category or function of business continuity and is the process of repairing, reestablishing, and returning the organization to all normal business functions and activities.

MANAGEMENT FUNCTIONS AND EMERGENCY MANAGEMENT FUNCTIONS

When managers identify management roles and responsibilities for emergency management, the structure is best explained by the POSDCoRB management acronym, which consists of planning, organizing, staffing, directing, coordinating, reporting, and budgeting.

Planning and Emergency Management Functions

Designing directions for annual or operational, multiyear, and/or master or strategic planning including strategies and activities that articulate what needs to be done to accomplish outcomes, goals, and objectives. Planning encompasses designing strategies and directions for communication, assessment, and emergency issues. Assessing includes identifying and using tools such as best practices, developing measures, and outcomes.

Planning for Prevention/ Mitigation

*   Library managers need to coordinate the creation and implementation of plans to put in place to prepare for critical incidents and disasters. Additional planning activities include assessments related to vulnerability, threats, facilities, employees, partners, and past events and activities.

*   There are literally dozens of ways to organize plans including by events, by seasons, by likelihood, by past events, and so on. Each manager has to decide what works best for planning for their geographic environment, and the size and type of library, to name just three areas.

- Prevention planning also includes implementing plans for stockpiling for employees, constituents, partners, shelter in place, and business continuity.
- Assessing risk includes any local or institutional mandate-specific risk assessments based on risk analysis and assessment methodology.

Planning for Business Continuity

- Business continuity plans position the organization to continue to deliver core services and resources critical to recovery as well as core services critical to continuing to meet constituent needs.
- Planning for continuity is embedded in daily, weekly, and monthly plans for operating through situations, as well through specific events and disasters.
- A critical element of planning in business continuity is data-gathering, assessment, and analysis of events, and analysis of incident and disaster impact. These data are used to evaluate continuity-plan rollout and then to assist in measuring recovery.

Planning for Recovery

- Recovery plans include assessment of incident or disaster impact, budget planning, significant planning for time, planning for change (both short term and long term), and the connection of recovery back to prevention, if possible, but at the very least recovery plans tied to mitigation or a reduction in impact of incidents and/or disasters.
- Successful prevention and/or mitigation plans contribute to a successful and, if possible, complete recovery.

Organizing and Emergency Management Functions

Organizing for emergency or critical incidents includes establishing structures for accomplishing work and organizational goals and outcomes, and identifying and defining levels and types of authority in the institution.

Organizing for Prevention/Mitigation

- Library managers must build in process owners to the organization for all aspects of prevention of critical incidents and disasters.
- These process owners might be within functional or service areas of the organization and then these individuals may form a response team, which operates as a whole to move the organization through events.

Organizing for Business Continuity

- Although the goal of business continuity is to have the organization's structure and standard operating procedures continued through events, continuity can include alternate, temporary structures, as well as different functions within existing structures to maintain resources and services.
- Overall authority is maintained but temporary authority can be identified during events to ensure, for example, safety and security.
- A specific example would be that the customer complaint process includes specific managers dealing with complaints in specific orders.
- During events, complaints to management might be redirected to specific managers to handle for expediting information-sharing and solutions.

Organizing for Recovery

- Unless events cause significant changes in resources and/or services or in facilities and/or tech infrastructure and delivery, the expectation is that organizational functions and authority return to normal levels.
- This might not happen as quickly as anticipated if the event is so significant as to alter business for a long period of time and/or changes to the organization have resulted in altering, for example, facilities and thus changing service delivery.

Staffing and Emergency Management Functions

This involves hiring, training, evaluating, firing, and all other human resources functions such as motivating, and organizational culture defines employee issues for managers. Other staff activities include orientation, training, continuing education and professional development, and all policies and procedures as they relate to employees.

Staffing for Prevention/Mitigation

- Prevention activities for employees focus on incident and disaster content integrated into orientation, training, and ongoing continuing education and professional development.
- This content includes not only behaviors expected and practices required, but also an employee commitment to prevention and mitigation.
- While all employees and partners are oriented, trained, and so on, select employees should be trained as process owners and response team members.

Staffing for Business Continuity

- Employees need a variety of activities and elements to assist in continuity activities.
- Managers must ensure that employees have what they need to alter, as needed, work functions, customer interactions, and so on, to ensure continuity is successful. They include:
  - specific scripts for customer/constituent questions and answers regarding providing services while dealing with events, articulation of employee roles, and responsibilities on event teams
  - communication created to ensure ad hoc/temporary changes are in place such as memos to employees, messages for partners, and content for customers such as signage and e-postings
- Alternate job functions need to be articulated for public-service-desk library employees, service and resource assistance interactions, and as needed for individual employees who need specific changes outlined.

Staffing for Recovery

- Employees serve on recovery teams as individuals responsible for implementing training as well as individuals responsible for managing internal and external approaches to recovery.
- Employees may work with vendors as resident experts during recovery.
- Managers need to track alternate job responsibilities for employee performance issues, compensation issues, and quality control.

Directing and Emergency Management Functions

Manager roles and responsibilities include not only working with and leading others to make decisions and contribute to decision-making, but also making their own management decisions on choosing from alternatives presented by employees.

Directing for Prevention/Mitigation

- Managers must ensure standards are met by conducting organizational audits for preparedness profiles, designing prevention activities such as drills, and auditing organizational policies and procedures on all aspects of emergency management.
- Managers are also responsible for identifying and designing roles and responsibilities for constituents and ensuring standards are met for safety and security.

- Managers must manage and lead the organization by working alone and with others to make decisions regarding event avoidance, event mitigation, and—if events do occur—preparedness.

Directing for Business Continuity

- Managers address decision-making that must take place during continuity and how those decisions might be made differently than during pre-event activities. Changes in decision-making may be different because of:
  - time/immediacy
  - expertise needed
  - safety and security issues
- Managers ensure standards are met in tandem with the organization's and/ or community's emergency management or continuity team.
  - Managers work with teams to ensure that during continuity activities policies and procedures are adhered to.
  - Managers must take the primary and final responsibility for all decisions made for the organization after events occur.

Directing for Recovery

- Managers are responsible for designing and directing recovery content, in tandem with larger organization or community team PR and safety professionals, communiqués for library employees, partners, constituents, and the broader continuity team of vendors and continuity workers.

Coordinating and Emergency Management Functions

Managers' coordinative responsibilities interrelate work functions, institutional infrastructure work, and library employee roles and responsibilities.

Coordinating for Prevention/Mitigation

- The nature of emergency management in today's organization is a team- and partner-driven management role and responsibility. Managers must identify and coordinate library employees, stakeholders, and other institutional peers and partners, as well as community or other institutional "players."
- Emergency activities are also integrated with area first responders as well as vendors who have been vetted and added to institutional-approved emergency management support.

Coordinating for Business Continuity

- While pre-event coordinating activities are key areas for managers focusing on emergency management, a manager's primary coordinating role takes place during continuity activities.
- Continuity coordinating activities often take up 100 percent or more of a manager's time due to the fact that few standard operating policies and procedures are in play, but rather primarily unique policies and procedures tailored to continuity activities are in play.
- Activities for managers include:
  - maintaining infrastructure
  - maintaining resources
  - maintaining services
  - oversight of facilities (if affected by event)
  - oversight of employees maintaining operations

Coordinating for Recovery

- Coordinating stakeholders, community members, other institutional members, and so on, involved in or supporting recovery
- Coordinating recovery activities for managers includes:
  - facility recovery issues caused by event
  - coordinating vendors in recovery
  - coordinating first responders in recovery

Reporting and Emergency Management Functions

The reporting function for managers includes basic and advanced management activities, including keeping employees informed and creating and disseminating contents throughout the institution and community as well as to stakeholders, first responders, and partners. Managers should expand beyond basic communication to include records and data from research, and records should include assessment content to be used throughout the emergency management event and process. Reporting should also include both awareness and knowledge of needs for signage through the event, continuity, and recovery.

Reporting and Prevention/Mitigation

- Pre-event reporting focuses on managers reporting to teams and establishing parameters for teams reporting back on policies and procedures, standards, and so on.

- A major part of the success of prevention and mitigation activities includes reporting out of all plans for preventing, continuity, and recovery for events, and reporting out of training roles and responsibilities.

Reporting and Business Continuity

- Additional critical reporting is the data-gathering of all assessment measures, the analysis of measures, and the dissemination of information to library employees, stakeholders, partners, constituents, community members, and first responders.
- A key element of the success of continuity is ongoing communication and reporting between and among groups/teams as well as communication flows internal and external to the institution.

Reporting and Recovery

- Reporting during recovery contributes to communication dissemination, expedites successful recovery, and aids in assessment for prevention and mitigation for reoccurring activities and events.

Budgeting and Emergency Management Functions

Budgeting roles and responsibilities for managers include planning, requesting, negotiating, allocating, tracking, and reconciling or accounting for hard money and soft money, as well as, when appropriate, entrepreneurial activities. In general, managers are responsible for all aspects of control for institutional dollars.

Budgeting and Prevention/Mitigation

- Managers must design budgets for pre-event needs that include stockpiling for events, as well as dollars to be spent for both avoidance and mitigation such as:

  ○ facilities design
  ○ facilities maintenance
  ○ training to address needs
  ○ assessment/audits of issues

- Managers are also responsible for identifying return-on-investment possibilities for investing in prevention to mitigate and/or reduce the impact of both critical incidents and disasters.

Budgeting and Continuity

- Dollars must be allocated annually to manage costs such as alternate infrastructures to maintain services and resources during events; increased communication, including increased signage and publications; as well as additional dollars to assist employees in meeting constituent needs.

Budgeting and Recovery

- Budget dollars are integrated into event budget lines for assuming costs for larger issues, unexpected issues, and discreet cost needs (e.g., unexpected single issues).
- Budget dollars are integrated into ongoing budget lines to support operating dollars such as supplies and vendor costs.

CRITICAL ISSUES/INCIDENTS

Critical incidents are defined as incidents that are of significance to someone, an institution, an organization, and so on, but not, in general, everyone. A critical incident could be of importance in general, or important to many, or may be based on an individual or organization, and so on, and have major significance only to specific or particular people. Library management of critical incidents is time-consuming and can take up much of contemporary managers' work time (see Paradigm Shift 16.2).

PARADIGM SHIFT 16.2.
Classic vs. Contemporary Management of Critical Incidents in Libraries

Sorting out emergency from critical incident situations is an important part of a manager's job in contemporary libraries. Just as in emergency management, classic handling has been primarily a first responder's role as well as the role of external departments and individuals. Library managers today identify critical incidents (as well as emergencies) and have policies and procedures for preventive measures, business continuity, and recovery.

Classic	Contemporary
• Incidents are managed as they arise and handled in primarily a reactive manner.	• Incidents are listed and identified prior to occurrence, and management plans are proactive and designed to handle these incidents.
• Dollars are not added to the budget for unforeseen occurrences other than "contingency" money.	• Dollars are slotted into emergency-management and critical-incident budget lines for preventive as well as recovery and business continuity costs.
• Critical incident activities are not parsed out among different categories.	• Critical issue and incident activities are parsed out among categories such

(continued)

PARADIGM SHIFT 16.2.
(continued)

Classic	Contemporary
	as natural and man-made and levels of urgency and magnitude such as emergency vs. critical issue or critical incident.

Examples of some common critical issues from three management areas are:

- financial issues
  - cash box imbalance
  - theft of resources by constituents
  - shortfalls in public service dollars
  - shortfalls in other operating accounts

- human resources
  - employees misbehaving
  - conflict among/between employees
  - employee conflict with constituents
  - illness
  - employee discipline
  - employee firing
  - new management
  - poor management

- facilities
  - displacement
  - remodel/renovations
  - shared spaces/issues

Examples of some less common critical issues from three management areas are:

- financial issues
  - theft of cash box resources by employees
  - embezzlement of funds (operating, grant, etc.)
  - counterfeit money passed by constituents

- human resources
  - employee death—natural causes
  - employee death—accident

- ○ employee death—homicide
- ○ employee injury—by constituents
- ○ employee injury—by peers/employees
- ○ employee injury—natural disasters/on the job
- ○ employee injury—external to work

- facilities

- ○ new facilities
- ○ shared spaces issues—major conflict

Although critical incidents are of importance to a specific audience, management of diverse critical incidents is challenging; preparing for and preventing these issues, as well as managing, continuity, and post-issue management, is now a requirement of twenty-first-century library managers.

DISASTERS (PREVENTION, RECOVERY, BUSINESS CONTINUITY)

Disasters

Depending on what you read, categories of "emergencies" include emergencies, disasters, and often other topical or profession-centric titles. For example, meteorologists might categorize a situation as a natural or man-made disaster, or a weather emergency. Although library managers have always had to deal with weather and weather-related emergencies, as well as fire and smoke with a focus on disaster planning that was unique to collections, contemporary management of these issues has now become all inclusive. Management of this diverse "disaster" environment is challenging, and preparing for and preventing as well as managing, continuity, and post-disaster handling is now a requirement of twenty-first-century library managers (see Paradigm Shift 16.3).

PARADIGM SHIFT 16.3.
Managing Disasters Affecting Library Environments—Classic vs. Contemporary

Disasters occur in libraries and within library communities. Library managers—now a part of many first-responder teams within communities—have roles and responsibilities for not only emergency management in general but also critical incidents and disasters. Although disasters have always occurred and affected libraries, library services, and library constituents, libraries now play a major role not only in their own disaster management but also in the recovery of others affected by disasters.

(continued)

PARADIGM SHIFT 16.3.
(*continued*)

Classic	Contemporary
• Most of the proactive treatment of disasters in libraries is focused on collections.	• Disasters are listed and identified prior to occurrence, and management plans are proactive and designed to handle this wide range of possible disasters.
• Most of the proactive treatment of disasters in libraries is focused on water, smoke, fire, and pestilence.	• Disasters are listed and identified prior to occurrence, and management plans are proactive and designed to handle this wide range of possible disasters.
• Dollars are added to the budget for primarily collection and facilities issues related to collections.	• Dollars are slotted into disaster budget lines for preventive as well as recovery and business continuity costs.
• Disaster activities are not parsed out among different categories.	• Disaster activities are parsed out among categories that are expanded beyond collections and facilities and include infrastructure, technology, and so on.

Risk Management Issues in Emergency Management

Risk management offices and functions (including critical incidents and disaster planning) strive to manage risks through proactive management rather than reactive management. These employees play a significant role in the management activities of organizations and, while most institutions do *not* have their own risk management office, managers must work with umbrella organization risk management employees as well as first responders for risk assessment, data-gathering, and training. Risk management personnel identify what could go wrong in general as well as the impact and consequences of natural events and manmade events. In addition, risk experts identify strategies for risk management within institutions and provide guidance on the institutions' required policies and procedures.

The importance of risk management has grown exponentially in the past fifteen-plus years and, although many institutions do not have a full-time employee trained in emergency management or extensive dollars for all necessary emergency management initiatives, risk issues should be a primary role of all managers. Library risk management elements include in general:

- assessment of the value and/or worth of print, media, software collections design, implementation, and oversight of environmental/facilities needs
- managing the design and maintenance of the critical issues planning and a disaster recovery plan

INDISPENSABLE RESOURCES FOR LIBRARY MANAGERS REGARDING EMERGENCY MANAGEMENT

Library managers have rich content available on disasters and emergencies regarding collections and a growing body of literature on emergency management in general. One of the most important aspects of emergency management is the need to learn the terminology of the field in order to "speak the same language" as emergency management experts and first responders. While more typical terms are used to search library literature, the profession now has a significant number of resources that are specific to the emergency management field with the literature of library and information science.

"American Library Association (ALA)." Accessed September 23, 2013. www.ala.org.
"Designing Libraries." Accessed October 27, 2013. www.designinglibraries .org.uk.
"EDUCAUSE." Accessed September 15, 2013. www.educause.edu.
"Federal Emergency Management Agency." Accessed October 27, 2013. www.fema.gov.
"Free Management Library." Accessed October 24, 2013. www.freemanage mentlibrary.org.
"Internet Public Library." Accessed October 15, 2013. www.ipl.org.
"Libguides Community." Accessed September 21, 2013. www.libguides.com.
"Special Library Association (SLA)." Accessed September 23, 2013.www .sla.org.
"State Libraries." Accessed October 27, 2013. www.publiclibraries.com/ state_library.htm.
"State and Regional Chapters." Accessed October 27, 2013. www.ala.org/ groups/affiliates/chapters/state/stateregional.
"WebJunction." Accessed October 21, 2013. www.webjunction.org.
"The Whole Building Design Guide." Accessed October 27, 2013. www .wbdg.org.

DISCUSSION QUESTIONS FOR CHAPTER 16

1. Should library managers take a leadership role in emergency management within their umbrella organizations?
2. Where can library managers find education and/or training for emergency management in general? For emergency management in libraries?

3. Should library managers integrate emergency management into the organization's policies and procedures or use the umbrella organization's policies and procedures?
4. Should library managers integrate emergency management into employee roles and responsibilities?
5. How should a library manager integrate emergency management into the library's budget?

Readers are reminded that a case method is intended to be used in conjunction with this chapter. The case designed to be used with this chapter is case 16, "Building Tomorrow's Future on Today's Expertise," located in part II, p. 330.

Part Two

THE CASES

Introduction to the Case Method

Effective techniques that provide a variety of approaches for teaching and training for management as well as managing in the workplace include: using models or comparisons through best (or effective) practices; outlining standards of practices through building and discussing paradigms; scanning the environment; illustrating change in practice through building and discussing paradigm shifts; thinking ahead or answering the "what if" or "what's next" questions using scenarios; and—one of the most recommended techniques for teaching and learning management when dealing with complexity, identifying issues, solving problems, and making decisions—the case method.

Using the case method technique in management education and training in general, in education for library and information science, or in the workplace is not new. Telling "stories" or using past examples to discuss issues has a rich tradition not only in management study but also in general culture and folklore. Although this method is better used in some disciplines or fields of study (e.g., law) rather than in more exact sciences or when "one answer" is the norm, use of the case method has expanded into almost all forms of higher education and training and is well-suited to many discussions in the library and information science profession.

As with any technique, however, a number of decisions are required when using the case method. Educators and managers must choose when to use a case, find an appropriate case, and decide how to use the case. Once these decisions are made, using the case method is an easy process. Case method elements provided for readers include: variations in case methods, variations in case content, variations for using case method in classroom settings, variations and ways for using case methods in workplace settings, case method pros and cons, case method steps, and specific considerations for using case methods in the workplace.

In addition, to assist readers in using cases provided in this book, a table is provided (page 235) with a list of cases for each chapter. The table also identifies, case by case, the types of libraries the cases "cover," a primary and secondary focus of each case, and multiple general and library management issues to suggest the variety of ways cases might be used.

VARIATION IN METHOD

There are a variety of ways cases can be designed and organized for discussion. Typically cases include a narrative with a "story" that describes the environment; the individuals or characters involved, such as employees (e.g., full- and part-time employees, student workers, or other types of workers), stakeholders (e.g., donors, boards of directors), clients (e.g., constituents, faculty, students), and constituents; and the outline of a situation, issue, or decision that needs to be addressed, or problem that needs to be solved. Some cases reveal much information on the environment, characters, or the situation, and in other cases, very little is revealed. Cases can be subtle or obvious in their telling of the story or in the identification of case elements, issues, or activities. There is no magic order for using cases; that is, shorter or less revealing cases aren't necessarily the ones to begin or end with. Instead, instructors should begin with the structure; no matter the length, the same structure or sets of questions should be applied to discussion. This structure can be:

- a set of steps (anywhere from five or six to ten) for research, analysis, and discussion
- a request for questions to be designed or identified, then answered
- a list of questions to be answered

VARIATION IN CONTENT

Cases are created and/or selected by managers or educators to meet a variety of needs. Case content can provide:

- opportunities for personalizing a work situation that has or will come up
- content that is designed to clarify workplace expectations such as employee behaviors, changing policies and procedures, or workplace elements

- opportunities for discussions to assist in teaching management for potential managers
- opportunities for discussions to assist in leadership teaching and learning content
- structures that provide for integrated shared or collegial decision-making
- processes to assist in data-gathering
- examples to illustrate visions and values (ethics, and so on) of the profession, of the workplace, or of a specific situation
- opportunities to discuss change in general

VARIATION IN CLASSROOM (OR TRAINING) SETTINGS

As a teaching and learning technique, the case method offers the classroom instructor or the trainer opportunities for active learning, lecture enhancement, real-world experience in a classroom setting, experience in applying critical-thinking skills, and practice in decision-making and problem-solving. These opportunities illustrate uncertainty, ambiguity, and complexity; highlight the importance of research in problem-solving and decision-making; and offer a systematic process for recognizing and dealing with change. Cases in the classroom (both digital and in person) can include but are not limited to:

- students study general content independently and then read a case for small-group or large-group discussion (in person or in an online forum)
- students read a case (in person or in an online forum), assess it or answer case questions as individuals, and then come together (in person or in an online forum) to discuss issues
- students receive a case in the classroom (in person or online, synchronous), discuss it as a group, and then a panel of experts addresses case issues
- students receive a case in the classroom (in person or online, synchronous), a panel of experts addresses case issues, and then the students discuss their panel discussion as a group and answer case questions
- students receive a case in the classroom, they discuss it in small groups, and then a panel of representative students is assembled to address case issues and answer case questions

VARIATIONS IN WORKPLACE SETTINGS

Although managers use techniques to manage in the workplace, a variety of techniques is critical to reach the diverse type and levels of employees and the (almost-incalculable) number of situations that can and do occur in every workplace. Not every technique works the same across all situations, and the reality is that managers, with their own preferences, styles, time constraints, and legalities, typically settle on a few techniques that work best, for the most part, with *all* of their employees. Then, they handle or manage individual issues with employees as each situation arises, and, if possible, choose techniques unique to that employee's needs. Good managers, however, must seek a variety of ways to handle current and future workplace issues, solve the more traditional as well as new or unique problems, make the hard decisions, and find appropriate and even perfect solutions for the workplace.

As a teaching and learning technique in the workplace, the case method technique offers a manager and/or facilitator or trainer opportunities for active learning; experience in applying critical-thinking skills; opportunities for decision-making and problem-solving; and opportunities to illustrate uncertainty, ambiguity, and complexity in safe, nonpersonal, or nonthreatening "work" discussion. In addition, using case method emphasizes the importance of continuing to use research methods in workplace problem-solving and decision-making as well as a systematic workplace process for recognizing and dealing with change.

Although the case method is typically thought of as a tool for teaching management in education and training, it is a successful tool for use in practice and offers a wide variety of approaches not only to traditional, usual, or classic situations, but also to unique or constantly changing situations. Specifically, case method consists of the content review or reading of the case itself and the discussion of that content. Typically, a case is a narrative in which individuals or groups are presented with a variety of elements in a "story" or description of a situation, and—given the content within the narrative of the situation—these individuals or groups must solve one or more problems or make a decision. Cases provide opportunities for teaching and learning about complex situations, with a description of the situation, content that includes context and description of the elements of the situation, and analysis of those elements within that context.

The logistics of using the case method in the workplace can vary dramatically. Following are some examples of specific ways to use the case method in workplace settings.

- Media can be used to introduce an issue or tell a story—followed by a facilitated general discussion with general questions asked during, for example, a staff development event. (Employee panels can discuss; all employees can discuss; breakout sessions can follow panels or precede panels.) YouTube videos can illustrate how others handle issues such as a constituent conflict at the circulation desk or public service desks, and employees can then critique the exhibited behaviors and performance. Managers would then follow up by working with employees (large or small group) with a document that clarifies what behaviors are expected of employees.

- Media can be used to introduce an issue or tell a story, followed by a facilitated or group open discussion with specific questions asked or specific steps outlined for discussing case elements during staff development. Feature movies are shown to the participants with a brief introduction such as, "The focus of this movie is the competencies needed for leadership under times of great stress." Following the movie (or at discrete parts of the movie), questions are posited about possible outcomes or perceptions of plotline outcomes. (Examples of movies: *High Noon* and *Twelve O'Clock High* are used to illustrate leadership, ethical behavior, and adhering to standards.)

- A case can be selected and personalized to illustrate an issue for discussion during a staff meeting. A general case about "new managers" can be chosen and then personalized with case characters or players altered to reflect the organization. For example, a case can be about a popular retiring manager and a Gen X replacement. Case questions could include: "How do we adjust to a new manager?" and "How do others adjust to having younger managers?" Besides characters, locations can be shifted; for example, "ongoing patron conflicts at the public service circulation desk" might be altered to focus on "patrons causing conflict at a public service reference desk" or "patrons causing problems in a library program." Levels of employees could be shifted from a reference public service desk with a new, younger manager to a very new, young branch manager for a branch in a traditional older neighborhood.

- Poor performance or bad behavior can be introduced during an all-library, all-departmental, or all-location/branch training with general case content, so all employees can be "on the same page" as to expectations without singling anyone out. This is important when a manager isn't sure of the actual service problem and may only have hearsay complaints. Instead of a manager working with one employee who may or may not be the problem, the manager can introduce a general related case for all employees. Cases can offer the basics of the "new, younger manager" overall, then a discussion of expectations. Managers can insert specific poor customer service examples such as specific characters' dialogue heard in the workplace but found lacking. Examples could be general dialogue overheard by a manager or dialogue reported by a constituent or another employee and could include a circulation desk assistant helping constituents with technology that librarians are responsible for or examples of librarians moving patrons between public service desks incorrectly. Managers can also use a case to review service behaviors at public service desks such as, "What customer service experience does the teenager have at the adult reference/information services desk?"

- Cases can be used to orient employees to an organization's vision and values in general or how they are in contrast to another organization. Case content can illustrate the difference in services and resources for an employee moving from a public library to a school library or a school library to an academic library. Similar uses include the discussion over an institution's mission statement with an employee who works in a partnership environment of a shared school and public library or a part-time librarian who moves between different types of libraries and needs direction on, for example, the reference interview in each setting and the need for in-depth assistance for employees.
- Cases can be used to illustrate issues for orienting, training, and educating, for example, governing or advisory boards, umbrella organization upper-level administrators, the media, and peer managers throughout the organization. Case content can illustrate the profession's commitment to intellectual freedom, the issues surrounding filtering, the debate over authentication, or the debate for open access to information.

CASE METHOD PROS AND CONS

Can case method be used in all situations? Absolutely not. Discussions of the pros and cons in the management literature typically focus on cases used in primarily academic settings; however, many of the pros and cons apply to both settings.

Pros

- Non-decision-makers can gain experience as decision-makers both through suggesting evidence, solutions, and so on, *and* through observation of others in the roles of decision-makers.
- Decision-makers can exhibit preferred decision-making for the organization, can observe other decision-makers, and can try alternate decision-making techniques.
- Participants gain experience in evaluating and assessing evidence and exercising judgment for contributing to activities within the organization.
- Participants (new hires in general, new hires from different types or sizes of organizations, hires from those new to the profession, employees moving from one department to another, etc.) can observe operations through the lens of the organization's vision, values, mission, and goals.

- Participants explore complex situations and the processes used to address complexity in organizations as well as alternative ways to deal with complexity in the workplace.
- Participants learn about classic structures and patterns that can be used to address workplace situations and experience positive ways to deal with change and ambiguity for continuously evolving workplaces.
- Participants experience successful ways to sort out issues and deal with uncertainty, incomplete information, and even chaos in changing organizations as well as organizations with a multitude of issues.
- Participants experience situations where a number of answers may "work" for individual situations, and experience decisions made and the variety of outcomes and repercussions of those outcomes.
- Participants experience working in groups or teams with others in the organization with whom they typically don't work.

Cons

- Case method is an exploratory tool. As the nature of exploration is often the discovery of a variety of elements rather than just one, employees may need more explanation to balance the ambiguity.
- Although case method is designed to sort out complicated issues, it is less appropriate in situations where there is—no matter how complicated the situation—only *one* answer due to, for example, legal, medical, or ethical elements.
- Establishing ways to deal with a situation through case method can be time-consuming and managers may not have the time to spend on a specific situation.
- Using cases intermittently may not be as effective in workplace settings, as having too many initial *unproductive* case sessions (while learning how to use case method) may be too difficult to overcome to use this method as an ongoing tool.

CASE METHOD STEPS

The steps for assessing case content can vary, depending on the process chosen. Having six steps to ten steps is common; for analysis of cases presented in this book, the ten-step case method will be used. The ten-step case assessment focuses on participants viewing the process of case discussion as a series of deliberate fact-finding steps that dissect the case and its components without necessarily identifying the research questions and specifically not identifying research questions at the initial stages of case discussion. The ten steps are as follows.

1. Read the case thoroughly without underlining or noting case elements. Take no immediate position or role. Then, during the second reading, note elements of the case by underlining and/or circling case individuals or "characters," case facts as stated, case suppositions, and implied as well as clearly stated issues and/or actual, perceived, or possible problems. Also make note of the following.

   a. If the case has a title, consider it part of the elements of the case.
   b. Pay close attention to the opening paragraphs of the case by identifying primary and secondary characters, and any outstanding elements of the work environment.
   c. Identify the time elements of the case mentioned, any location issues, and consider if the case elements are related to any standard management documents such as policies and/or procedures.
   d. Note any data that is needed for a final solution, for example, but is not available.

2. Prepare lists of the important or relevant facts and/or statements in the situation.
3. List the characters or "players" in the situation, and, if possible, list them in relevant categories such as those directly involved, those indirectly involved, and those affected by the situation. Other categories or descriptors for characters can be: decision-makers, primary vs. secondary characters in the case, and so on.
4. Review the underlined, marked case elements and list the primary or most important issues, elements, and/or problems in the case/situation.
5. Prioritize the most important and/or least important issues or problems in the situation. At this point in case review, the timelines indicated by the case should be taken into consideration; however, other aspects of the case may contribute significantly toward prioritizing case elements. Other ways to prioritize could include now vs. later, immediate vs. can wait, and so on.
6. After review/discussion of the prioritized situation content, and given the players, elements of the organization, and so on, list "what can be done."
7. After review/discussion of the prioritized situation content, and given the players, elements of the organization, and so on, list "what can't be done."
8. Choose the best one or two solutions.
9. Speculate on the outcome(s) and/or impact if the solutions are used/put into effect.
10. Build in an evaluation mechanism.

CASE METHODS FOR EACH CASE STUDY

The first case study in this book, "A Difficult Path of Moving Up and Out," is analyzed in detail to illustrate how the ten-step case method is used. Refer to this more detailed analysis when evaluating and working with the other cases in the book.

Many cases can be used for more than one discussion or focus, or a multiuse case can have a number of discussions taking place in one case method analysis. The following table includes the chapter number and name, the case number and name, the type or types of library settings relevant to the case, and the primary and secondary focuses of the case.

After the case grid, all cases include introductory information on case content and outlines of how the case might be discussed by participants. Finally, prior to using any case, educators, managers, or facilitators should read the detail provided in all ten steps for case #1 for application in each case.

Summary of Cases

Chapter/Case # and Case Name	Type of Library and Information Setting *(listed alphabetically)* Academic Public School Special All	**Primary Focus** *The primary design of the case and case solutions was intended to be problem-solving and decision-making in these areas in order of listing.*	**Secondary Focus** *The case can also be used to solve problems and make decisions in secondary areas. These secondary foci are in no particular order.*
1. A Difficult Path of Moving Up and Out	• Academic • Public • Special (larger)	• Manager moving up from the ranks/now managing their peers • New manager	• Younger manager • Repairing a dysfunctional organization • Importance of communication in management
2. Building Your Own Management Training Program	• Public (larger) • School/High School	• Transitioning from in-person management only to virtual and in-person management • Using virtual modes and methods in management	• Transitioning a function from one manager to another • Managing intermittent employees

Chapter/Case # and Case Name	Type of Library and Information Setting	Primary Focus	Secondary Focus
3. Rumor Has It	• Academic • Public • Special (larger)	• Addressing rumors in the workplace • Assessing organizational climate including using data • Need for flexibility in management	• Managing organizational and human resources issues during freeze; potential cutback issues • Models for organizing technical services
4. Do You Have Any Change on You?	• Public	• Management planning for a new facility	• Planning a new, larger, accessible, and tech-ready facility • Transitioning from a retiring, long-standing manager to a new manager
5. Racking Up the Library Pool Table	• Academic • Public • School	• Management reporting in a variety of types of libraries	• Self-analysis involved in finding a job/the perfect job
6. Manuals, Handbooks, Policies, Procedures, Budgets, Minutes, and Plans, Oh My!	• School • Web environments of any type and size of library	• Issues related to management document upkeep in multiple modes and deliveries	• Balancing new technologies
7. What's Old Is New—If the Money Is There	• Public • Special Collection	• Budget shortfalls • Budget processes such as time management • Gifts and donations	• Supporting special collections
8. But Enough about Me—What Do *You* Think about Me?	• Special	• Library/information center relationships with IT • Establishing and maintaining departmental partnerships	• The importance of communication

Chapter/Case # and Case Name	Type of Library and Information Setting	Primary Focus	Secondary Focus
9. Suffering from Past Mistakes	• Academic • Public • School • Special	• Internal communication; the importance of a communication plan for all issues, but especially facilities issues • Employee negativity regarding remodel and the expression of negativity to each other but also, more importantly, to their constituents	• Employee negativity overall • Facilities remodel
10. What You Don't Know *Can* Hurt You	• School	• Lack of leadership • Ethics in the workplace • Working with external groups	• Making career decisions
11. A Fixer Upper	• Academic • Public • School • Special	• Technology renovation • Planning for and scheduling change in the workplace	• Time management
12. Penny's Partners Proliferate due to Punctual, Prioritized and Positive Planning	• Academic • Public • School • Special	• Importance of partnerships • Roles and responsibilities of partnerships • Planning for partnerships	• Communicating with disparate groups
13. Keeping Up with the "Joneses"	• Academic • Public • School • Special	• Assessing constituent needs • A new manager returning • A new manager	• Keeping up with change • The new technologically advanced library

Chapter/Case # and Case Name	Type of Library and Information Setting	Primary Focus	Secondary Focus
14. Torture the Data	• Public • Academic • School • Special	• Identifying modes and methods of collecting data • Processes for maintaining management information • A new boss	• Keeping up with assessment practices • Translating library data into umbrella organization data/ meaningful data
15. Matching Data to Data Requests	• School • Academic • Public • Using data to justify new employees applicable to any type of library	• Managing new technologies • Justifying new employee requests	• Transitioning from older spaces to newer spaces
16. Building Tomorrow's Future on Today's Expertise	• Public • Academic • School	• Managing co-location partnerships • Managing relationships with first responders	• Planning for partnership activities • Planning for first-responder relationships

Case One

A Difficult Path of Moving Up and Out

Chapter/Case # and Case Name	Type of Library and Information Setting	Primary Focus	Secondary Focus
1. A Difficult Path of Moving Up and Out	• Academic • Public • Special (larger)	• Manager moving up from the ranks/ now managing their peers • New manager	• Younger manager • Repairing a dysfunctional organization • Importance of communication in management

THE CASE

Jennifer Carter was reluctant to assume what she felt was the difficult management role of head of reference at the Richards Library after having been a member of the department's reference team for three years. She was, however, assured by her manager that he believed that—despite her younger age—her first-hand knowledge of the department, her use of and commitment to communicating with and implementing technological solutions, her past education, her experience in her previous institution, and the training and mentor relationship available and promised to her would serve her well as she assumed the new role.

In preparation for Jennifer assuming the management role in the next week, her manager was planning a formal introduction of her to the reference department. She was asked to update her résumé and prepare a summary of her relevant work and post it to the library's general internal online forum. She was also asked to have an initial goal of recommending immediate technological support changes (online meetings with remote reference employees at smaller locations and the design of a reference management wiki) but to *not* change reference department structure for at least six months as the department had been identified as dysfunctional in the last organizational development survey. Jennifer had been reassured, however, that the department employees—considered an entrenched group—would know that ultimately things needed to be different in reference. She and the administration discussed the benefits of an established technology-driven communication structure being layered on the existing department with assessment of impact for future reorganization discussions.

Jennifer's plans for assuming her new role included informal meetings with peer managers through Skype; the design of an outline of steps she needed to take before/as she was being introduced as the new manager; a plan for gathering information about perceptions on and data about the reference department; and a need to have management's promises to her in writing.

CASE COMMENTS

This case represents a variety of issues in workplaces that are common problems or issues. That is, becoming a team or group manager after having been a member of that team or group can be a difficult issue and should always be planned carefully by the new manager, peer, and senior-level management. In addition, this move may be exacerbated by the "new" manager being younger than most of the other employees in that department and—as this case outlines—the fact that the most recent assessment of the department climate has been more negative than desired. Finally, this case illustrates not only that careful preparation for moving this new manager in should be done with the great care suggested but also that the management processes and expectations in this situation should be communicated to employees throughout the process.

CASE METHOD ANALYSIS

1. Underline Case Elements

The first step in the case method for "A Difficult Path of Moving Up and Out" includes reviewing and—if appropriate—underlining content in the title of the case, underlining characteristics of those involved with a focus on the (possibly Gen X) individual in question (and his or her credentials), and how the administration is taking care to put a number of elements in place or take significant steps to facilitate—if at all possible—a smooth transition. Case elements indicating that data-gathering is needed should be included in underlined content.

A Difficult Path of Moving Up and Out

Jennifer Carter was reluctant to assume what she felt was the difficult management role of head of reference at the Richards Library after having been a member of the department's reference team for three years. She was, however, assured by her manager that he believed that—despite her younger age—her first-hand knowledge of the department, her use of and commitment to communicating with and implementing technological solutions, her past education, her experience in her previous institution, and the training and mentor relationship available and promised to her would serve her well as she assumed the new role.

In preparation for Jennifer assuming the management role in the next week, her manager was planning a formal introduction of her to the reference department. She was asked to update her résumé and prepare a summary of her relevant work and post it to the library's general internal online forum. She was also asked to have an initial goal of recommending immediate technological support changes (online meetings with remote reference employees at smaller locations and the design of a reference management wiki) but to *not* change reference department structure for at least six months as the department had been identified as dysfunctional in the last organizational development survey. Jennifer had been reassured, however, that the department employees—considered an entrenched group—would know that ultimately things needed to be different in reference. She and the administration discussed the benefits of an established technology-driven communication structure being layered on the existing department with assessment of impact for future reorganization discussions.

Jennifer's plans for assuming her new role included informal meetings with peer managers through Skype; the design of an outline of steps she needed to take before/as she was being introduced as the new manager; a plan for gathering information about perceptions on and data about the reference department; and a need to have management's promises to her in writing.

2. List the Facts

Identifying facts of the case can be done in the order in which the facts are presented or in the order of importance of the facts. In addition, facts listed can be those intuited or suggested; that is, the case content mentions Jennifer uses technology to address this situation and it can be intuited that she uses technology to address problems in general. It is unlikely, however, that at step 2, the order of importance of facts is clear or even able to be determined.

- Jennifer is taking over soon.
- She has been internal and known to the department but as a peer.
- She is young, possibly younger than her peers, and will be their manager.
- She is a techie and uses technology to address problems.
- The department has been identified as a problem by upper-level management.
- Promises from management will be in writing regarding her new position and include the introductory letter and the mentor training.
- Management has indicated support for change after six months.

3. List the Characters

Not all characters mentioned in the case are necessarily included as part of case discussion. Characters *not* mentioned, however, should be considered for listing. That is, Jennifer's new peers—or other managers at this level in the organization—are not specifically mentioned, but they could be consulted for opinions on survey data or for suggestions on introducing her to her new role, or they could play a role in addressing issues with a younger manager—if they are knowledgeable about this issue or may have been in this situation or if they are younger than their employees themselves. While primary and secondary categories can be established, the list could begin as a general noncategorized list or could use the categories "work with first" and "work with later."

Primary

- upper management
- Jennifer in her previous role/as people know her now
- the new Jennifer/Jennifer as head of reference in her new role
- the members of the reference department
- peer managers in general
- peer or other managers who have employees younger than themselves or are Gen X
- Jennifer's mentor "to be"

Secondary

- other higher-level administrators other than her direct supervisor
- constituents or reference "customers"
- those who have negative perceptions of reference (in general and if possible from survey respondents)

4. Review

After discussion of facts and characters, participants in the case should be ready to provide opinions and suggestions and list issues they see emerging in the case. That is, Jennifer appears to have support from her administration; however, if the level of support needs to be documented, then readers may want to list this as an issue in and of itself. "Review" may bring up obvious omissions that must be addressed or list assumptions of what *should* be happening so that recommendations can include a list of obvious and nonobvious steps that must be taken. Participants should be encouraged to think broadly and many elements may be listed early in this review that would not—given review of other considerations—end up in final recommendations.

- The department is at a deficit but administration is willing to "invest" and make changes.
- Jennifer has been encouraged to make some tech/communication and management changes now.
- Jennifer is a "known" but has support from the administration.
- The administration has a plan for introducing change.
- Jennifer has a plan for the future that includes change.
- Although Jennifer has "baseline data" on the department—which is good— the administration will be seeking (as will Jennifer) future data that changes perceptions. It's good to have data, but always challenging to change data.

5. Prioritize

When considering issues and characters for prioritization, as in other steps, different categories can be established. While "now" and "later" are natural categories, "first" and "second" or categories that are specific to a timeline can be used such as "fall" and "spring" or even a more narrower "before Jennifer begins her new role" and "after Jennifer begins her new role."

Now

(If the discussion concurs that this case is really about the new manager, Jennifer, rather than so much about the department.)

- Jennifer is a "known" but has support from the administration.
- Jennifer is younger and tech oriented.
- The administration has a plan for introducing change.
- The administration is supportive of tech changes now.

Later

- The department is at a deficit but administration is willing to "invest" and make changes.
- Jennifer has a plan for the future that includes change.
- Although Jennifer has "baseline data" on the department—which is good— the administration will be seeking (as will Jennifer) future data that changes perceptions. It's good to have data, but always challenging to change data.

6. What Can Be Done

Case discussion typically combines content gathered for steps 1–5 and considers—given priorities—what *can* be done. While this can never be considered a perfect assessment, by step 6, the elements outlined should include those things that—given generally held opinions—can be accomplished.

- Jennifer can verify and communicate her credibility with content.
- Jennifer can introduce tech changes to illustrate better communication and management infrastructure.
- Through both in-person and tech solutions, Jennifer can communicate her plans (e.g., a Paradigm Shift on the wiki) to the department to include her study and thoughtful processes regarding timeline for any changes needed.
- Jennifer can request to work with the administration on her introductory letter so that her content is presented in concert with her own plan of introducing her "new" self as manager to her previous peers.
- Jennifer can ask the administration to articulate their support/promises to her regarding the introduction and mentorship in writing on the online forum and—for those not used to technology-based communication—in a print memo and in an in-person departmental or library-wide meeting.
- Jennifer's plan must include working *with* department members for the transition and immediate future.

7. What Can't Be Done

Often considered by many educators, trainers, and managers to be one of the most important steps in the case method (especially in workplace settings,) what *can't* be done should be generally agreed on by participants with typically more input from educators, trainers, or managers. As a critical step, it asks participants to make hard decisions about what is possible given stated facts. Valuable discussions take place when managers introduce—if not mentioned before—any legal issues or policies that participants may not be aware of. Many teachable moments occur when students or employees have chosen specific directions that cannot be taken given legal issues or policies. Clearly this step provides "big moments" that make big impressions on those participating, and this step often contributes to accelerated learning that serves to keep some choices from being repeated.

One additional strength of this step is stating an obvious point in a case. For example, while participants already know that the poor morale or possible discomfort with a new manager from "one of their own" can't be ignored, stating it ensures that what's obvious to some, which may not be obvious to others, is critical to success.

- The administration can't ignore the importance of the careful introduction of Jennifer, her credibility, and her transition from peer to manager.
- Jennifer can't make changes within the time period discussed *unless* she uncovers egregious issues that must be addressed (and would then work with the administration on changing that timeline).
- Jennifer can't ignore the data or choose to address that later in that she must establish pathways to identify, measure, and illustrate change under her management and leadership.
- Jennifer can't ignore not only the importance of her shift from peer to manager but also the importance of involving the entire department in the process.

8. Choose Solutions

Solutions can be varied, and there may be more than one set of solutions if the case indicates more than one issue.

- Jennifer can request to work with the administration on documentation for what should be completed (concerning her) prior to her assuming her role as manager such as her introductory letter so that her content is presented in concert with her own plan of introducing her "new" self as manager to her previous peers.
- Jennifer and the administration can identify specific changes and the timeline needed for required and requested changes for the reference department such as increased positive responses on the organizational-development survey.
- Jennifer's plan must include working *with* department members for the transition and should communicate her (first-six-months, first-year) plans (such as a Paradigm Shift) for the department to include her study and thoughtful processes for any activities and changes needed.

- Jennifer should create a personal management plan for her own needs and activities for transitioning to reference manager including professional development, work with peer managers, and work with the administration.
- Jennifer and the administration should assess the department's survey data and choose appropriate questions and a timeline for administering a follow-up survey after Jennifer's transition into management.

9. Speculate on Outcome(s)

Case discussion should include participants speculating on both general outcomes and—as needed—outcomes to specific solutions chosen. Educators, managers, or facilitators can have participants speculate on outcome-by-outcome solutions for further assessment or can have participants look broadly by answering questions like "What should the reference department look like after six months of Jennifer's management?" and "What should the reference department look like after the first year of Jennifer's management?"

- Jennifer—with proper introduction and transition—should be able to have a smooth transition that includes a position with a *new* relationship with the reference department employees.
- A post-first-year survey should indicate a more positive morale (with a specific increase indicated such as "significantly more pleased with reference department management" as a goal or a higher numerical choice overall on a chosen Likert scale).

10. Evaluate

Evaluation should be a part of the case in a variety of ways. For example, all evaluative data present "prior to the case" should be used to provide background to assist in identifying case recommendations and proposed outcomes. Protocols should be identified or designed to evaluate case recommendations and proposed outcomes. In addition to using data to discuss and evaluate steps and activities in the case, varieties of types of evaluation should be considered and recommended for such concerns as: preventing any problems in the case from occurring again, assisting in related case issues and solutions, and using evaluation mechanisms—such as standard performance evaluation and customer service feedback forms, and so on—as needed.

- Jennifer needs to study the organization data available as well as the measurements used to gather the information.

- Jennifer should work with the last survey to design a survey for a six-month and a post-first-year "how am I doing" for employees, peer managers, and the administration.
- Jennifer should clearly establish and communicate measures for her performance for her first year as head of reference that includes data from her employees and from the administration.
- Evaluation data should be integrated into six-month, first-year, and any longer-range plans for the reference department.

Case Two

Building Your Own
Management Training Program

Chapter/Case # and Case Name	Type of Library and Information Setting	Primary Focus	Secondary Focus
2. Building Your Own Management Training Program	• Public (larger) • School/High School	• Transitioning from in-person management only to virtual and in-person management • Using virtual modes and methods in management	• Transitioning a function from one manager to another • Managing intermittent employees

THE CASE

Assistant director Frank Sumner had supervised the library's summer employees since his arrival three years ago. These workers—hired annually to assist with general stack management—were now also asked to work with the annual book sale, the teen comic collectors club, and the summer reading program. Their meetings had been primarily face to face; however, increasing numbers of participants and reduced time for training now dictated that in-person training and communication (meetings, etc.) would be replaced primarily by e-mails, online training content under the "volunteer" section of the library's website, YouTube training videos, and content placed on the internal wiki for use with these valuable volunteers.

The number of summer employees had increased in the last year and would be increasing again that coming summer because of the increase in programming. Sumner realized that, given the migration to the library's new online system, he would not have time to work with the summer employees. In discussions with director Alison Davis, Frank and Alison decided that he needed to train, at the very least, another employee to manage summer employees.

CASE COMMENTS

This case represents both contemporary technology issues as well as classic issues of managing intermittent employees. In addition, educators, managers, or facilitators can include this case in discussion of the challenges of intermittent workers who may be volunteers or, for example, workers who are assigned to the library through educational programs or court-mandated work. While the case can have both a broad focus of technology *and* movement from in-person to virtual or digital management, the case can also have a single focus of in-person to digital management or a single focus of the challenges of managing intermittent workers such as volunteers.

CASE METHOD ANALYSIS

1. Underline Case Elements

<u>Building Your Own</u> Management Training Program

Assistant director—<u>Frank</u> Sumner had <u>supervised</u> the library's summer employees since his arrival <u>three years ago</u>. These employees—hired annually to assist with general stack management—were <u>now also asked</u> to work with the annual book sale, the teen comic collectors club, and the summer reading program. Their meetings had been primarily face to face; however, <u>increasing numbers of participants and reduced time for training now dictated that in-person training and communication</u> (meetings, etc.) would be <u>replaced</u> primarily <u>by e-mails, online training content under the "volunteer" section of the library's website, YouTube training videos, and content placed on the internal wiki for use with these valuable volunteers.</u>

The <u>number</u> of summer <u>employees</u> had <u>increased in the last year and would be increasing again</u> that coming summer because of the increase in programming. Sumner realized that, given the migration to the library's new online system, he would not have time to work with the summer employees. In discussions with <u>director</u> Alison Davis, Frank <u>and Alison</u> decided that <u>he needed to train, at the very least, another</u> employee to manage summer employees.

2. List the Facts

- Sumner is a long-standing supervisor who should be familiar with the summer program employee roles and responsibilities.
- Employees in the summer have been asked to expand their work and move among a variety of roles and responsibilities, many of which are new.
- Technology is needed to provide different organization for this population of employees.
- There are more summer workers than there have been in previous years.
- Summer workers need training for their library roles and responsibilities.
- Sumner needs to identify another staff person to train.
- Sumner needs to identify and deliver training materials to train another employee.

3. List the Characters

Directly Involved/Primary

- Sumner (decision-maker)
- summer workers new to the library
- summer workers returning to the library
- the employee who will be trained to manage summer workers

Indirectly Involved/Secondary

- Director Davis
- other employees who need to work with summer workers

4. Review

- Sumner is a long-standing supervisor who should be familiar with the summer program worker roles and responsibilities.
- Sumner needs to identify and deliver training materials to train another employee.
- Sumner needs to identify another employee to train.
- The employee to manage should be tech savvy.

5. Prioritize

- Sumner needs to identify another tech-savvy employee to train.
- Sumner needs to verify with the director that the person chosen can be the person to take on this responsibility given—the level of the person chosen, their salary grade, their previous experience, and more specifically their

ability to manage as well as their interest/commitment to the management of these employees.

- Once approved, Sumner needs to approach the person approved and verify they do accept the role and responsibility.
- Sumner needs to identify and deliver training materials to train another employee.
- Sumner needs to establish a training schedule and timeline.
- Sumner needs to prepare the content (Paradigm Shift, introductory information for the new manager) to inform other library employees of the change in management.
- Sumner needs to prepare the content (Paradigm Shift, introductory information for the new manager) to inform summer employees of the change in management.

6. What Can Be Done

- Sumner needs to identify another employee to train.
- Once approved, Sumner needs to approach the person approved and verify they do accept the role and responsibility and that they have the tech skills to infuse technology into the training/organization.
- Sumner needs to establish training content, schedule, and timeline.
- Sumner needs to prepare the content (Paradigm Shift, introductory information for the new manager) to inform other library employees of the change in management.
- Sumner needs to prepare the content (Paradigm Shift, introductory information for the new manager) to inform summer employees of the change in management.

7. What Can't Be Done

- Summer employees can't go unmanaged.
- The new manager can't begin untrained.
- They can't choose someone to manage who doesn't have tech skills.
- The situation should not occur without employees being informed of the change.
- It should be clear if the new manager will be compensated for increases in work or will forgo other responsibilities to take on new responsibilities.

8. Choose Solutions

- Sumner needs to identify another employee who is tech savvy to train and establish training content, schedule, and timeline.

- Sumner needs to prepare the content (Paradigm Shift, introductory information for the new manager) to inform other employees and the summer employees of the change in management.
- Sumner needs to prepare the content (Paradigm Shift, introductory information for the new manager) to inform summer employees of the change in management.

9. Speculate on Outcomes

- Employees should clearly understand who will manage other employees and how that management will be handled as well as the infusion of technology.
- Employees will understand the transition of current manager to new manager and feel comfortable with the change.
- The new manager should feel comfortable in and be successful with his or her new role and set of responsibilities.

10. Evaluate

- Sumner will design training outcomes for the management training and measure outcomes at the end of training.
- Sumner will design an evaluation tool for summer employees to assess the new manager's performance throughout the summer to identify and correct problems in a timely fashion.
- Sumner will compare last summer's evaluation against the new manager's evaluation in general but give special attention to the employees who are returning to the library.
- The new manager will complete a self-assessment of his or her management performance midway through the summer.
- Sumner will identify ways for peer employees to assess the new management of the summer employees.

Case Three

Rumor Has It

Chapter/Case # and Case Name	Type of Library and Information Setting	Primary Focus	Secondary Focus
3. Rumor Has It	• Academic • Public • Special (larger)	• Addressing rumors in the workplace • Assessing organizational climate including using data • Need for flexibility in management	• Managing organizational and human resources issues during freeze; potential cutback issues • Models for organizing technical services

THE CASE

The Technical Services employees—supervised by assistant manager Cleo Rowan—was an interesting group of librarians and library employees. The team consisted of librarians, paraprofessionals, hourly employees, and a half-time administrative assistant. In addition, service-learning interns and field experience students rotated in and out of the department at a variety of times each year. Two openings were frozen due to budget shortfalls, and Rowan had been working with her peers to gather data to assess Technical Services functions and employee roles and responsibilities to determine if the department needed a temporary or permanent reorganization until the frozen positions could be filled.

Rowan's meeting with her peer library managers on the Technical Services data she had been gathering, however, began in an unexpected way with one of her peers sharing a rumor she had heard about Rebecca, one of Rowan's Technical Services employees. The rumor had been told to her by one of Rebecca's Technical Services department/team members and included the information that the team atmosphere in the department was strained due to Rebecca. Rowan knew that Rebecca's history with the department was one of excellent customer service and respectful relationships with her peers. She had also heard, however, that the universal feeling was that Rebecca's past year of service to her constituents had continued to be exemplary, but her peer relationships were strained.

Rowan thanked her peer for sharing the rumor and changed the meeting conversation to the primary purpose of the meeting—a review of the organizational data gathered. At the end of the meeting, Rowan turned her attention to her next steps for Technical Services.

CASE COMMENTS

This case represents typical or general human resources issues as well as issues in Technical Services—what is typically identified as a nonpublic-services workplace. The reality is, however, that Technical Services may not have standard public-services roles and responsibilities, but they do have customers who are not their own departmental employees; that is, they provide services to other library employees and even partners, and so on. In addition, this case focuses on communication issues surrounding rumors in the workplace; the case can be used to discuss only rumors by personalizing or changing the department from Technical Services to Reference Services or Children's Services.

One additional use of this case could include the importance of flexibility in management as well as how to remain calm and productive as plans change, for example, from one agenda to another.

CASE METHOD ANALYSIS

1. Underline Case Elements

<u>Rumor</u> Has It

The Technical Services employees—supervised by assistant manager Cleo Rowan—was an interesting group of librarians and library workers. The team consisted of librarians, paraprofessionals, hourly employees, and a half-time administrative assistant. In addition, service-learning interns and field experience students rotated in and out of the department at a variety of times each year. Two openings were frozen due to budget shortfalls, and Rowan had been working the her peers to assess services and employee roles and responsibilities to determine if the Technical Services department needed a temporary or permanent reorganization until positions could be filled.

Rowan's meeting with her peer library managers on the Technical Services data she had been gathering; however, began in an unexpected way with one of her peers sharing a rumor she had heard about, Rebecca, one of Rowan's employees. The rumor had been shared by one of Rebecca's Technical Services team members and included the fact that the team atmosphere was strained due to Rebecca. Rowan knew that Rebecca's history with the department was one of excellent customer service and respectful relationships with her peers. She had also heard, however, that the universal feeling was that Rebecca's past year of service to constituents had continued to be exemplary, but her peer relationships were strained.

Rowan thanked her peer for sharing the rumor and changed the meeting conversation to the primary purpose of the meeting—a review of the organizational data gathered. At the end of the meeting, Rowan turned her attention to her next steps for Technical Services.

2. List the Facts

- Some of the content to be addressed is based on rumors and second-hand information.
- There are a variety of people (jobs, levels of employees, types of members who are *not* employees) on the team. We don't know much about the team such as which positions are frozen.
- We don't know what position Rebecca has on the team.
- Rowan is managing and supervising the team and is addressing issues such as: assessing Technical Services, identifying roles and responsibilities of Technical Services, scheduling reference employees, and/or gathering general and specific information to use in deciding on the future of the team.
- Rowan is hearing team information from others in rumor form and—possibly—in front of others in the organization.
- Rebecca has an excellent record in customer service and with her peer/team members.
- Recent activities have identified Rebecca as having issues within the department.
- Recent activities have identified Rebecca's behaviors as causing a strain within the Technical Services team.
- Rowan hasn't made any decisions but knows she needs to focus on next steps.

3. List the Characters

Directly Involved/Primary

- Rowan
- Rebecca
- Technical Services team members
- those/the person who started what might be the rumor (talking about the situation)
- those who perpetuate (what might be) the rumor

Indirectly Involved/Secondary

- library administration
- other departments in the organization
- Technical Services constituents

4. Review

- Rebecca has an excellent record in customer service and there appears to be a history of positive interactions with her peer/team members. It's not clear what position Rebecca holds on the team; however, recent activities and information have identified Rebecca as having issues within the department—specifically behaviors identified as causing a strain within the Technical Services team.
- Some of the information about what has/is happening in Technical Services that needs to be addressed is—apparently—based on rumors and second-hand information.
- There are a variety of people (jobs, levels of employees, types of members who are *not* employees) on the team. We don't know much about the team such as which positions are frozen.
- Rowan is managing the team and performing some supervisory functions and is addressing issues such as: assessing Technical Services, identifying roles and responsibilities of Technical Services, and/or gathering general and specific information to use in deciding on the future of the team as well as assigning responsibilities as needed and scheduling employees and signing time sheets.
- Rowan is hearing team information from others in rumor form (as stated above); however, this information may have been shared with others in the organization.
- Rowan hasn't made any decisions but knows she needs to focus on next steps for managing as well as next steps for leading the group.

5. Prioritize

Now

- Recent activities have identified Rebecca as having issues within the department and recent activities have identified Rebecca's behaviors as causing a strain within the Technical Services team but Rebecca has an excellent record in customer service and with her peer/team members. (We don't know what position Rebecca has on the team.)
- Some of the content to be addressed is based on rumors and second-hand information. Rumors should be identified separately from information and second-hand information.

Later

- There are a variety of people (jobs, levels of employees, types of members who are *not* employees) on the team. We don't know much about the team such as which positions are frozen.
- Rowan is managing the team and is addressing issues such as: assessing Technical Services, identifying roles and responsibilities of Technical Services, and/or gathering general and specific information to use in deciding on the future of the team.
- Rowan is hearing team information from others in rumor form and—possibly—in front of others in the organization.
- Rowan hasn't made any decisions but knows she needs to focus on next steps.

6. What Can Be Done

- Rowan must investigate recent activities of issues within the Technical Services team and the strain reported within the Technical Services team.
- Rowan must clarify information or fact from rumor.
- Rowan must continue her assessment of Technical Services, identifying roles and responsibilities in the team and which are those of the frozen/open positions.
- Rowan must communicate to others about her handling of the situation with the goal to stop rumors.
- Rowan must focus on next steps/make a plan.

7. What Can't Be Done

- Rowan can't ignore the information/rumors.
- Rowan can't investigate the rumors as she investigates facts/gathers data.
- Rowan can't ignore the fact that the rumors are widespread.

8. Choose Solutions

- Rowan should sort out fact from rumor and add that information to the Technical Services team assessment.
- Rowan should use her Technical Services team information to work with Rebecca on Technical Services team issues that relate to her and on a plan to—if the information is verified—identify areas for Rebecca's improvement.
- Rowan should work with Technical Services employees to identify scenarios for how the team might be improved (Possible strain reduced? Temporary reorganization? More permanent reorganization?).

9. Speculate on Outcome(s)

- The Technical Services team has its issues addressed and rumors lessen or cease.
- Rebecca's behaviors—if the rumors have validity—return to previous levels of excellence.
- The Technical Services department has an organization (temporary or permanent) that meets employee and constituent needs with two fewer employees and possible changed roles and responsibilities.

10. Evaluate

- If the rumors have validity, Rowan works with Rebecca on a plan for returning to previous levels of excellence with a specific timeline and measurable outcomes.
- No matter the outcome regarding Rebecca, Rowan establishes a date for a second round of data-gathering to compare with previous data gathered and assessed.
- If the Technical Services department and/or team has a temporary or permanent reorganization, Rowan establishes a timeline for assessing those changes for impact on the library and its employees, the Technical Services team, and the employees in the Technical Services department.
- Rowan pays close attention to organizational rumors and establishes a process for gathering and addressing rumors.
- Rowan attaches a cover memo on rumors and disseminates the library's communication policy on sharing information.

Case Four

Do You Have Any Change on You?

Case for use with chapter 4, "New Management of Change"

Chapter/Case # and Case Name	Type of Library and Information Setting	Primary Focus	Secondary Focus
4. Do You Have Any Change on You?	• Public	• Management planning for a new facility	• Planning a new, larger, accessible, and tech-ready facility • Transitioning from a retiring, long-standing manager to a new manager

THE CASE

After five decades the Varney Community Library was getting a new facility. The current library was too small, had inadequate infrastructure for technology, was not ADA/ADAAA compliant, and had an unusable basement. The attorney who contacted the Library Board stated that an endowment was funding the new library from a "wills and estates" donor; however, there was a tight timeline for expending funds.

Director Carter—who had been there for thirty years *and* was scheduled to retire in eighteen months—did not want to plan the new facility. *Who* could and would plan it, though, was the big question and Carter sat down to prepare for the first discussion with the board on how the next eighteen months might be handled. What should Carter prepare? So far he had identified:

- donor content
- data/an environmental scan on the "community" (profiles, usage, other "community" members, umbrella organization needs)
- an employee list (with strengths, weaknesses, opportunities, threats)
- a current timeline for retiring
- a building timeline so far

CASE COMMENTS

This case provides not only an area for focus that is typically not a focus for educators, trainers, or managers, but also levels of complexity of content for either small or large organizations. Specifically, although the majority of libraries have many changes taking place, and while these libraries are dealing with changes on a daily basis, most libraries do not deal with change in and of itself, including: What is change, how do employees deal with change, what can managers do to assist employees in making necessary changes, and how do managers prevent future problems with change?

In addition, this case deals with not only change but also a change in facilities and management, which imposes change on employees, services, and resources, as well as all constituents, partners, stakeholders, and so on. To add to the complexity, the case has a focus on donors and giving (with strict timelines) as well as new technologies and the integration of technology, which could easily cause a redesign of the majority of services and resources. This level of complexity provides educators, managers, or facilitators with multileveled opportunities for both discussing and proposing solutions; one or more levels of complexity can be taken by themselves and/or can be personalized to an organization.

CASE METHOD ANALYSIS

1. Underline Case Elements

Do You Have Any <u>Change</u> on You?

After five decades the Varney Community Library was getting a <u>new facility</u>. The current library <u>was too small, had inadequate infrastructure for technology, was not ADA/ADAAA compliant, and had an unusable basement</u>. The attorney who contacted the Library Board stated that an endowment was funding the new library from a "wills and estates" donor; however, there was a tight timeline for expending funds.

Director Carter—who had been there for thirty years *and* was scheduled to retire in eighteen months—did not want to plan the new facility. *Who* could and would plan it, though, was the big question and Carter sat down to prepare for the first discussion with the board on how the next eighteen months might be handled. What should Carter prepare? So far he had identified:

- donor content
- data/an environmental scan on the "community" (profiles, usage, other "community" members, umbrella organization needs)
- an employee list (with strengths, weaknesses, opportunities, threats)
- a current timeline for retiring
- a building timeline so far

2. List the Facts

- This case is complex and educators, managers, or facilitators can choose to focus on all topics or one or fewer topics.
- The case is about "change."
- The case is about integrating new technology.
- This change is occurring after half a century so change does not come often to this community regarding the library.
- The library has a number of problems, and some need to be fixed based on law (such as ADA/ADAAA).
- The existing location may be a problem regarding technology, basement problems.
- The money is a gift.
- The money has a timeline.
- The timeline is a tight timeline.
- The person who should be planning the library is leaving.
- The person who should be planning the library doesn't want to plan the new library.
- The board will be in discussions on the project/who/timeline with the outgoing director.

3. List the Characters

Directly Involved/Primary

- director
- another employee (specifically one person who might be the one to step in to build the library)

- family of the donor
- attorney representing donor
- board

Indirectly Involved/Secondary

- employees who are not going to be running the project/building the library
- other possible or needed donors
- library constituents of the new facility

4. Review

- The person who should be planning the library is leaving.
- The money has a timeline.
- The timeline is a tight timeline.
- The board will be in discussions on the project/who/timeline with the outgoing director.
- The library has a number of problems, and some need to be fixed based on law (such as ADA/ADAAA).
- The existing location may be a problem regarding technology, basement problems.
- The money is a gift.
- The person who should be planning the library doesn't want to plan the new library.
- The case is about "change."
- The case is about "technology."
- This change is occurring after half a century so change does not come often to this community regarding the library.

5. Prioritize

Now

- The person who should be planning the library is leaving.
- The board will be in discussions on the project/who/timeline with the outgoing director.
- The money has a timeline.
- The timeline is a tight timeline.
- The person who should be planning the library doesn't want to plan the new library.
- The case is about "change."
- The case is about "technology."

Later

- The library has a number of problems, and some need to be fixed based on law (such as ADA/ADAAA).
- The existing location may be a problem regarding technology, basement problems.

6. What Can Be Done

- The director can gather information from employees, stakeholders, partners, and so on (survey results, brainstorming, scenarios, etc.).
- The attorney should be consulted as to donor information, dos, and don'ts.
- The director can consider making recommendation on who might manage the project and who might take over a building project (including employees, consultants, etc.).
- A timeline should be drafted to reflect issues, building issues.

7. What Can't Be Done

- The director can't ignore the donor issues/tight timeline.
- The board can't decide to avoid putting someone else in charge of the project.
- The director can't ignore the fact that "change" will be an issue in and of itself.

8. Choose Solutions

- The director should schedule a meeting with the attorney.
- The director should gather content and prepare a packet for the board with issues, questions. Packets should include:
  - employee strengths, weaknesses, opportunities, and threats
  - attorney/donor answers and unanswered questions
  - ideas from employees on how to proceed/scenarios

9. Speculate on Outcome(s)

- The director's search for content and data should assist her in a successful final eighteen months of change.
- The board should be prepared to make the decision on how to assign the new facilities project.

- Employees should feel like a part of the decision-making process by preparing scenarios for change.
- The process should be in place for the transition to the change of new facilities.

10. Evaluate

- The director should assess the scenarios for board discussion and identify strengths and weaknesses of each.
- The board should assess the packet and select a scenario.
- The director should present scenarios chosen to employees so they can work together to design a timeline, and so on, for the next eighteen months.
- The director should consider appointing a transition team for the upcoming changes and assess progress (surveys, etc.).
- The director should include reports of progress in quarterly board/director reports.

Racking Up the Library Pool Table

Case for use with chapter 5, "New Managers Designing New Organizations"

Chapter/Case # and Case Name	Type of Library and Information Setting	Primary Focus	Secondary Focus
5. Racking Up the Library Pool Table	• Academic • Public • School	• Management reporting in a variety of types of libraries	• Self-analysis involved in finding a job/the perfect job

THE CASE

Carter Stevens had worked in a number of library settings including a medium-sized public library, a community college, a high school, a four-year private college, and as an online researcher for the largest online (proprietary) university in North America. He served in a variety of roles within each setting—respectively as the director, the head of reference, special collections librarian, the learning resources manager, and reference and information literacy librarian. In each environment he experienced a different management structure and through the years found himself reporting to a city manager (directly, but then to the city council as well), a dean of libraries, the associate director and the collection management coordinator, the principal, the district-wide learning resources coordinator, and the vice president for Student Support Services.

While he had enjoyed the variety of settings, his service roles and responsibilities, and his constituents in these positions, he found dealing with the management structures frustrating as—literally—at every turn he reported to not only a different person within the institution or entity, but also in some locations to more than one person at a time.

With his current temporary position in Martinville Public Library ending, Carter found himself back on the job market and as exciting as that always was to him, he began to review the job postings to see what the best match might be for him—given the variety of experiences he had and the plusses and minuses he had been compiling on diverse library management structures and reporting protocols.

CASE COMMENTS

The more open-ended the case, the more varied the discussion, and this case is very broad and open-ended with a variety of types of libraries included in the description of the situation. Discussion for this case could include the importance of comparing and contrasting management structures in a variety of types and sizes of organizations and could also include the engagement of participants in discussions for preparation for job-seeking and interview processes at the beginning of or during careers. Obviously case content can also be used for asking questions of discussion participants about how libraries are the same and how libraries are different, as well as how different managers manage differently overall as well as in certain settings. This case discussion should illustrate the fact that a variety of factors affect the design of the organization and the management of the organization. The variety of management issues, based on the type and structure of the library, include but are not limited to: who reports to whom; who is in charge; how communication takes place; what management styles are more prevalent given the environment; and how many managers employees and functions have.

This case can also be used in workplace settings when, for example, orienting new employees or building teams, especially when employees or team members are from a variety of types of backgrounds. This discussion is also valuable when institutions are designing or coordinating partnerships with other institutions and there is a need for educating employees and partners about how organizations are managed overall as well as in the partnership.

Those generating discussion can also ask participants to identify (on many of the ten steps) who has experience with exact or similar areas. That is, on step 2, after the list of facts, which include where Stevens has worked, participants might be asked where they might have worked. On step 7 when "what can't be done" is listed, participants can be asked, given their knowledge, for examples of what can't be done given the locations where they have worked.

Finally, while one might think that Stevens "moves around too much" or "he must be unsuccessful in these positions to make these many changes," the case doesn't mention the number of years at each position or the number of years in a profession or whether or not—as is often common—Stevens is full time in some and may also be working part time in another. No matter these issues, Stevens is doing something *all* professions should do prior to looking for a new position—asking the tough questions in an effort to find a good fit.

CASE METHOD ANALYSIS

1. Underline Case Elements

Racking Up the Library Pool Table*

Carter Stevens had worked in a number of library settings including a medium-sized public library, a community college, a high school, a four-year private college, and as an online researcher for the largest online (proprietary) university in North America. He served in a variety of roles within each setting—respectively as the director, the head of reference, special collections librarian, the learning resources manager, and reference and information literacy librarian. In each environment he experienced a different management structure and through the years found himself reporting to a city manager (directly, but then to the city council as well), a dean of libraries, the associate director and the collection management coordinator, the principal, the district-wide learning resources coordinator, and the vice president for Student Support Services.

While he had enjoyed the variety of settings, his service roles and responsibilities, and his constituents in these positions, he found dealing with the management structures frustrating as—literally—at every turn he reported to not only a different person within the institution or entity, but also in some locations to more than one person at a time.

With his current temporary position in Martinville Public Library ending, Carter found himself back on the job market and as exciting as that always was to him, he began to review the job postings to see what the best match might be for him—given the variety of experiences he had and the plusses and minuses he had been compiling on diverse library management structures and reporting protocols.

The phrase "racking up the pool table" is chosen as the title for this case to illustrate how—given the variety of constituents, organizations, services, and resources—the same elements may have different parameters. That is, libraries may have the same resources and services (pool balls) yet different structures or needs or constituents (racks) will necessitate different outcomes.

2. List the Facts

Relevant Facts

- Stevens has worked in a number of library settings.
- Stevens's experience includes a medium-sized public library, a community college, a four-year private college, and a proprietary school.
- Stevens has experience as a director (public), the head of reference (college), special collections librarian (college), and reference and information literacy librarian (online proprietary).
- Stevens has experienced a variety of management structures.
- Stevens has reported to a wide variety of bosses including city management, a higher education dean and administrators, and a coordinator.
- Stevens has been frustrated with a number of management structures including structures when he reports to multiple managers.
- Stevens has created pro and con lists by location.
- Stevens has created pro and con lists by manager.

Unknown, but Needed Information

- overall management style and management success of managers in these locations
- Stevens's performance in these locations
- Stevens's performance either as a manager or working for a manager
- why Stevens moves around—specifically (may or may not be needed)
- what Stevens's pros and cons list covers for different entities
- what Stevens's pros and cons list covers for working for different types of managers

3. List the Characters

Directly Involved/Primary

- Stevens
- past managers (some more than others given the pros and cons lists)
- Stevens's next manager/management situation
- Stevens's employees in relevant environments (some more than others given the pros and cons lists)

Indirectly Involved/Secondary

- past managers (some more than others given the pros and cons lists)
- Stevens's employees in relevant environments (some more than others given the pros and cons lists)

4. Review

- What steps should Stevens take to make the decision he needs for the next job?
- Which elements on lists frustrated him the most and why?
- Which list frustrated him the most?
- Given his pros and cons lists (of which we don't know the content), what elements *might* be on the list? For example, multiple reporting structures appear to frustrate Stevens; therefore, which structures might be more likely to have multiple reporting structures? Which environments might tend to be more frustrating than others such as a primarily distance- or remote-learning position?

5. Prioritize

- Stevens should determine what frustrated him more—the structure or the manager or the management style—and work from that list and that data to determine his next position.
- Stevens should, upon deciding which structural issue, type of library, or management structure/management frustrated him the most, review the list of pros and cons to assess his next job possibilities.

6. What Can Be Done

- Stevens can identify structural issues for types and sizes of libraries.
- Stevens can review his lists to narrow down, for example, when he was the most frustrated.

7. What Can't Be Done

- Stevens cannot definitively determine if the next structure will be like the last structure; that is, not all colleges are organized in the same way.
- Stevens cannot determine if the next manager will manage in the same way (and should be aware that if the management style—no matter what—frustrates him the most, he may need a great deal of specific information about the next management/manager before accepting the position.

8. Choose Solutions

- Following his review of pros and cons lists, Stevens should use his greatest concerns/issues to design a set of questions he must answer prior to taking (and possibly prior to applying for) the next job.

- Stevens should review the job description but also design a process that allows him to find out more information (e.g., query potential managers, ask others in the area where the library is located, etc.).

9. Speculate on Outcome(s)

- Stevens's processes should provide him with information to narrow down the type of library in which he has been the least frustrated and possibly the happiest and most successful.
- Stevens's processes *should* provide him with more information to make the best decision for his next position.

10. Evaluate

- While a real-life example would include a vetting of Stevens's next position and whether or not he has been less frustrated or more successful (i.e., Did his processes find him the job he wanted?), the reality is one can't do that with a case. The significance of a case, however, is the realization of the importance and the design of the approach to problem-solving, and in this case the problem is how he should determine the next position.
- If the case has outlined what pros and cons people should look for in different types of libraries and with different managers, it has achieved a measure of success. Knowing that different types of libraries are managed differently is an important realization in the profession and in the world of work at large. Knowing that different managers may manage differently *and* that the differences may be from them *but also* driven by the type of library is equally important in the profession.

Case Six

Manuals, Handbooks, Policies, Procedures, Budgets, Minutes, and Plans, Oh My!

Case for use with chapter 6, "Management Infrastructure Documents in New Organizations"

Chapter/Case # and Case Name	Type of Library and Information Setting	Primary Focus	Secondary Focus
6. Manuals, Handbooks, Policies, Procedures, Budgets, Minutes, and Plans, Oh My!	• School • Web environments of any type and size of library	• Issues related to management document upkeep in multiple modes and deliveries	• Balancing new technologies

THE CASE

Serving on the school district's web team provided Olivia with opportunities to contribute to decisions for online content as well as opportunities to lobby for specific design and "digital real estate" for the learning resource center's web resources.

The web team's annual goals were being met and—on schedule—the complete remake of the district's website was launched with public pages and, for the first time, there was an online infrastructure for internal management content. Olivia was surprised to find her role chairing the subcommittee for the internal web content more difficult work than the external site.

What Olivia and other web team members discovered while trying to implement the internal management content included a morass of management content with little organization, diverse subject headings for files, a variety of publication dates, and little coordination with the school district's print content. In addition, documents that included policies and procedures placed on the family and parents' website outside the firewall were also in disarray and, instead of providing a public resource, it ended up being yet another location for mislabeled, disorganized, and out-of-date manuals, handbooks, budgets, minutes, plans, and policies and procedures.

Olivia pondered her next subcommittee's meeting agenda—scheduled for two weeks after the launch. What should she do to ramp up the process for the delivery of accurate and well-organized management documents on the internal web content area?

CASE COMMENTS

No matter how sophisticated the organization is, design and control of the organization's internal document content and structure is a challenge. Given the dynamic nature of the online world, the creation of an accurate, up-to-date set of sources is easily done; however, maintaining any print parallel document sets results in problems and these problems are compounded when web environments change for redesign, new software, or software updates.

This case provides a forum for discussing the management roles and responsibilities for design and maintenance of management documents.

CASE METHOD ANALYSIS

1. Underline Case Elements

Manuals, Handbooks, Policies, Procedures, Budgets, Minutes, and Plans, Oh My!

Serving on the school district's web team provided Olivia with opportunities to contribute to decisions for online content as well as opportunities to lobby for specific design and "digital real estate" for the learning resource center's web resources.

The web team's annual goals were being met and—on schedule—the complete remake of the district's website was launched with public pages and, for the first time, there was an online infrastructure for internal management content. Olivia was surprised to find her role chairing the subcommittee for the internal web content more difficult work than the external site. What Olivia and other web team members discovered while trying to implement the internal management content included a morass of management content with little organization, diverse subject headings for files, a variety of publication dates, and little coordination with the school district's print content. In addition, documents that included policies and procedures placed on the family and parents' website outside the firewall were also in disarray and, instead of providing a public resource, it ended up being yet another location for mislabeled, disorganized, and out-of-date manuals, handbooks, budgets, minutes, plans, and policies and procedures.

Olivia pondered her next subcommittee's meeting agenda—scheduled for two weeks after the launch. What should she do to ramp up the process for the delivery of accurate and well-organized management documents on the internal web content area?

2. List the Facts

Relevant Facts

- The organization is redoing their public and private or internal website.
- Two different groups (at the very least) are working on the various aspects of the design/redesign.
- The public design is on schedule.
- The private/internal design appeared to be on schedule, but recent issues have surfaced with variations of documents (different dates, different content) for both print and online content.
- Important public policies and procedures are also in disarray.
- Those in charge of the process must prepare an immediate plan of action to correct the content.

Unknown, but Needed Information

- Which documents must be done first and why?
- What are the specific timelines?
- Who are the process holders of the documents considered out-of-date?

3. List the Characters

Directly Involved/Primary

- Olivia
- Olivia's team
- the public team
- managers in areas with internal documents
- managers in areas with important documents that must be available to the public

Indirectly Involved/Secondary

- which content must be completed first
- which content must be available in both print and online form and why
- the audience for the public website content
- the audience for the private/internal website content

4. Review

- Olivia must work quickly to establish a plan to identify problems within documents and between different forms and formats of documents.
- Timelines for goals must be addressed and—if necessary—revised.
- A structure for finding and working with process owners must be designed.
- A structure for speeding up the design and delivery of inaccurate documents must be designed and implemented.
- A process for evaluating changes must be established.

5. Prioritize

- Timelines for goals must be addressed and—if necessary—revised.
- Olivia must work quickly to establish a plan to identify problems within documents and between different forms and formats of documents.
- A structure for finding and working with process owners must be designed.
- A structure for speeding up the design and delivery of inaccurate documents must be designed and implemented.
- A process for evaluating changes must be established.

6. What Can Be Done

- Olivia can call her team together and assign data-gathering to assess the amount of work that must be done and by when.
- Olivia can work with the other team to determine the extent of the problems.
- Olivia can survey the organization to determine the breadth of the issue and to determine process owners.

7. What Can't Be Done

- The differences between the print and online versions must not be ignored.
- The solution can't be "throw away the print documents" because—for example—the public content on the nonfirewall site is comprised of—among other things—policies and procedures.
- Timelines can't be ignored.

8. Choose Solutions

- Olivia can call her team together and assign data-gathering to assess the amount of work that must be done and by when.
- Olivia can work with the other team to determine the extent of the problems.
- Olivia can survey the organization to determine the breadth of the issue and to determine process owners.
- Timelines for goals must be addressed and—if necessary—revised.
- Olivia must work quickly to establish a plan to identify problems within documents and between different forms and formats of documents.
- A structure for speeding up the design and delivery of inaccurate documents must be designed and implemented.
- A process for evaluating changes must be established.

9. Speculate on Outcome(s)

- Olivia, Olivia's team, and the public website team will gather and use data to design a plan and a timeline for plan implementation.
- A process for evaluating website content (public and private) changes is established, is successful, and occurs within the revised timeline.
- Processes are established to maintain accurate, up-to-date online and print content.

10. Evaluate

- Online and print content is assessed—post-implementation—for accuracy.
- The revised completion timeline is vetted by internal and external individuals.
- Constituents using the website indicate a high level of satisfaction with the organization and availability.

Case Seven

What's Old Is New—
If the Money Is There

Case for use with chapter 7, "Managing New Services and Resources"

Chapter/Case # and Case Name	Type of Library and Information Setting	Primary Focus	Secondary Focus
7. What's Old Is New—If the Money Is There	• Public • Special Collection	• Budget shortfalls • Budget processes such as time management • Gifts and donations	• Supporting special collections

THE CASE

Barton Solomon, chief librarian for Beckwith County, was faced with choices going into (and two weeks away from) the new year. The county administration was suddenly projecting a budgeting shortfall and—surprising as it was—each county entity was now tasked with identifying and recommending at least two scenarios for their 17 percent cut and—the only good news—managers were given the latitude to choose their own areas for cuts.

Barton had planned to provide a number of new e-resources and, given the library's consortial membership timeline, had already committed to subscriptions two months previous to the new year. In addition, the new subscriptions focused on genealogy, and the county society—committed to the one-hundredth-year events coming up in two years—had promised a matching gift for refurbishing the county seat library's history room expansion.

Barton had two weeks before he turned in his budget.

CASE COMMENTS

While this case is primarily about budget shortfalls and timelines for dealing with shortfalls, a major component for concern is the potential for problems with gifts and donations, "giving" and the strings attached to giving and accepting gifts, and—in general—supporting special collections in public libraries. Designing budgets is a related issue.

Typically when cases have more details about timelines, the issue of time colors all case analysis. For example, in this case a difficult budget is due, but it is due in two weeks. This time restriction, the restriction on the gifts and donations, *and* the issue of restrictions on expenditures must become a significant driving force in recommendations and outcomes.

CASE METHOD ANALYSIS

1. Underline Case Elements

What's Old Is New—If the Money Is There

Barton Solomon, chief librarian for Beckwith County, was <u>faced with choices going into (and two weeks away from) the new year</u>. The county administration was suddenly projecting a budgeting shortfall and—surprising as it was—each county entity was now tasked with identifying and <u>recommending at least two scenarios for their 17 percent cut</u> and—<u>the only good news—managers were given the latitude to choose their own areas for cuts</u>.

Barton had planned to provide a number of new e-resources and, given the library's consortial membership timeline, <u>had already committed to subscriptions two months previous to the new year</u>. In addition, the new subscriptions focused on genealogy, and the county society—committed to the one-hundredth-year events coming <u>up in two years</u>—had <u>promised a matching gift for refurbishing the county seat library's history room expansion</u>.

<u>Barton had two weeks</u> before he turned in his budget.

2. List the Facts

- Resources and services are tied together.
- Resources are prepaid.

- Matching funds are tied to the provision of these resources.
- A 17 percent cut is significant to a budget.
- The chief librarian has choices.
- The chief librarian has two weeks.

3. List the Characters

Directly Involved/Primary

- the chief librarian
- the chief librarian's direct supervisor and/or county supervisor (one or more administrators such as elected officials, board of supervisors, commissions, judges, etc.)
- the genealogy society (specific leader[s])

Indirectly Involved/Secondary

- library employees
- county peers/department chiefs
- other genealogical leaders
- consortial managers
- vendors
- areas chosen to be cut (others needing to be involved might be those areas, departments, constituents affected by the choice of cuts)

4. Review

- A 17 percent cut is significant to a budget.
- Matching funds are tied to the provision of these resources.
- Resources and services are tied together.
- The resources are prepaid.
- The chief librarian has two weeks (time enough to speak with all parties involved, to be involved).

5. Prioritize

- A 17 percent cut is significant to a budget.
- There are significant numbers of people tied to these funding decisions.
- These funding decisions affect not only a number of people but also significant events planned.
- Matching funds are tied to the provision of these resources.

- Resources and services are tied together.
- The chief librarian has two weeks (time enough to speak with all parties involved, to be involved).

6. What Can Be Done

- The chief should list and plan for all meetings needed as well as—strategically—which meetings should come first, second, and so on.
- The chief needs to spend time with his employees and his budget to identify areas of possible cuts and list those affected by possible proposed cuts.
- The chief needs to apprise the county society of the cuts' issues and provide them with information and—if appropriate—assurance of the process and that—again, if appropriate—he is choosing to hold harmless the genealogy resources and services plans.
- The county society's discussions with the chief might be able to identify additional outside dollars to make the new resources and services happen.

7. What Can't Be Done

- Subscriptions can be cancelled, more than likely; however, the activities and the county society events appear to be locked in at this point.
- It is unlikely that the library will be able to propose fewer than 17 percent in cuts.
- The chief can't ignore other cut areas as to the process for establishing cuts.
- The chief should *not* plan in a vacuum; that is, he must bring in the county society, his employees, and so on.

8. Choose Solution(s)

- The chief should plan to work with his employees to identify areas for cuts to enrich discussions with employees, and so on. Presenting this data provides more of a leadership role and will assist him in retaining control of his areas to cut.
- The chief then needs to apprise the county society of the cut's issues and provide them with information and—if appropriate—assurance of the process and that—again, if appropriate—he is choosing to hold harmless the genealogy resources and services plans.
- The chief should list and plan for all meetings needed as well as determine strategically which meetings should come first, second, and so on.
- The chief needs to spend time with his employees and his budget to identify areas of possible cuts and list those affected by possible proposed cuts.

9. Speculate on Outcome(s)

- The library will present choices for cuts and—with the proper support—should retain control of the decision of choice.
- The chief will need to carefully explain the data and the data-driven decisions made for the choices for cuts.
- The chief will need to establish new measures for areas that have been cut as well as measures for tracking new services and resources.
- The chief needs to *carefully* market the new services and resources for the one-hundredth-year event, since other constituents' resources and services will have been cut.

10. Evaluate

- usage data for new resources
- usage data for new services
- detailed data for areas in the 17 percent cut
- deadlines increased (every six months rather than annually?) for measures taken, assessed, and reported with more frequency to determine impact of cuts as well as impact of new services and resources

Case Eight

But Enough about Me—
What Do *You* Think about Me?

Chapter/ Case # and Case Name	Type of Library and Information Setting	Primary Focus	Secondary Focus
8. But Enough about Me— What Do *You* Think about Me?	• Special	• Library/information center relationships with IT • Establishing and maintaining departmental partnerships	• The importance of communication

THE CASE

Although the director of Revco's information center (IC) (i.e., library) William Fortis knew that working with any company's organizational technology department (IT) was always challenging, he felt that over the past two years he had established a solid working relationship with the department. This relationship included a successful process of communicating needs and issues with Revco Inc.'s senior managing director/head of technology, Marcus Frank, and although Fortis had been criticized for including external departments so prominently in the IC's communication plan, he felt this inclusion and focus had reaped great rewards.

Fortis—in the midst of assessing specifically how his processes and the relationship with IT worked—got the news on Monday that another company had hired Frank away from Revco Inc. Fortis called a quick meeting of his full-time and part-time IC employees to see what else he needed to do to make sure he articulated the current and future needs of the department to IT in the midst of Frank's exit and the IC's preparation for a new IT director.

Overall, what should he do in the next month regarding the IT director position?

CASE COMMENTS

Support for technology is an issue in all libraries. These issues include: "We don't have anyone and must rely on ourselves"; "we don't have anyone specifically assigned to us, so getting attention to our needs is difficult"; "we have access to assistance but they do not use the same service model for support and it's hard to work with them"; and/or "we have support but training and keeping up is an issue *and* they aren't paid comparable salaries to tech support elsewhere so it's hard to keep them." Complicating issues revolve around technology designed "just" for library and information environments that others aren't aware of and/or trained on, and around older technology with the organization not being able to upgrade and tech support "patching things together."

This case—based on several of the premises above—focuses on education and communication. Discussion for this case focuses on what managers should do to connect with IT departments outside the library. An additional complexity is the existence defined as a special library with typically competing interests—that is, the library may not be viewed as revenue-generating support, and therefore their needs may be put after revenue-generating needs. The essence of the case, however, can be personalized to any type of library where a manager must plan carefully to establish, maintain, and—as needed—transition an effective working relationship to another individual. In addition, to illustrate the urgency that technology support always brings to the "management table," a one-month timeline is imposed for action.

CASE METHOD ANALYSIS

1. Underline Case Elements

But Enough about Me—What Do *You* Think about Me?

Although the director of Revco's information center (IC) (i.e., library) William Fortis knew that <u>working with any company's organizational technology</u>

department (IT) was always challenging, he felt that over the past two years he had established a solid working relationship with the department. This relationship included a successful process of communicating need and issues with Revco Inc.'s senior managing director/head of technology, Marcus Frank, and although Fortis had been criticized for including external departments so prominently in the IC's communication plan, he felt this inclusion and focus had reaped great rewards.

Fortis—in the midst of assessing specifically how his processes and the relationship with IT worked—got the news on Monday that another company had hired Frank away from Revco Inc. Fortis called a quick meeting of his full-time and part-time IC employees to see what else he needed to do to make sure he articulated the current and future needs of the department to IT in the midst of Frank's exit and the IC's preparation for a new IT director.

Overall, what should he do in the next month regarding the IT director position?

2. List the Facts

Relevant Facts

- The IC's "external" relationships—for example, IT—are often challenging.
- Fortis has established a solid working relationship with IT.
- The IC and IT's relationship includes a communication process with the IT director.
- Fortis was criticized for including IT, an external department, so prominently in the communication plan.
- Frank—the IT director—is leaving the company.
- Fortis is assessing his relationship with IT to see what "worked."
- Fortis is having a meeting of his full-time and part-time employees.
- The meeting's goals include the identification of current and future needs of the IC for IT.

Unknown, but Needed Information

- What is Revco going to do with the vacant IT position?

3. List the Characters

Directly Involved/Primary

- Fortis
- Fortis's departmental (IC) employees
- Frank and Frank's work with the IC specifically (even though he is leaving)
- upper-level management
- the interim IT director

Indirectly Involved/Secondary

- IT departmental employees
- the possible replacement for the IT director

4. Review

- Fortis has established a solid working relationship with IT.
- Frank—the IT director—is leaving the company.
- Fortis is assessing his relationship with IT to see what "worked."
- Fortis is having a meeting of his full-time and part-time employees.
- The meeting's goals include the identification of current and future needs of the IC for IT.

5. Prioritize

Now

- Fortis has established a solid working relationship with IT.
- The IC and IT's relationship includes a communication process with the IT director.
- Frank—the IT director—is leaving the company and the library manager has a one-month window to take action.
- Fortis is assessing his relationship with IT to see what "worked."
- Fortis is having a meeting with his full-time and part-time employees.
- The meeting's goals include the identification of current and future needs of the IC for IT.

Later

- Fortis was criticized for including IT, an external department, so prominently in the communication plan.
- The IC's "external" relationships—for example, IT—are often challenging.

6. What Can Be Done

- Fortis can plan for communicating with Revco management regarding their IT/IC integrated plans and his hopes for the interim director and hiring.
- Fortis can establish a plan for communicating to the IT employees and the interim director.
- Fortis can task his IC employees with reviewing the IC strategic plan for accuracy—in tandem with the IT employees being involved in the first plan-designing process.
- Fortis can meet with Frank to see if he is interested in outlining interim IC/IT plans and how they will continue to be met.

7. What Can't Be Done

- Fortis can't ignore the one-month timeline.
- Fortis should *not* remain silent regarding interim IT and IC plans and processes.
- Fortis and the IC can't ignore the existing strategic plan.
- Fortis should *not* cease regular, ongoing communication established between the IC and IT.

8. Choose Solutions

- Fortis can meet with Frank to see if he is interested in outlining interim IC/IT plans and how they will continue to be met.
- Fortis can plan for communicating with Revco management regarding their IT/IC integrated plans and his hopes for the interim director and hiring.
- Fortis can establish a plan for communicating to the IT employees and the interim director.
- Fortis can task his IC employees with reviewing the IC strategic plan for accuracy—in tandem with the IT employees being involved in the first plan-designing process.

9. Speculate on Outcome(s)

- Fortis will be able to maintain IC/IT relationships.
- The IT employees will continue to be made aware of joined plans and processes and assist in the communication of those to any interim director and the new director.
- The more visible Fortis and the IC plans are, the more likely Fortis will be officially involved in the immediate future of IT regarding the interim director and selection of the new director.

10. Evaluate

- Review the IC's strategic plan to see what has been accomplished in order to better brief new employees or managers of new employees.
- Assess Fortis's short-term plan to see if communication has been maintained.
- Assess IT's and the IC's joint or related processes in place to see if they were maintained in the interim.
- Consider a measure that includes a level of involvement by Fortis in the "life" of the IT interim director and the possible new director.

Case Nine

Suffering from Past Mistakes

Case for use with chapter 9, "New Management 'in Action' Communication"

Chapter/Case # and Case Name	Type of Library and Information Setting	Primary Focus	Secondary Focus
9. Suffering from Past Mistakes	• Academic • Public • School • Special	• Internal communication; the importance of a communication plan for all issues but especially facilities issues • Employee negativity regarding remodel and the expression of negativity to each other but also, more importantly, to their constituents	• Employee negativity overall • Facilities remodel

THE CASE

While getting ready for the remodel, Beatrice, the new associate director, was told by the director that the employees complained throughout previous renovations not only to other employees at their location, but also to employees throughout the system as well as constituents before, during, and after the remodel.

Given what she knew about the employees in her first six months, Beatrice was surprised that so much negativity was apparent. In an effort to determine why they were so negative, however, Beatrice pulled old memos to see how the previous associate director for facilities and operations prepared employees for similar and/or related situations.

Beatrice found five memos and fifteen e-mail updates about the five memos from the past decade and quickly read through them to see if she could determine how the employees were used to receiving information about upcoming building issues. Beatrice's goal became to determine past problems, avoid laying the same groundwork that might have yielded negativity, and have a successful employee environment for the upcoming recarpeting and painting remodel.

CASE COMMENTS

While this case directs the reader to Beatrice's goal in the closing content, there are a wide variety of issues for this situation and a significant number of steps for managers to take to correct the immediate situation and future behaviors. Although this case is complex in the number of things that need to be done, this case can easily be personalized to any type and size of environment and retain the need for managers to immediately address employee issues to mitigate similar future mistakes.

CASE METHOD ANALYSIS

1. Underline Case Elements

Suffering from Past Mistakes

While getting ready for the remodel, Beatrice, the new associate director, was told by the director that the employees complained throughout previous renovations not only to other employees at their location, but also to employees throughout the system as well as constituents before, during, and after the remodel.

Given what she knew about the employees in her first six months, Beatrice was surprised that so much negativity was apparent. In an effort to determine why they were so negative, however, Beatrice pulled old memos to see how the previous associate director for facilities and operations prepared employees for similar and/or related situations.

Beatrice found five memos and fifteen e-mail updates about the five memos from the past decade and quickly read through them to see if she could determine how the employees were used to receiving information about upcoming buildings issues. Beatrice's goal became to determine past problems, avoid laying the same groundwork that might have <u>yielded negativity,</u> and have a <u>successful employee environment</u> for the <u>upcoming</u> recarpeting and painting <u>remodel</u>.

2. List the Facts

Relevant Facts

- There are past mistakes.
- The director is aware of past mistakes/past employee complaints.
- The director is aware of apparent past negativity.
- Employee complaints were directed to not only staff but also constituents.
- The new associate director has been asked by her new boss to address past negativity and make sure the new remodel doesn't have employees repeating the same behavior.
- Old memos are being pulled and analyzed.
- Beatrice is going to design remodel communication that is designed to engender more positive communication from employees.

Unknown, but Needed Information

- Were all employees negative or were specific employees negative?
- Were the same employees negative for each event?
- How did senior employees find out about the continuing negativity?
- Did employees know they were negative?
- If they knew they were negative, do they know the director knows they were negative?

3. List the Characters

Directly Involved/Primary

- negative employees at the remodel location
- the new associate director
- the director
- nonnegative employees at the remodel location
- constituents using the facilities during the remodel (if possible)

Indirectly Involved/Secondary

- negative employees at other locations
- the previous associate director
- nonnegative employees elsewhere
- constituents not using the facilities during the remodel

4. Review

- There was negativity before, during, and after past remodels.
- Another remodel is coming up.
- Beatrice is charged—by her boss—with managing the situation to avoid negativity.
- Communication in general must be addressed.
- The damage to constituents must be assessed and remediated.

5. Prioritize

- Employee complaints were directed to not only employees but also constituents.
- The director is aware of apparent past negativity.
- The director is aware of past mistakes/past employee complaints.
- The new associate director has been asked by her new boss to address past negativity and make sure the new remodel doesn't have employees repeating the same behavior.
- Employee complaints were directed to other employees throughout the library.
- Beatrice is going to design remodel communication that is designed to engender more positive communication from employees.

6. What Can Be Done

- The upcoming situation must be addressed immediately and differently, and the difference in handling more facilities issues should be directly addressed with employees as well as expectations of their behaviors.
- Negativity can be addressed with employees for their past behaviors.
- A positive communication piece can be designed for the upcoming remodel.
- Managers should create a broader communication plan for the employees with successful elements of the plan designed and implemented for the immediate renovation.

7. What Can't Be Done

- Negativity shared with constituents can't be ignored.
- Past negativity—in general—can't be ignored.
- Past communication (and the faults in that past communication) can't be ignored.
- Beatrice can't ignore her supervisor.

- Employees can't ignore the management's expectations of their behavior in general and during the next remodel.

8. Choose Solutions

- A positive communication piece can be designed for the upcoming remodel.
- Negativity can be addressed with employees for their past behaviors.
- A PR initiative should be designed to reach constituents regarding past negativity and different behaviors for the new remodel.
- Employees will be given an outline of how to work with managers on proactive communication for workplace issues to rechannel and replace internal and external negative communication.

9. Speculate on Outcome(s)

- Employees will be made aware of management concerns of past negativity shared with the public and will be aware of their roles and responsibilities in the PR initiative for the public during the new remodel.
- Employees will be made aware of management concerns of past negativity and will be aware that there are standard behaviors expected for upcoming remodels.
- The positive communication will specifically address overall communication that is acceptable and unacceptable.

10. Evaluate

- The associate director will present an analysis of past communications to the director and speculate on causes, effects, and needed changes.
- The director will review a draft of the upcoming remodel communications.
- The associate director will prepare an observation rubric and an exit interview for constituents leaving the library following employee interactions and during the remodel.
- The associate director will draft language to be used to inform staff immediately of issues surrounding their negative communication to constituents and of expected behavior change outlined during employee performance evaluations in three months.

What You Don't Know
Can Hurt You

Case for use with chapter 10, "New Managers within Classic and New Organizations"	

Chapter/Case # and Case Name	Type of Library and Information Setting	Primary Focus	Secondary Focus
10. What You Don't Know *Can* Hurt You	• School	• Lack of leadership • Ethics in the workplace • Working with external groups	• Making career decisions

THE CASE

When Carrie accepted the middle school librarian position in the district based on its location and her commitment to the neighborhood, she knew that she was leaving behind her unique high school PTA, Friends of the Library, and supportive principal who not only had provided her with resources but also had taught her the best possible model for the library's role in teaching and learning. She did not know that her new school's situation was far different than what she had been told or what she had anticipated and far from standards of practice as well as what she felt it should be.

In the first month of her contract she confirmed (although she had heard earlier) that her principal was spending a great deal of time away from campus working on his PhD, and the assistant principal—concerned that she made half the salary the principal made—was passive due to the principal's absence and unannounced expectation that as the next in charge, she would manage the school in his absence.

In the first two months of her contract, Carrie confirmed that her new PTA was almost nonexistent in their organization and operation and that they had not fully functioned—including few meetings, no fundraising, and little interest in anything other than the school's small gifted and talented program—for the past four years.

Much of what she heard—then confirmed—she learned from curriculum team leaders in the school, and from the small Friends of the Library group she contacted two weeks after her arrival. Initially unaware of the group's existence, during her first week of work she found a flyer in her desk asking parents and families to join the Friends group from three years before. After contacting last year's Friends president, he apprised her of the opinions the Friends group had and of their lack of interest given the problems in the school.

Following general comments she was hearing, she listened in the lounge and lunchroom, reviewed the last two years of minutes from school meetings, interviewed the assistant principal, and spoke with someone at the district office she trusted with confidential discussion.

At Thanksgiving, Carrie received a call from her previous high school principal asking her to return due to the recent exit of the librarian who had been hired to replace Carrie.

CASE COMMENTS

This case presents several difficult situations for professionals that range from choosing a difficult work situation over an easy work situation; communication and miscommunication issues; and ethical issues. In addition, the work environments described include work environments with little leadership as well as managers with possible inappropriate behaviors and a need for employees to work with a variety of groups and colleagues to verify behaviors and document issues.

Discussions for this case will be wide-ranging, and there is clearly no one correct answer or set of answers for how professionals might or might not choose to gather evidence, report or not report inappropriate behavior, and make or not make major choices on how to conduct themselves, as well as the major choices for a final selection of options. Lessons learned—no matter the varieties of choices made—include not only those directions or decisions for case issues but also recommendations for making career decisions.

CASE METHOD ANALYSIS

1. Underline Case Elements

<u>What You Don't Know *Can* Hurt You</u>

When Carrie <u>accepted</u> the middle school librarian <u>position</u> in the district <u>based on its location and her commitment to the neighborhood</u>, she knew that she was <u>leaving</u> behind <u>her unique high school PTA, Friends of the Library, and supportive principal who not only had provided her with resources but also had taught her the best possible model</u> for the library's role in teaching and learning. She <u>did not know</u> that her new school's <u>situation was far different than what she was told or than she anticipated</u> and far from standards of practice as well as what she felt it should be.

In the first month of her contract <u>she confirmed</u> (although she had heard earlier) that her <u>principal was</u> spending a great deal of time <u>away from campus</u> working on his PhD, and <u>the assistant principal</u>—concerned that she made half the salary the principal made—<u>was passive</u> due to the principal's absence and unannounced expectation that as the next-in-charge, she would manage the school in his absence.

In the first two months of her contract, Carrie confirmed that her new <u>PTA was almost non-existent</u> in their organization and operation and that they had not fully functioned—including few meetings, no fundraising, and little interest in anything other than the school's small gifted and talented program—for four years.

Much of what she heard—then confirmed—she learned from curriculum team leaders in the school, and from the small Friends of the Library group she contacted two weeks after her arrival. Initially unaware of the group's existence, during her first week of work she found a flyer in her desk asking parents and families to join the Friends group from three years before. After contacting last year's Friends president, he apprised her of the opinions the <u>Friends group</u> had and of their <u>lack of interest given the problems in the school</u>.

Following their general comments, <u>she listened in the lounge and lunchroom, reviewed the last two years of minutes from school meetings, interviewed the assistant principal, and spoke with someone at the district office she trusted with confidential discussion.</u>

At Thanksgiving, <u>Carrie received a call from her previous high school principal asking her to return</u> due to the recent exit of the librarian who had been hired to replace Carrie.

2. List the Facts

Relevant Facts

- The problems are spread throughout the school infrastructure at every management and advisory level.

- The problems appear to be long-standing, antiquated, and unethical ways of doing business.
- The problems in the school were confirmed from a variety of reputable sources.

Unknown, but Needed Information

- Is the district office fully aware of the situation?
- Are any changes in school management forthcoming?

3. List the Characters

Directly Involved/Primary

- the school librarian
- the principal in the new school
- the assistant principal in the new school

Indirectly Involved/Secondary

- the students in new school
- those indicated as part of the problem (e.g., principal, assistant principal, heads of groups such as PTA, Friends)
- those indicated as being part of a possible solution (e.g., curriculum team leaders, district employees aware of and speaking with the school librarian)
- other teachers
- students in the new school

4. Review

- There are multiple problems in the school.
- The problems appear at all levels and specifically all management levels.
- The problems have been happening for some time.
- The number and type of problem appear to be pervasive and unsolvable by one person.

5. Prioritize

- The problems have been happening for some time. Why haven't they been reported? Or have they been reported but not handled? Certainly a wide variety of people know bits and pieces and with so many informed on a number of levels it would stand to reason that someone higher up knows something (one would hope).
- The problems appear at all levels and specifically all management levels.

- The number and type of problem appear to be pervasive and unsolvable by one person.
- The librarian should carefully decide on how to handle her existing situation as well as immediately prepare pros and cons for her own career and offer to return to her previous school.

6. What Can Be Done

- The librarian can return to her old school.
- The librarian can work within the district office to see if there are changes coming to the school.
- The librarian can work within the school to see how she might turn the Friends group around to benefit the library.
- The librarian can work within the school with curriculum team leaders to see if they can improve the situation.

7. What Can't Be Done

- The librarian cannot ignore her own career or her own happiness and job satisfaction for something that she herself cannot easily correct.
- The librarian cannot turn the situation and the various problems around by herself given the amorphic nature and complexity of the issues.
- The librarian cannot expect that the situations will turn around by themselves or have natural endings such as "things will be better next year when _____ leaves," as no exit strategies have been identified or are known.
- Confronting school management does not seem to be an appropriate strategy for a new professional.

8. Choose Solutions

- The librarian can accept her previous principal's offer and return to her previous high school position.
- Following her return, the librarian can consult HR on how to (or if she should) provide an exit report for the previous school's situation.
- The librarian can stay and work within the system to change the school given her reasons for choosing the new school including her commitment to the neighborhood.

9. Speculate on Outcome(s)

- Although most cases don't and shouldn't end with "runaway" or "give up"—in this case, the issues may appear to be and might be interpreted as overwhelming for one person to attempt the major change(s) needed to turn the school around. What is to be learned from this case includes:

- ○ the variety of avenues to explore to not only investigate but also validate the information
- ○ the pervasiveness of the issues including top management, second level of management, advisory group, and front-line individuals—all aware and all seemingly burned out or uninterested in making changes
- ○ the level of the employee coming into the environment is low within the organization and is lower level even within the flatter building-level organizational structure of a middle school

- Oftentimes the best strategy is a clean exit strategy if all *known* avenues for an individual do not meet either short-term or long-term needs. Other interesting issues for this situation include:

- ○ Should the librarian reveal all issues confirmed to the district office within the confines of the confidential employee discussion?
- ○ Should the librarian stay and report everything formally to the district?
- ○ Should the librarian leave and report everything formally to the district?
- ○ Should the librarian leave and report everything to her previous principal (the principal to whom she is returning)?

10. Evaluate

- There are a variety of evaluation issues that can be applied to this case. They should include concern for the impact to the middle school, the librarian's professional life, the impact to the high school (if she returns to that base and reports the middle school issues), and the impact at the district level.
- The librarian can report the situation in any number of configurations and then establish a mechanism to find out if things have changed, including: her high school principal can inform her of news within the district; a curriculum team leader can communicate to her; and/or the district employee can report back to her. As with any situation (most often referred to as a whistleblower situation), individuals must weigh the impact of reporting issues as well as the way issues are reported and weigh the impact of *not* reporting issues.
- While many employees struggle with ethical and moral dilemmas at work, some have the opportunity to report from outside the institution rather than as an employee. In this case, however, the individual returning to the high school must realize:

○ they are still within the district and thus still considered internal
○ they would be involving not only themselves but also the high school in the process
○ the high school principal must be consulted, as his employee would be spending time on the issue (more than likely) during a workday
○ given the variety of ways the issue might be "solved," if the middle school principal is *not* found culpable, this principal remains within the district and—as such—would have to be part of the ongoing network of the librarian's professional life

Case Eleven

A Fixer Upper

Case for use with chapter 11, "New Managers in Classic and New Facilities and Environments"

Chapter/Case # and Case Name	Type of Library and Information Setting	Primary Focus	Secondary Focus
11. A Fixer Upper	• Academic • Public • School • Special	• Technology renovation • Planning for and scheduling change in the workplace	• Time management

THE CASE

Jennifer got the news late in the week that, beginning the next Monday, her ongoing request for a redesign of the leisure reading space to accommodate extensive technology support would be honored. Excited about the possibility of change but concerned about the timeline, Jennifer called an emergency meeting of employees to determine what they had/what they needed to produce or what was "ready" for the upcoming situation.

Complicating the issue was the upcoming programming planned for the leisure space, expanded constituent use in general at that time, the weather, and upcoming employee vacations.

CASE COMMENTS

Although at first glance this case might appear to be a facilities and/or re-model or renovation issue or even a technology issue, the case is really about business continuity in service and resource delivery. In addition, this case can easily be personalized to any type of library or information setting.

CASE METHOD ANALYSIS

1. Underline Case Elements

A Fixer Upper

Jennifer got the news <u>late in the week</u> that, <u>beginning the next Monday</u>, her ongoing request for a <u>redesign</u> of the leisure reading space to accommodate <u>extensive technology support</u> would be honored. Excited about the possibility of change but concerned about <u>the timeline</u>, Jennifer <u>called an emergency meeting of employees</u> to determine <u>what they already had</u>/<u>what they needed to produce</u> or what was "ready" for the upcoming situation.

Complicating the issue was the <u>upcoming programming planned</u> for the lei-sure space, <u>expanded constituent use</u> in general <u>at that time</u>, <u>the weather</u>, and <u>upcoming employee vacations</u>.

2. List the Facts

Relevant Facts

- Construction news came late in the week with a very tight timeline (the next Monday).
- The leisure reading space will be changed.
- Space will be modernized for extensive technology support and the re-model must take place given the general changing nature of technology.
- The timeline is tight but primarily unknown.
- An emergency meeting of employees has been called.
- There is upcoming programming planned for the space to be remodeled.
- Jennifer is taking an inventory of what they already have for the remodel.
- Jennifer is taking an inventory of what they need for the remodel in terms of employees, programming, and services.
- The weather might be problematic.
- There are upcoming employee vacations.

3. List the Characters

Directly Involved/Primary

- management/leadership—Jennifer
- management—Jennifer's manager
- management—governing or advisory groups
- the manager of the space to be changed (if applicable)
- employees—general
- employees—public relations
- constituents who currently attend and will be attending the events and using the area to be changed
- other constituents of the library
- design/construction professionals
- design/construction workers
- maintenance employees for the library

Indirectly Involved/Secondary

- management—Jennifer's manager
- management—governing or advisory groups
- employees
- other constituents of the library

4. Review

- There isn't much time between "now" and facilities changes.
- Extensive technology support—no matter if it is a redesign, remodel, renovation, and so on—means electrical interruptions, among a variety of other invasive issues relating to both constituents and employees.
- The project timeline for duration isn't stated/isn't yet known.
- Jennifer is unclear of what is available or "ready" based on what is needed for the upcoming facility changes.
- Jennifer is unclear of what is needed but not available based on upcoming facility changes.
- Programming planned for the specific area must be determined.
- Weather issues given the timeline and area must be determined as well as the possible impact of weather issues.
- Employee vacation plans need to be built into the building timeline.

5. Prioritize

Now

- There isn't much time between "now" and facilities changes.
- The project timeline for duration isn't stated/isn't yet known and must be determined.
- Jennifer is unclear of what is available or "ready" based on what is needed for the upcoming facility changes.
- Jennifer is unclear of what is needed but not available based on upcoming facility changes.
- Programming planned for the specific area must be determined and moved.

Later

- Extensive technology support—no matter if it is a redesign, remodel, renovation, and so on—means electrical interruptions, among a variety of other invasive issues relating to both constituents and employees.
- Weather issues given the timeline and area must be determined as well as the possible impact of weather issues.
- Employee vacation plans need to be built into the building timeline.

6. What Can Be Done

- A list of questions regarding electrical interruptions and issues can be identified.
- A project timeline for duration can be drafted for discussion with project employees.
- A list of content/issues identified that are available or "ready" based on what is needed can be identified.
- A list of content/issues identified that are *not* available or "ready" based on what is needed can be identified.
- Programming planned for the specific area can be identified and moved.
- Employee vacation plans can be built into the building timeline.

7. What Can't Be Done

- Planned programming can't be ignored.
- Planned employee vacations/time off can't be ignored.
- There can be speculation on weather issues given the timeline, but weather is unpredictable.

- There isn't much time between "now" and the facilities changes and the timeline shouldn't be delayed.

8. Choose Solutions

- Jennifer's employees must meet immediately to gather information and recommend action.
- Programming should be either cancelled or moved.
- Jennifer must create a business continuity assessment plan for communicating regarding the programming and marketing any changes in the situation to users.
- A new project timeline must be created immediately.
- An inventory should be done of what is available regarding content for the project, immediately.
- A list of what is missing and how to create that information must be worked into the first items on the timeline.

9. Speculate on Outcome(s)

- Jennifer should be able to create an initial plan of action even with such a short timeline.
- The project will begin on time with minimal interruption in overall services but with some changes to programming.
- Effective marketing of service interruption and upcoming changes benefitting constituents (in the long term) should be emphasized.
- A back-up manager should be selected to support Jennifer on the project and to lend a second pair of eyes and intellect to vet and assist in managing the project timeline, and so on.

10. Evaluate

- Ask administration to approve the business continuity plan(s).
- Design and implement a streamlined reporting form for employees to use during the project to evaluate situations, expedite problems and issues, and solve problems.
- Have marketing employees design a user feedback and assistance form for project evaluation during the activities.

Case Twelve

Penny's Partners Proliferate due to Punctual, Prioritized, and Positive Planning

Case for use with chapter 12, "New 'Landscapes' for Library and Information Settings"

Chapter/Case # and Case Name	Type of Library and Information Setting	Primary Focus	Secondary Focus
12. Penny's Partners Proliferate due to Punctual, Prioritized, and Positive Planning	• Academic • Public • School • Special	• Importance of partnerships • Roles and responsibilities of partnerships • Planning for partnerships	• Communicating with disparate groups

THE CASE

Penny returned from her workshop committed to bringing both digital and in-person partnerships to her organization. She began by re-reading the workshop curriculum and listing what needed to be done. Her list included the following.

- Identify current and previous in-person and tech-driven partnerships.
- Identify current and previous in-person and tech-driven partnerships in her greater community.
- Create a constituent benefits list from in-person and digital partnerships.

- Prepare a plusses and minuses list based on her own experience (which included her work prior to coming to her present position).
- Begin a list of librarians in her area that she had worked with on other projects.
- Begin a list of other individuals and entities she had worked with on other projects.
- Begin a list of new librarians she felt would make good partners and presented "win-win" possibilities.
- Begin a list of new organizations and entities she felt would make good partners and presented "win-win" possibilities.

Penny also knew that her friend James, a school librarian, had worked with several other professionals in higher education and could identify who might work for future projects and additional names for partnerships.

First, Penny called James, who thought it was a great idea, and she asked for and received permission to share the workshop content with him. Together they blocked out times for possible meetings at the community center (recommended as neutral territory), chose three possible planning meeting dates, created an e-mail list of names and addresses they had gathered, and sent out a summary of the ideas and an "invitation to discuss" to the area librarians and external or nonlibrary partners.

For their introductory information, Penny and James decided to include basic partnership information and examples of benefits of in-person and digital partnerships and attached several of the discussion threads that began to appear on an e-list she belonged to. She also recommended that the e-mail group make online visits to at least two of the additional sites linked from the partnerships website and asked for RSVPs. Finally, James and she created a draft agenda, went to her favorite online environment for great ideas for planning—Big Dog—and selected a fun but meaningful "get to know each other" exercise and arranged for the flip charts and markers as well as the media set-up with web access.

Prior to the meeting, Penny printed off documents from the web content she had identified, and began to research and identify people/groups (local city and county employees, the hospital and health care groups, local service organizations and employers) who she felt should be in the group that would move beyond the first discussion group for a steering committee or more formal planning group. She met with James once to count RSVPs, go over handouts, decide on presentation and facilitation roles, and go over her ideas for the more formal group of leaders for the partnership. They planned for a distribution of a reminder e-mail with directions and parking information and included a list of who had RSVP'd so far.

The First Meeting

Penny and James:

- passed out nametags
- welcomed the area librarians
- circulated agendas
- distributed a signup sheet
- conducted the icebreaker "get to know you" exercise
- passed out sets of the latest documents posted to the website for those who had not brought them

Penny and James began by establishing their interest and experience in partnerships and presented an overview of the goal of partnerships and took questions and answers on the content the group had reviewed. In addition, James included city and county data he had gotten from the new census data for his presentation and several local directories from several bureaus around town, feeling these could provide some ideas and names and addresses for partnership ideas as well as for the larger group to be formed.

Following their presentations, Penny and James did a "reality check" of the group to see if a partnership was an idea they wanted to pursue and why, and then led a brainstorming session of what size group was needed, the group members or other "players" and stakeholders who needed to be in on basic planning, and finished with a discussion on dates when people could meet next.

Penny and James facilitated the group to several decisions.

1. They did want to better inform people on libraries and library value (all sizes and types) and therefore provide a mechanism for educating a larger group on the importance of their partnership idea.
2. They were hopeful that, once educated, a larger group would see the value of discussing what their community was doing and what they could *all* do in the future to partner to reach their goal.
3. They decided they did *not* want, at this time, to talk money or finalize any processes.
4. The group adjourned with each attendee taking four names of people to contact, a list of sites to look at, and a worksheet for putting goals, strategies, and outcomes as well as general and specific ideas down for sharing on their local e-list.

The Second Meeting

The group (of now thirty interested people) assembled with their previously e-mailed documents in hand. Penny and James conducted a "get to know you" with the larger group and identified credentials of each group member to post to the online partnership site being planned.

James presented a Prezi presentation on their partnership idea and on the benefits to the community. Penny led the group through examples of other partnerships forming and the sample mission and vision statements found through reviewing benchmark partnerships.

The group broke into smaller groups, led by initial group members, and followed a process of group discussion with forms and guides. Group members picked their best ideas and reported back to the larger group and then Penny led the group through a prioritizing of the list and the choice of keywords for a vision and mission statement. Penny agreed to draft both—with the words chosen—and to post to the e-list.

The group then discussed what they wanted to accomplish in their next meetings through both short-term and long-term goals, they chose another date to meet, group members chose to become involved on a primary, secondary, or support or information-sharing only level, and group co-leaders for each were chosen.

Each of the three groups then met to discuss what their roles might be, project what they thought they could accomplish with costs and support mechanisms, and discuss future activities. Group note-takers completed their forms and got instructions on posting them to the e-list.

CASE COMMENTS

This case provides discussion participants with extensive information including clearly defined activities and action steps being taken for the partnership project in question. The focus of the case, therefore, is less about determining a course of action, but rather it has participants reading an "almost" best-practice partnership process and identifying a few—but critical—missing steps and issues, one of which is completely contemporary (technology) and the other is classic (evaluation).

Case discussion should include a focus on project managers using technology to include but taking great care not to use it to exclude. In addition, while the project managers have clearly evaluated all options for the design of the project, case discussion should determine that post-meeting evaluation should be used as a tool to determine levels of satisfaction with the project rather than just a "head-counting" measurement. While people returning or joining is absolutely a testament to the project planners, time should be spent identifying *who* is returning and why—which is done through post-meeting evaluation. Once the concern for broadening communication beyond "just technology" has been integrated as well as evaluation mechanisms, case content can be used as a model or best practice for planning partnerships.

CASE METHOD ANALYSIS

1. Underline Case Elements

Penny's <u>Partners Proliferate</u> <u>due to</u>
<u>Punctual</u>, <u>Prioritized</u>, and <u>Positive Planning</u>

Penny returned from her workshop committed to bringing <u>both digital and in-person partnerships</u> to her organization. She began by re-reading the workshop curriculum and listing what needed to be done. Her list included the following.

- <u>Identify current and previous in-person and tech-driven partnerships.</u>
- <u>Identify current and previous in-person and tech-driven partnerships in her greater community.</u>
- <u>Create a constituent benefits list from in-person and digital partnerships.</u>
- <u>Prepare a plusses and minuses list based on her own experience (which included her work prior to coming to her present position).</u>
- <u>Begin a list of librarians in her area that she had worked with on other projects.</u>
- <u>Begin a list of other individuals and entities she had worked with on other projects.</u>
- <u>Begin a list of new librarians she felt would make good partners and presented "win-win" possibilities.</u>
- <u>Begin a list of new organizations and entities she felt would make good partners and presented "win-win" possibilities.</u>

Penny also knew that her friend James, <u>a school librarian,</u> <u>had worked with</u> several other professionals in <u>higher education</u> and could identify who might work for future projects and additional names for partnerships.

First, Penny called James, who thought it was a great idea, and <u>she asked for and received permission to share the workshop content</u> with him. Together they blocked out times for possible meetings at the community center (recommended as <u>neutral territory</u>), chose three possible planning meeting dates, created an e-mail list of names and addresses they had gathered, and <u>sent out a summary of the ideas</u> and an "<u>invitation to discuss</u>" to the <u>area librarians</u> and <u>external or nonlibrary partners</u>.

For their <u>introductory information,</u> Penny and James decided to include <u>basic partnership information</u> and <u>examples of benefits of in-person and digital partnerships</u> and attached several of the discussion threads that began to appear on an e-list she belonged to. She also recommended that the e-mail group make on-line visits to at least two of the additional sites linked from the partnerships website and <u>asked for RSVPs</u>. Finally, <u>James and she</u> created a <u>draft agenda</u>, went to her favorite online environment for great ideas for planning—Big Dog—and selected a <u>fun but meaningful "get to know each other" exercise and arranged for the flip charts and markers as well as the media set-up with web access</u>.

   <u>Prior to the meeting</u>, Penny printed off documents from the web content she had identified, and <u>began to research and identify people/groups (local city and county employees, the hospital and health care groups, local service organizations and employers) who she felt should be in the group that would move beyond the first discussion group for a steering committee or more formal planning group. She met with James once</u> to count RSVPs, go over handouts, decide on presentation and facilitation roles, and go over her <u>ideas for the more formal group of leaders for the partnership</u>. They planned for a <u>distribution of a reminder e-mail with directions and parking information and included a list of who had RSVP'd so far.</u>

The First Meeting

Penny and James:

- <u>passed out nametags</u>
- <u>welcomed the area librarians</u>
- <u>circulated agendas</u>
- <u>distributed a signup sheet</u>
- <u>conducted the icebreaker "get to know you" exercise</u>
- <u>passed out sets of the latest documents posted to the web site for those who had not brought them</u>

Penny and James began by <u>establishing their interest and experience in partnerships</u> and presented an overview of the goal of partnerships <u>and took questions and answers on the content the group had reviewed</u>. In addition, James included <u>city and county data he had gotten from the new census data for his presentation and several local directories from several bureaus around town feeling these could provide some ideas and names and addresses for partnership ideas as well as for the larger group to be formed</u>.

   Following their presentations, Penny and James did a <u>"reality check" of the group</u> to see if a partnership was an idea they wanted to pursue and why, and then led a <u>brainstorming session</u> of what size group was needed, the group members or other "players" and stakeholders who needed to be in <u>on basic planning and finished with a discussion on dates when people could meet next</u>.

   Penny and James facilitated the group to several decisions.

1. They did want to better inform people on libraries and library value (all sizes and types) and therefore provide a mechanism for educating a larger group on the importance of their partnership idea.
2. They were hopeful that, once educated, a larger group would see the value of discussing what their community was doing and what they could *all* do in the future to partner to reach their goal.
3. <u>They decided they did *not* want, at that time, to talk money or finalize any processes.</u>

4. The group adjourned with each attendee taking four names of people to contact, a list of sites to look at, and a worksheet for putting goals, strategies, and outcomes as well as general and specific ideas down for sharing on their local e-list.

The Second Meeting

The group (of now thirty interested people) assembled with their previously e-mailed documents in hand. Penny and James conducted a "get to know you" with the larger group and identified credentials of each group member to post to the online partnership site being planned.

James presented a Prezi presentation on their partnership idea and on the benefits to the community. Penny led the group through examples of other partnerships forming and the sample mission and vision statements found through reviewing benchmark partnerships.

The group broke into smaller groups, led by initial group members, and followed a process of group discussion with forms and guides. Group members picked their best ideas and reported back to the larger group, and then Penny led the group through a prioritizing of the list and the choice of keywords for a vision and mission statement. Penny agreed to draft both—with the words chosen—and to post to the e-list.

The group then discussed what they wanted to accomplish in their next meetings through both short-term and long-term goals, they chose another date to meet, group members chose to become involved on a primary, secondary, or support or information-sharing only level, and group co-leaders for each were chosen.

Each of the three groups then met to discuss what their roles might be, project what they thought they could accomplish with costs and support mechanisms, and discuss future activities. Group note-takers completed their forms and got instructions on posting them to the e-list.

2. List the Facts

Relevant Facts

- The planners are committed to the idea of partnerships.
- The planners are extremely well organized with an emphasis on diverse participation, communication, and opportunities for planning for a shared vision.
- It appears that—given the meeting of a number of planner outcomes—the first meetings were successful.
- It appears that all individuals involved must be technology-ready for successful participation.

Unknown, but Needed Information

- What are the opinions of participants after group meetings (although subsequent attendance can indicate satisfaction with the project)?

- Was attendance at follow-up meetings of the same or different people or a combination of people?
- Are there people who should be at the table but aren't due to technology? Expertise?

3. List the Characters

Directly Involved/Primary

- co-planners—Penny and James
- attending area librarians
- attending potential partners (which may or may not be area librarians)
- meeting participants (for each meeting)

Indirectly Involved/Secondary

- invited potential partners (which may or may not be area librarians)
- invited area librarians
- participants unable to participate given the technology-driven approach
- constituents identified in benefits presentations
- unidentified possible partners
- unidentified possible constituents

4. Review

- The planners are committed to the idea of partnerships.
- The planners appear to have enough introductory content and process to initiate interest.
- Because it appears that all individuals involved must be technology ready for successful participation, the planners should take great care to *not* be dependent on technological delivery of information or communication for success in outcomes.

5. Prioritize

- Planners appear to have enough introductory content and process to initiate interest.
- Was attendance at follow-up meetings of the same or different people or a combination of people?
- The opinions of participants after group meetings are unknown—although subsequent attendance (aggregated information is known at this point) can indicate some measure of satisfaction with the project.
- Because it appears that all individuals involved must be technology ready for successful participation, planners should take great care to *not* be de-

pendent on technological delivery of information or communication for success in outcomes.

- Are there people who should be at the table but aren't—due to the technology-driven process or due to their lack of expertise?

6. What Can Be Done

- The co-planners can continue to organize the partnership project.
- Project participants can continue to meet, investigate, and plan partnerships.
- The planners can assess who was invited, who is attending, and who needs to attend.
- The planners can expand the group and infrastructure communication plan to include nontechnology-driven participants.
- The planners can integrate evaluation into the process.

7. What Can't Be Done

- Original invitees who did not attend should not be discounted (but should be recontacted).
- Technology should not remain the only method of delivery for communication for the partnership project.
- Evaluating the partnership process should not be discounted, nor should it only be conducted at the end of the project.
- The partnership project should not shortcut the established process but should continue the detailed approach to investigating and establishing partnerships.

8. Choose Solutions

- Planners should integrate evaluation into the partnership project.
- Planners should assess who was invited but not attending partnership meetings and identify reasons for them not attending.
- Planners should scan the partnership environment throughout the project to determine additional partners.
- Planners should integrate nontechnology communication into the partnership project.

9. Speculate on Outcome(s)

- Appropriate partners will attend and participate in the partnership project meetings.
- Tech and nontech partners will participate and be successful in the partnership project.

10. Evaluate

- Evaluation measures will assist project co-planners in determining appropriate partner attendance and activity.
- Evaluation measures will assist project co-planners in assessing successes to include diverse partners and benefits for partnership constituents.

WORKS CITED

"Big Dog's & Little Dog's Performance, Learning, Leadership and Knowledge." Accessed October 27, 2013. http://nwlink.com/~donclark.

"Prezi, Inc. Prezi—Ideas Matter." Accessed November 8, 2013. http://prezi.com.

Case Thirteen

Keeping Up with the "Joneses"

Case for use with chapter 13, "Managing the Balance to Meet New Constituent/Customer Expectations"

Chapter/Case # and Case Name	Type of Library and Information Setting	Primary Focus	Secondary Focus
13. Keeping Up with the "Joneses"	• Academic • Public • School • Special	• Assessing constituent needs • A new manager returning • A new manager	• Keeping up with change • The new technologically advanced library

THE CASE

After a ten-year hiatus from the profession, Jeanette Proud returned to library work at a small college in Michigan as the director of the Williams Library. In her first week of work, she realized—and was surprised—that although the library was small and the employees only adequate in number, it provided a wealth of technology, cutting-edge resources, and services for the small student and faculty population. Other surprises for her in the first week included the myriad of budget lines from operating, capital, and grants and especially from partnership agreements; the library's brand and social media presence not only for students, faculty, and employees but also for alumni and families enrolled in the First Year Experience program; the in-depth talents of the small number of employees; and—above all else—how the library constituents had changed in the past decade.

Proud recognized her challenge in the coming months wasn't only learning the new library but also identifying ways to keep up with employees as well as with constituents; ways to get ahead of/out in front of constituent needs given the upcoming budget cycle; *and* a scheduled meeting with the development officer. After her realization of her biggest issues, she met with her employees to discuss how they had identified constituents in general, how they identified constituent *needs* in the past, and how they maintained a level of knowledge to meet existing needs. She was hopeful there was a process in place to continue identifying and meeting existing and/or future needs.

CASE COMMENTS

The "Joneses" case is typical not only for those returning to work after a hiatus but also for those who may move from a library that is *not* so technologically connected to one that is technologically connected. In addition, a major component of the case is how a library assesses constituent needs and uses that data for designing resources and services.

Although many elements of the case focus on a medium-sized to small academic library, this case can be personalized to a larger academic library or a large public library by identifying the new manager as, for example, the new manager of the reference department. In addition, either the medium-sized to smaller library or the larger library can be personalized to be a public library setting.

CASE METHOD ANALYSIS

1. Underline Case Elements

Keeping Up with the "Joneses"

After a ten-year hiatus from the profession, Jeanette Proud returned to library work at a small college in Michigan as the director of the Williams Library. In her first week of work, she realized—and was surprised—that although the library was small and the employees only adequate in number, it provided a wealth of technology, cutting-edge resources, and services for the small student and faculty population. Other surprises for her in the first week included the myriad of budget lines from operating, capital, and grants and especially from partnership agreements; the library's brand and social media presence not only for students, faculty, and employees but also for alumni and families enrolled in the First Year Experience program; the <u>in-depth talents of the small number of employees</u>; and—above all else—how the <u>library constituents had changed in the past decade</u>.

Proud recognized that <u>her challenge</u> in the coming months wasn't only learning the new library but also <u>identifying ways to keep up</u> with employees as well as with constituents; ways to get <u>ahead of/out in front of constituent needs</u> given the upcoming budget cycle; *and* a scheduled meeting with the development officer. After her realization of her biggest issues, she met with her employees to discuss how <u>they had identified constituents in general, how they identified constituent *needs* in the past,</u> and how they maintained a level of knowledge to meet existing needs. She was hopeful there was a process in place to continue identifying and meeting existing and/or future needs.

2. List the Facts

Relevant Facts

- "Keeping up" is an important aspect of management.
- A manager is trying to recover from a ten-year hiatus.
- Employees are only adequate in number.
- The library has a wealth of cutting-edge resources and services for students and faculty.
- There are a myriad of budget lines for operating, capital, and grants and especially for partnership agreements.
- Employees have in-depth talent.
- The library constituents have changed in the past decade.
- The director wants to identify ways to keep up with technology.
- The director wants to get ahead of/out in front of constituent needs.
- There is a budget cycle coming up.
- The director is scheduled to meet with the development officer.
- The director has met with her employees to discuss how constituents in general and constituent needs have been identified.
- The director is seeking a process to continue identifying and meeting existing and/or future needs.

Unknown, but Needed Information

- The director does not know how she is going to catch up.
- The director realizes she does not know today's constituents.
- The director realizes she does not know tomorrow's constituents.
- The director is hopeful that the employees know how they planned for constituents.
- The budget cycle is "coming up" but specific timelines aren't known.
- There is a meeting with the development officer but it isn't clear what the agenda of the meeting will be.

3. List the Characters

Directly Involved/Primary

- the director
- library employees
- administrators/managers directly over the library
- administrators/managers in umbrella institutions/organizations "over" the library
- library constituents using the library in general
- library constituents using the library for a specific need/designed for their use
- those who can help the director with the budget process

Indirectly Involved/Secondary

- other employees in the organization
- library constituents who are *not* using the library but should be/are identified as being unaware of library services designed to meet their needs
- Development Office employees/development officer (depending on the outcome of the meeting, this may move to the "Directly Involved/Primary" category)

4. Review

- The library constituents have changed in the past decade.
- The director realizes she does not know today's constituents.
- The director realizes she does not know tomorrow's constituents.
- There is a budget cycle coming up.
- Employees have in-depth talents.
- The library should/the director wants to identify ways to keep up with constituents.
- The director wants to get ahead/out in front of constituent needs.
- The director is scheduled to meet with the development officer.
- The director met with her employees to discuss how constituents in general and constituent needs had been identified.
- The director is seeking a process to continue identifying and meeting existing and/or future needs.
- The director is hopeful the employees know how they planned for constituents.

5. Prioritize

- There is a budget cycle coming up.
- The library constituents had changed in the past decade.

- The director wants to identify ways to keep up with constituents.
- The director wants to get ahead/out in front of constituent needs.
- The director met with her employees to discuss how constituents in general and constituent needs had been identified.
- The director is hopeful that employees know how they planned for constituents.
- The director is seeking a process to continue identifying and meeting existing and/or future needs.
- Employees have in-depth talents.
- The director is scheduled to meet with the development officer.
- The director realizes she does not know today's constituents.
- The director realizes she does not know tomorrow's constituents.

6. What Can Be Done

- The director can first identify all specific information on the budget process and let those timelines guide her other research.
- The director should work with her employees to identify the process they went through to identify library constituents.
- The director should study constituent profiles to discuss current and future constituents.

7. What Can't Be Done

- The director should not wait to "catch up" or update her knowledge of the profession before she identifies the organization's budget processes.
- The director should not ignore all profile information before putting the next budget together.
- The director should not put off discussions with the development officer.

8. Choose Solutions

- The director should not wait to "catch up" or update her knowledge of the profession before she identifies the organization's budget processes.
- The director should not ignore all profile information before putting the next budget together.
- The director should gather constituent assessment data and compare it to existing services and resources and any organizational plans to see how goals have been met and how future goals might be impacted.
- The director should work with employees to identify additional staffing needs as well as additional training for existing employees.

- The director should outline a professional-development plan for herself.
- The director should outline a trending plan for keeping up for herself and her employees.

9. Speculate on Outcome(s)

- The director should not wait to "catch up" or update her knowledge of the profession before she identifies the organization's budget processes.
- If the director moves ahead without waiting to figure out how to "catch up," she can focus on what is critical for now, that is, identifying the budget process for the organization. In addition, given the newness of the director, and the need to focus on justifying budget requests representing large amounts of funding and high-priority needs (such as identified needs of today's patrons), the director is wise to ask employees about and then use the same process used in the past to identify constituent needs for this new and rapidly advancing budget request.

10. Evaluate

- Constituent data should be continuously updated and evaluated against the organization's resources and services and upcoming plans.
- As a new director, a measurement of success should *not* be whether or not the budget requests are approved. Instead, this first year's measure of success for the new director should be for the budget process to be completed and for the director to begin to build a team with a "first project" to determine the appropriate processes for identifying constituents for immediate needs to be used in the first year's requests.

Case Fourteen

Torture the Data

Case for use with chapter 14, "Accountability, Measurement, and Assessment in New Management Organizations"

Chapter/Case # and Case Name	Type of Library and Information Setting	Primary Focus	Secondary Focus
14. Torture the Data	• Public • Academic • School • Special	• Identifying modes and methods of collecting data • Processes for maintaining management information • A new boss	• Keeping up with assessment practices • Translating library data into umbrella organization data/ meaningful data

THE CASE

Torture the data, and it will confess to anything.

—Ronald Coase, Economics, Nobel Prize Laureate

In identifying content to go into the annual report to be distributed at the August board meeting, Bertram, the library director, began his usual search for statistics and pulled out the hash mark, input, and usage numbers from collections, services, and programs. He then read—for the first time—the new assistant city manager's May memo with instructions for completing

319

departmental annual reports and realized that report requirements for this past year were dramatically different from the year before.

As he studied the instructions, he began to list those elements requested and who he should consult with and tried to indicate what he thought he did and didn't have given the content and format requested. As Bertram completed the list, he realized he couldn't answer approximately one-third of the questions the assistant city manager wanted and began to wonder how he should approach the required report.

CASE COMMENTS

It is not unusual for organizations to change their processes from year to year. These processes can include reporting, budgeting, and communication, to name only a few. While some of these processes are driven by management, others, such as human resources, can be driven by new or changed local, state, regional, or federal changes. This case can be used in any setting and for any size of environment. That is, the focus is on the change needed, the timeline, and the importance of the documents. In addition, the importance of this case also lies in the fact that the manager has a new supervisor (the assistant city manager, or associate vice president of academics, assistant principal, or assistant vice president of business operations) and must move quickly to conform. Of additional importance, but a subtext, is the fact that library data must routinely be translated into meaningful data for those outside the library field and in many cases stakeholders and supporters within the library field. This need for translation often makes moving from one form to another more difficult.

CASE METHOD ANALYSIS

1. Underline Case Elements.

Torture the Data

Torture the data, and it will <u>confess to anything</u>.

—<u>Ronald Coase</u>, Economics, Nobel Prize Laureate

In identifying content to go into the annual report to be <u>distributed at the August</u> board meeting, Bertram, the library director, began his usual search for statistics and <u>pulled out the hash mark, input, and usage numbers from collections, services, and programs</u>. He then read—<u>for the first time</u>—the <u>new</u> assistant city manager's May memo with instructions for completing departmental annual reports and realized that report <u>requirements for this past year were dramatically</u> <u>different</u> from the year before.

As he studied the instructions, he began <u>to list those elements requested</u> and <u>who he should consult with</u> and tried to indicate what he thought <u>he did and</u> <u>didn't have</u> given the content and format requested. As Bertram completed the list, he realized <u>he couldn't answer approximately one-third of the questions</u> the assistant city manager wanted and began to wonder <u>how he should approach</u> <u>the required report</u>.

2. List the Facts

Relevant Facts

- The assistant city manager is new.
- Changes are expected in the required report.
- The library director is behind in preparing the report.
- The library director has not prepared adequately by reading his new boss's instructions.
- The library director is estimating a significantly incomplete report.

Unknown, but Needed Information

- The exact amount of time is unclear.
- The missing data is unknown and must be identified quickly.
- The list of people to speak with should be finalized.

3. List the Characters

Directly Involved/Primary

- the library director
- the new assistant city manager

Indirectly Involved/Secondary

- individuals identified as sources for data needed
- other peer report authors (how they are interpreting data for the new assistant city manager)

4. Review

- There is a short timeline for when the required information is due.
- Missing information is needed for the required report.

- The library director must report to a new supervisor (the assistant city manager).
- The library director got a late start in the budget preparation—for whatever reason.

5. Prioritize

- There is a short timeline for when the required information is due.
- The library director got a late start in the budget preparation—for whatever reason.
- Missing information is needed for the required report.
- The library director must report to a new supervisor (the assistant city manager).

6. What Can Be Done

- The director can prepare two-thirds of the report or the amount of information needed with the information readily at hand and appropriate for the report.
- The director can contact other individuals to identify data needed.
- The director can request an extension.
- The director can clarify what is needed.

7. What Can't Be Done

- The director can't turn in an incomplete report.
- The director can't ignore the new instructions and/or the timeline.
- The director can't do the report in isolation/without people to assist.

8. Choose Solutions

- The director can clarify what is needed.
- The director can request an extension.
- The director can contact other individuals to identify data needed.
- The director can prepare two-thirds of the report or the amount of information needed with the information readily at hand and appropriate for the report.

9. Speculate on Outcome(s)

- The director should be able to clarify expectations.
- The director should be able to have a successful initial relationship with his new assistant city manager.

• The director should complete the entire report and confirm that this situation will not occur in the future.

10. Evaluate

• The director should design a process for vetting this year's report once it is completed.
• The director should build a timeline for the coming year that includes data needed, creation of forms not yet available, forms in place, training needed for those responsible for data needed, and a process for approaching next year's creation of the report.

Matching Data to Data Requests

Case for use with chapter 15, "New Budgeting with (Mostly) Classic Budgeting Issues"

Chapter/Case # and Case Name	Type of Library and Information Setting	Primary Focus	Secondary Focus
15. Matching Data to Data Requests	• School • Academic • Public • Using data to justify new employees applicable to any type of library	• Managing new technologies • Justifying new employee requests	• Transitioning from older spaces to newer spaces

THE CASE

The Franklin High School Library Media Center is in a recently renovated space that now includes a coffee bar; a laptop, e-reader, and iPad check-out service; a production lounge for individual and small-group design of media product for school assignments; and a stage and raked seating area for demonstrating media produced in the lounge as well as drama/theater performance and author and book talk readings.

Given that the new space (recently opened in September) was paid for by bond money and given that bond money would not pay for staffing (not even as an initial hire), the puzzle for Geneva Frost—the new school librarian/

media specialist—was to figure out how to obtain approval from the district-wide media specialist, the principal, and the school board for, at the very least, one new librarian position and, if possible, an additional position of a media tech or instructional designer.

CASE COMMENTS

Through the past decades the profession of library and information science has experienced great challenges in funding. These challenges include no money for anything, no money for mandated initiatives, no money for critical issues, money earmarked for other things, money for building but no money for renovation, money with conditions for expenditures, and finally (but certainly not the last issue) money for other things but no money for employees.

This case illustrates the conundrum of having some money to drive design, resources, and services but having no money to staff or support either in new hires, additional hires, or expanded employee hours or—more than likely—no training dollars for updating current employees.

This case has additional complex issues including management of new technologies in general and transitions from the old to the new. Other unstated but soon-to-be-realized issues include availability of dollars for sustainability of the new environment. Finally, this case can be personalized for another type of library—specifically academic—and public for either general services or age-level services.

CASE METHOD ANALYSIS

1. Underline Case Elements

Matching Data to Data Requests

The Franklin High School Library Media Center is in a recently renovated space that now includes a coffee bar; a laptop, e-reader, and iPad check-out service; a production lounge for individual and small-group design of media product for school assignments; and a stage and raked seating area for demonstrating media produced in the lounge as well as drama/theater performance and author and book talk readings.

Given that the new space (recently opened in September) was paid for by bond money and given that bond money would not pay for employees (not even an initial hire), the puzzle for Geneva Frost—the new school librarian/media specialist—was to figure out how to obtain approval from the district-wide media specialist, the principal, and the school board for, at the very least, one new librarian position and, if possible, an additional position of a media tech or instructional technologist.

2. List the Facts

Relevant Facts

- The library/media center has a variety of new services and resources, several of which are typically mediated for services (e.g., production of media, tech check-out, newer tech items for use, event space that needs oversight, etc.).
- No bond funding can be spent on employees.
- The timing is early fall so there is time (more than likely) for preparing budget requests.
- There are three different people Geneva must work with for approval for employees.
- Geneva is new so she does not yet know how to get approval for new positions.

Unknown, but Needed Information

- Geneva needs information on the school's budgeting/hiring processes, including a specific timeline.
- It's not clear from the information how many employees are in the library/media center.
- It's not clear what skills Geneva or any current employees have.
- It's not clear who needs to be convinced of the need for new employees first or who is the most important to convince.
- It's not clear how the district manages justification for new employees.

3. List the Characters

Directly Involved/Primary

- Geneva Frost
- any other staff currently in the library/media center
- the district-wide media specialist
- the principal
- the school board (specific members who might be identified as supporters of the new staff)
- the school board (all members)
- students (or constituents) identified as using the new areas/those projected as needing assistance

Indirectly Involved/Secondary

- all students who use the library
- other students who don't use the library, but may use the new services

- other groups involved in supporting school budgets and school activities such as parents and the school library Friends group
- parents of students who are identified as users and potential users of the library in general and the library's new areas
- other librarians in the district in general
- other librarians in the district seeking new employees
- other librarians with similar environments with similar services

4. Review

- The library/media center has a variety of new services and resources, several of which are typically mediated for services (e.g., production of media, tech check-out, newer tech items for use, event space that needs oversight, etc.).
- No bond funding can be spent on staff.
- There are three different people Geneva must work with for approval for staff.
- Geneva is new so she does not yet know how to get approval for new positions.
- It's not clear from the information how many staff are in the library/media center.
- It's not clear who needs to be convinced of the need for new staff first or who is the most important to convince.

5. Prioritize

Now

- Geneva is new so she does not yet know how to get approval for new positions.
- Geneva needs information on the school's budgeting/hiring processes, including a specific timeline.
- The timing is early fall so there is time (more than likely) for preparing budget requests.
- It's not clear who needs to be convinced of the need for new staff first or who is the most important to convince.

Later

- It's not clear what skills Geneva or any current staff have.
- There are three different people Geneva must work with for approval for staff.

- It's not clear from the information how many staff are in the library/media center.
- It's not clear how the district manages justification for new staff.

6. What Can Be Done

- Geneva can and should find out the process and timeline.
- Geneva can and should immediately find out who she needs to convince and by when.
- Geneva can determine staffing needs for assisting students and faculty with the new services.

7. What Can't Be Done

- Geneva can't/shouldn't use the same justification for the position for each person she needs to convince.
- Geneva shouldn't ignore the timelines necessary to participate in the process.
- Library/media center staff should not ignore the assistance needed to support students in the new service(s).

8. Choose Solutions

- Geneva should immediately find out what the budget and process timeline is.
- Geneva can and should immediately find out who she needs to convince and by when, including finding answers to the questions, "How do the three individuals/groups each learn?" and "What kind of justification data is needed to convince the three individuals/groups?"
- Geneva should gather as much data as possible, including: who else in district libraries has these services; how many staff are in library and media center environments in the district; and research on how these services are integrated into library and media center services.

9. Speculate on Outcome(s)

- Data will be gathered, assessed, and then integrated into the process of asking for new staff.
- Justification data should be individually designed to meet the "persuasion" needs of the three groups in the process.
- It is likely no new staff will be approved; therefore, a variety of scenarios for service should be identified so the space isn't "running as it should even though no new staff are hired."

10. Evaluate

- Geneva's data should be shared with other district staff to compare against other data used in successful human resources requests.
- Data should be vetted to determine how it matches the learning and persuasion needs of the three individuals/groups needing convincing.
- Geneva should establish recordkeeping and assessment for the new space designed to gather information on (should they get new staff) how the space is used and designed as well as (should they not get new staff) how the staff is *not* being used.

Case Sixteen

Building Tomorrow's Future on Today's Expertise

Case for use with chapter 16, "Emergency Management Roles and Responsibilities of New Managers"

Chapter/Case # and Case Name	Type of Library and Information Setting	Primary Focus	Secondary Focus
16. Building Tomorrow's Future on Today's Expertise	• Public • Academic • School	• Managing co-location partnerships • Managing relationships with first responders	• Planning for partnership activities • Planning for first-responder relationships

THE CASE

In preparation for opening the new branch in the northwest quadrant of the county, Jennifer Remington, the county branch coordinator, hired a new manager from the city library system, Ruby Leigh Carmichael. Ruby Leigh had varied in-depth experience in city branches and had managed a library near Riverdale—the small community in the northwest quadrant where the new county library was located. Her experience in city co-located branches was anticipated as a major element of the success of the new county branch as the new county branch was co-located with Riverdale police, fire, and city hall.

In planning for the first community meeting of co-location managers, Jennifer began to gather the community information from her files that included the partners who had participated in early focus groups who met to plan the county co-located facility. She decided not to create the agenda by herself, but chose instead to meet with Ruby Leigh to work with her on creating the agenda, but Ruby Leigh was unavailable to meet until the day of the community meeting. Thus, their meeting was scheduled for the next morning with an agenda needed for the same afternoon.

CASE COMMENTS

Although most emergency management cases outline preparation for and responses to emergency situations—as they should—cases should also be included that assist entities in establishing positive, working, and, in this case, co-location protocols for relationships with first-responder and emergency management environments.

While all professions use standards and benchmarks, there are a variety of standards and benchmark environments that should be assessed for relevance. First responders use benchmarks and best practices in all facets of the emergency management discussion.

This case can easily be personalized for other types of libraries.

CASE METHOD ANALYSIS

1. Underline Case Elements

Building <u>Tomorrow's Future</u> <u>on</u> Today's <u>Expertise</u>

In preparation for opening the <u>new branch</u> in the northwest quadrant of the county, Jennifer Remington, the county branch coordinator, hired a new manager from the city library system, Ruby Leigh Carmichael. Ruby Leigh had <u>varied in-depth experience</u> in city <u>branches and had managed a library</u> near Riverdale—the small community in the northwest quadrant <u>where the new county library was located</u>. Her <u>experience in city co-located branches</u> was anticipated as a <u>major element of the success</u> of the new county branch as the <u>new county branch was co-located</u> with Riverdale police, fire, and city hall.

In planning for the first community meeting of co-location managers, Jennifer began to gather the community information from her files that included the <u>partners who had participated in early focus groups who met to plan the county co-located facility</u>. She decided not to create the agenda by herself, but <u>chose instead to meet with Ruby Leigh to work with her on creating the agenda</u>, but Ruby Leigh was unavailable to meet until the day of the community meeting. Thus, their meeting was scheduled for the next morning with an <u>agenda needed for the same afternoon</u>.

2. List the Facts

Relevant Facts

- A new manager has been hired with a unique type of library and partner-ship/co-location expertise.
- A new branch with a new community team must be formed immediately.
- There is a short timeline for an upcoming, imminent meeting.
- Some preliminary content identifying partners is available.

3. List the Characters

Directly Involved/Primary

- the new branch director, Ruby Leigh Carmichael
- co-location first responders including partners and police, fire, and city hall managers and/or representatives
- the branch library staff who will be working in Riverdale
- the branch library coordinator
- community constituents instrumental in the funding and design of the new library

Indirectly Involved/Secondary

- other co-location county branch managers
- other county branch managers
- benchmark environments for co-location with first responders

4. Review

- There is a need for an agenda to be created immediately.
- The partners will be first responders.
- A new partnership must be formed with co-locators and first responders.
- Employees are all new to the location.
- The employees will have a manager new to the specific system.

5. Prioritize

- There is a need for an agenda to be created immediately. .
- The employees will have a manager new to the specific system.
- The partners will be first responders.
- A new partnership must be formed with co-locators and first responders.
- Employees are all new to the location.

6. What Can Be Done

- A quick agenda can easily be created in the morning for the afternoon meeting.
- Partners can be identified for a successful co-location.
- Ruby Leigh can use her expertise for success in the new co-location.
- The first meeting can lay a significant foundation with little initial information.

7. What Can't Be Done

- The agenda can be but shouldn't be created without the new branch manager's input.
- The meeting of partners should not be postponed.
- The managers should not forget to address the unique aspects of co-location with first responders (it is recommended to contact benchmark/other co-location first-responder library environments to be knowledgeable about possible unique issues).
- Managers should not forget to include other new branch employees in discussions.

8. Choose Solutions

- The new managers should address the unique aspects of co-location with first responders by contacting other co-location libraries who partner with first responders.
- The new managers should—if possible—speak by phone or e-mail on the draft first agenda and then create the final agenda that morning.
- Benchmark issues should be outlined for participants.
- The new manager should be credentialed for those attending the meeting and afterward—for all first responders/partners.

Prioritize

- The new managers should—if possible—speak by phone or email on the draft first agenda and then create the final agenda that morning.
- The new managers should address the unique aspects of co-location with first responders by contacting other co-location libraries who partner with first responders.
- Benchmark issues should be outlined for participants.
- The new manager should be credentialed for those attending the meeting and afterward—for all first responders/partners.

9. Speculate on Outcome(s)

- Although Ruby Leigh has extensive experience in co-location, issues relating to co-location with first responders are legion and have impact on all partners.
- The first meeting should serve to introduce partners and identify issues and outline a plan for establishing relationships.

10. Evaluate

- Ruby Leigh should create goals and outcomes for her first-six-month/first-year performance.
- Ruby Leigh should work with her staff to create goals and outcomes for the first six months of branch activity.
- Ruby Leigh should work with her new employees to create individual employee goals and outcomes.
- Jennifer and Ruby Leigh should plan a series of meetings to determine progress on the co-location of first responders near the Riverdale Branch, Ruby Leigh's progress, the progress of goals/outcomes for the new branch, and the progress on individual goals and outcomes.

Part Three

APPENDIXES

Appendixes are additional information typically located at the end of re-search, a monograph, or a report. As supplementary materials, they are designed to illustrate content, give examples, and expand information previously introduced. Although appendixes are often said to contain nonessential information, the content here includes:

- appendix A: Annotated Master List of "Indispensable" Resources—a list of documents and websites
- appendix B: Examples of Paradigms—to identify specific elements and activities within the organization for review
- appendix C: Additional Paradigm Shifts—additional general paradigm shifts to supplement chapter content

Appendix A

Annotated Master List of "Indispensable" Resources

"Alison." Accessed September 10, 2013. http://alison.com.

Alison, advertised as "a new world of free certified learning," is free web-based curriculum delivered in courses, but with a variety of forms and formats. Website content can be searched by topic, subject, and date and includes some coursework that can be personalized to meet individual and organizational need. Alison requires sign-in; however, a vast amount of information is available and searchable in different ways. Accessing "Courses by Subject" offers learners hundreds of options in general business (including specific to as well as applicable to nonprofit), communication, presentation skills, instructional technology, and general teaching and learning.

"American Library Association (ALA)." Accessed September 23, 2013. www.ala.org.

ALA offers website guests and visitors significant content on general information on the profession of library and information science including standards and guidelines. ALA offers members visiting the website extensive professional support, guidance, and content through a variety of modes and methods. Library managers find valuable general content to support the management of libraries throughout the website, including the websites of ALA's functional divisions and specialized organizations (by type of library). Some examples are:

- AASL. "American Association of School Librarians." Accessed September 23, 2013. www.ala.org/aasl. AASL provides extensive links for school librarians and school library managers ("Essential Links: Resources for School Library Program Management: Library Management." Accessed

June 2, 2013. http://aasl.ala.org/essentiallinks/index.php?title=Library_
Management).

- ACRL. "Association of College & Research Libraries." Accessed September 23, 2013. www.ala.org.acrl. Specific management by type and size of library can be found in ACRL with—among other resources—current and back issues of the association's journal that provides managers with extensive content for higher education and academic libraries.
- LLAMA. "Library Leadership & Management Association." Accessed September 23, 2013. www.ala/llama. General management content is available from LLAMA.
- PLA. "Public Library Association." Accessed September 23, 2013. www .ala.org/pla. PLA provides extensive links for public library managers. Additional extensive areas for librarians and library managers include advocacy and the value of libraries, as well as in-depth information on library functions and activities.

"American Society for Training & Development" (ASTD). Accessed August 10, 2013. www.astd.org/Search?q=management.

ASTD is the premier website for the profession of training and development. Although the site offers fee-based content, users can register (or not) for free online content. Searching ASTD for "management" yields hundreds of articles for managers wishing to retool or retrain, as well as content for new managers and those wishing to achieve management positions.

"Big Dog's & Little Dog's Performance Juxtaposition." Accessed October 27, 2013. http://nwlink.com/~donclark.

Big Dog's site—a must for every manager, employee, and volunteer developer/trainer—offers hundreds of training and learning sites, "Links to HRD Sources" and human resources sites, and examples and best practices of human resources documents such as performance content and employee manuals.

"Designing Libraries." Accessed October 27, 2013. www.designinglibraries .org.uk.

Designing Libraries offers extensive visual information with design and building ideas for academic, public, school, and special libraries. This site has global content and information for managers as well as architects, supporters, and stakeholders.

"EDUCAUSE." Accessed September 15, 2013. www.educause.edu.

EDUCAUSE offers unique content to educators, librarians, and managers including conferences and research, as well as stand-alone training and education. While the focus of the association is higher education, educators seeking content on, for example, P–16 educational initiatives will find both general and specific information. While many publications are for sale, extensive research is available online for free along with annual research overviews (e.g., Horizon, EDUCAUSE Learning Initiatives).

"Federal Emergency Management Agency" (FEMA). Accessed October 27, 2013. www.fema.gov.

Library managers can access extensive content on emergency management and critical incidents, including content and links not only for facilities but also for constituents, resources, and services. In addition, FEMA content illustrates what partnerships organizations can form to provide local, regional, and statewide support in times of emergency and for non-emergency assistance.

"Free Management Library." Accessed October 24, 2013. www.freemanagementlibrary.org.

Free Management Library offers consistently excellent, expanding web content and the ability for keyword searching. A dynamic web environment for managers, the depth and breadth of this online resource is extensive with multiple layers of content, pathways to determining relevance, annotations, and recommended lists. A manager seeking updated, contemporary information can search by date for extensive "new" information. The website can be accessed through http://managementhelp.org as well as the www.freemanagementlibrary.org.

"The Future of Libraries." Accessed September 12, 2013. www.davinci institute.com.

The institute's website offers current and future trends applicable for all types and sizes of libraries as well as scenarios, white papers, presentations, and a newsletter. Although librarians and library managers can use this material, it is also helpful for informing and inspiring supporters and stakeholders as well as administrators in umbrella organizations.

"Internet Public Library" (IPL). Accessed October 15, 2013. www.ipl.org.

IPL (now IPL2) has remained one of the most vital and dynamic library environments on the web for all types and sizes of librarians in general, and certainly for library managers. Searching for "management" yields hundreds of hits and—of these—over 50 percent are related to general management. An additional search of "nonprofit management" and "library management" yields helpful citations as well with some overlapping, but also a number of good, on target, discrete links. Links from IPL2 are vetted, and annotations provide the user with a clear understanding of the resource.

"Ken Haycock & Associates Inc. Blog." Accessed June 23, 2013. http://kenhaycock.com/blog.

Haycock's blog offers contemporary leadership and management comments and content from experts; a number of presentations are also archived and available with critical information such as types of employees (millennials) and the immediate future of libraries.

"Libguides Community." Accessed September 21, 2013. www.libguides.com.

The primary focus of the Libguides community is access to thousands of clients' pages with bibliographies and weblinks; however, the community includes links to several hundred pages designed for librarians and library managers.

"Library and Information Science—A Guide to Online Resources." Accessed October 27, 2013. www.loc.gov/rr/program/bib/libsci/guides.html.

Although there are a number of "keeping up" techniques and pathfinders on the web, this Library of Congress guide offers an excellent list of management tools for managers seeking ways to retrain, retool, and—once updated—keep up with their profession and management.

"Librarylawblog." Accessed September 30, 2013. http://blog.librarylaw.com/librarylaw.

Librarylaw web content offers librarians and library managers the opportunity for an overview of laws and legislation as well as comments and interpretation by a lawyer-librarian. The blog provides topical information, follows a blog archive format, and offers users keyword searching. Not only is the information helpful for librarians and managers, but also this site's content is invaluable for library supporters and stakeholders.

"Library Networking: Journals, Blogs, Associations and Conferences." Accessed October 27, 2013. www.interleaves.org/~rteeter/libnetwork.html.

This website maintains over fifteen categories of links of web content. Both the breadth and depth of content provide a manager with the "latest" from a variety of resources. A particularly helpful list is the list of blogs— institutional and from individuals—with brief annotations as well as links to blog directories. Managers should visit this specific blog regularly, and a number of these links should be favorites on the manager's bookshelf.

"Library Research Service (LRS)." Accessed September 23, 2013. www .lrs.org.

LRS is a primary web environment for data for all types and sizes of libraries. LRS provides extensive data for library managers, supporters, and stakeholders for library measurement, assessment, and accountability to support data-driven decisions.

"Library Success: A Best Practices Wiki." Accessed October 27, 2013. www .libsuccess.org.

Although this wiki is updated intermittently, the organization is extensive with many management categories and a growing body of links.

"Library Technology Guides." Accessed October 27, 2013. www.librarytech nology.org/LibraryTechnologyReports.pl.

Library Technology Guides offers not only links to pathfinders on technology but also a number of reports and links to more contemporary library technology information for librarians and library managers.

"OCLC." Accessed October 27, 2013. www.oclc.org.

OCLC conducts and disseminates extensive research for all types and sizes of libraries. Research includes environmental scan data, constituent profiles and user data, and content on facilities and materials. Many of the profession's most extensive and relevant research reports are provided for data-driven decision-making by not only librarians and library managers but also umbrella organization administrators, supporters, and stakeholders.

"The Pew Charitable Trusts." Accessed October 27, 2013. www.pewtrusts.org.

Pew Content provides invaluable "thought" pieces of contemporary experts on primarily public libraries and the role of the public library in the "community." Although content focuses more on larger libraries, papers are excellent informative and supporting information for not only smaller public libraries but also all types and sizes of libraries.

"Resources for School Librarians." Accessed October 27, 2013. www.sl directory.com/index.html.

School librarians have rich collections of web resources to assist managers. This site offers extensive content, simply arranged for all sizes of school libraries. The management content located here (see "Program Administration") is one of the best sets of information for "manager bookshelves" on the web.

"Special Library Association (SLA)." Accessed September 23, 2013. www
.sla.org.

The SLA website offers content primarily to members only; however, there
is basic information freely accessible for not only special librarians but also
those in other types of libraries where librarians are in solo practice such as
school libraries or departmental librarians in public or academic libraries.

"State Libraries." Accessed October 27, 2013. www.publiclibraries.com/
state_library.htm.

State Libraries offers incredibly rich environments for not only information
specific to the laws and practices of individual states but also general best-
practice information on libraries. This list—a list of all state libraries—is a
one-stop location for links to all state library sites. Users will link to all state
library homepages and then be able to access content in a variety of locations
within each state library's website categorized as library developments or
library services. For additional information, "State and Regional Chapters"
(accessed October 27, 2013, www.ala.org/groups/affiliates/chapters/state/
stateregional) offers users connections to ALA-related organizations state by
state. Some of these environments are formally affiliated with the ALA.

"Stephen's Lighthouse." Accessed October 22, 2013. http://stephenslight
house.com.

The Lighthouse is an important web environment for keeping up with
trends, future discussions, and best practices.

"Steven Bell's Resource Center." Accessed October 27, 2013. http://steven
bell.info.

Bell's content is carefully chosen and discussed or commented on and can
be used by all types of libraries, although the primary focus is academic.

"Tame the Web." Accessed October 27, 2013. http://tametheweb.com.

An older site, Tame the Web remains relevant and a "must see" web environment for all types and sizes of libraries and especially for library managers. Although technology has always been a primary focus of the site, managers should bookmark this site for not only technology but also management
of technology and trends and future discussions.

"Top Technology Trends." Accessed September 21, 2013. http://litablog.org/
category/top-technology-trends.

This annual tech trends list represents a collective expertise from ALA's
LITA experts, who offer ongoing technology trend information in this valu-

able website. Updates typically occur around midwinter and identify trends to track. Although these trends focus on technology, the list is invaluable for driving other discussions and decisions. In addition, the site archive provides a rich perspective on "what was" as well as "what is" and "what might be."

"Urban Libraries Council." Accessed October 27, 2013. www.urbanlibraries .org.

While all sizes of libraries do not have the same issues, much can be said about larger libraries of all types facing similar issues as well as urban academic libraries having the same issues as urban public libraries. The Urban Libraries Council website provides good information on trends, activities, and events for public libraries in metropolitan areas and the corporations that serve them. In addition, extensive content on outcomes assessment for public libraries is available. Outcomes assessment, available under the Library Edge umbrella, provides significant content for managers to assess. While metrics do not always transfer across all sizes of libraries, much of the Edge outcomes data can be applied to libraries other than urban libraries. Edge content can be accessed through the council's website as well as from "Library Edge" (accessed October 27, 2013, www.libraryedge.org).

"WebJunction." Accessed October 21, 2013. www.webjunction.org.

WebJunction has been the premier web-based content-delivery site for libraries for many years, and although there is fee-based continuing education, there is an enormous amount of content for all types of libraries on all aspects of library management. Website users can register for access, but many materials are available without registration. Additional substantive and relevant free management content can be found in the "Catalog of Free Online Courses."

"The Whole Building Design Guide." Accessed October 27, 2013. www .wbdg.org.

Library managers *must* bookmark this guide not only for new or renovation projects but also for best practices for a variety of facilities issues.

"Workforce." Accessed October 27, 2013. www.workforce.com.

Workforce is a resource for news, trends, tools, and information about human relations topics including compensation/benefits, HR management, legal insight, recruiting/staffing, software/technology, and training/development. The site provides articles, research, and case studies.

Appendix B

Examples of Paradigms

Paradigms assist planners in the categorization of areas/functions and activities among libraries in a system or partners within a consortia or library branches, etc., through data and opinion gathering and projecting area, function or activity, outcome, and timelines for change.

Paradigm Shifts provide planners not only with categorizations of areas/functions and activities but also with comparisons of, for example, the classic to the new, one location to another, a best practice to a current practice or services, activities with and without money. Other ideas for Paradigm Shifts are listed below.

Old vs. New
Right Way vs. Wrong Way
We Spent Money This Way, and Now We Spend Money This Way
We'll Do It This Way, and You'll Do It This Way
The Old System vs. the New System
Old Way to Handle Reference vs. New Way to Handle Reference
The Old Service vs. The New Service
Now . . . Later

Appendix C

Additional Paradigm Shifts

Example 1. Twenty-First-Century Library Paradigm Shift

THEN	NOW
All services available only when library was "open"	Many services available 24/7
Limited technology for individual use by public	Greatly expanded technology for individual constituents
Single or individual product workstations	One workstation or network now multitasks
Change in library services hardware, software and constituent need occurs once a year or eighteen months	Change occurs anywhere from every month to every two to three months—constant reassessment is needed
Strong reliance on print resources	Strong reliance on electronic and print Resources
Most things available in print, only indexes available electronically	Full text available electronically and some things now available only electronically
Constituents have easily identified needs and levels of learning and knowledge	Constituents have dramatically different needs *and* dramatically diverse levels of learning and knowledge, often hard to identify and rapidly changing
Constituents spend moderate time with print materials and indexes	Constituents spend expanded time on library hardware
Traditional services available such as copying	New services added *on top of* old services such as printing, downloading, and basic computer skills such as keyboarding
Standard budget categories for buying and record-keeping	Additional/expanded categories relating primarily to hardware and software resources
Offer library instruction in traditional ways such as tours, one-on-one, handouts	Expanded offerings on top of traditional ones, such as signage, small-group instruction, virtual instruction

Example 1. (*continued*)

THEN	NOW
Planning qualitative and quantitative	Planning very data driven, emphasis on strategic
Planning for resources annual or biannual updates	Rapid change in products drives more frequent updating/greater expenditures
Limited technology for employees	Greatly expanded technology for employees
Not much time spent teaching the tool, rather locating and using content	Now much time spent teaching the tool or method of finding, and so on.
Reference in person	Reference in person, virtual, digital, synchronous, asynchronous
Offer only those things we purchase	Offer access to selective resources *freely*
Library a quiet place with individual seating for study	Noise! Equipment! One-on-one teaching of hardware/software, vying for seating and finding seats without computers at them!

Example 2.   Twenty-First-Century Library and Information Center Employees

THEN	NOW
Librarians and library professionals could provide reference and information services and have a few specialty areas.	Librarians and library professionals must provide a variety of kinds of reference and information services *and* specialize *and* have many general areas.
Librarians and library professionals serve on few internal workgroups/committees.	Librarians and library professionals serve on a wide variety of committees for their expertise and to integrate libraries into the organization.
Teaching was point-of-use in-person and some small group/tour presentation.	Teaching is now point-of-use in-person and virtual and small group and large group in class and virtual. It is both asynchronous and synchronous.
Librarians select materials and create some print material guides and handouts and make them accessible.	Librarians now select, make accessible, *and* create print and online documents, guides, and resources to meet constituent needs.
Librarians and library professionals need to possess and maintain traditional personal instructional technology tools/competencies such as overheads/word processing.	Librarians and library professionals must maintain all traditional and also add twenty-first-century toolbox for employees such as html, java scripting, web-based products, and PowerPoint.
Librarians' and library professionals' continuing education has been typically more library-related such as resource based and selection based.	Librarians and library professionals now must more broadly address training in hardware, software, and teaching and learning and general management issues
Employee continuing education has been in traditional formats for learning.	Employee continuing education and development has been expanded into additional formats, web based, teleconferences, and so on.

THEN	NOW
Professional development and learning have been sporadic, periodic, and often issue or product specific.	Learning and development are now continuous, ongoing, and often more general.
Librarians and library professionals have worked on committees and groups on some projects with some decision-making.	Librarians and library professionals now have more of a smaller-team approach to general work functions with more team recommendations and decision-making.
People have been working together in person on projects and committees.	People are also now working together virtually.
People could share workspaces, hardware, and environments.	People now need their individual workstations to be able to customize hardware and software to ergonomic and intellectual needs.
Librarians and library professionals have been more reactive.	Librarians and library professionals must be proactive.
Librarians and library professionals create PR for their services and activities.	Librarians and library professionals must market themselves.
Librarians and library professionals justify needs with general goals and aggregate data.	Librarians and library professionals justify needs with general and targeted goals and outcomes statements. Usage data must be designed to match goal statements.

Example 3. Twenty-First-Century Library and Information Center Reference

THEN	NOW
Library employees provide basic reference services and may have specialty areas.	Librarians now must provide a variety of kinds of reference *and* specialize *and* have many general areas in a wide variety of formats.
Constituents need help in finding information, analyzing information, applying information, and using resources where information is located.	Constituents need help in finding, analyzing, and applying or thinking critically about information and in using the hardware to read/view/locate (PC, keyboard, mouse, other), using the software, and using printing devices, and so on.
Teaching or helping constituents use the library has been point of use or in person and some small-group presentation primarily.	Teaching/helping constituents is now point of use, in person, virtual, small group, and large group in classroom, in-person settings for a wide variety of ages and levels and styles of learning. It can be both asynchronous and synchronous.

(continued)

Example 3. *(continued)*

THEN	NOW
Librarians and library employees only count use by in-person or door count and contact such as call-in.	Librarians and library employees now count in-person, call-in, and virtual usage both locally and remotely.
Librarians and library employees count reference questions as in person or by phone.	Librarians and library employees now count in person, call-in, fax, email, and web based.
Librarians and library employees typically had few usage categories that seldom varied.	Librarians and library employees now have *many* more things to count as well as usage categories, such as searching an item, searching and finding, or a "hit."
Librarians and library employees have only aggregate or input stats such as: How many did we buy? How many were checked out?	Librarians and library employees now still count how many were purchased but also count use in general, types of use input, and in some cases outcome such as use of an online resource.
Counts or statistics typically are steady or growing, or they grow at the same pace.	Now there is a national decrease in some areas that we see locally and an increase in alternative uses/counts such as electronic resources, printing, use of interactive software, or tutorials.
Employees weren't worried about finding information people shouldn't see or didn't have to worry about teaching people "not to" do something (e.g., .gov or .org or .net and not .com for some websites).	Constituents must be taught (sometimes) what to do and what not to do.

Example 4. Twenty-First-Century Library and Information Setting Paradigm Shift

EXISTING LEARNING	NEW CONTINUOUS LEARNING
Was/is	Should be/will be
Random learning opportunities	Systematic planning for continuous learning
Training/education/development blurred	Identification and differentiation of each independently
Annual planning	Short-term planning (two to three years)
Random learning locations	Specifically designated learning stations and designated environments
Learning at varied times	Self-directed, standardized, and scheduled learning times
Competencies and skills not addressed	Identification of core and specialized skills needed
Change addressed randomly or not at all	Change being recognized, defined, and a training and education topic
People learning alone	Self-directed, team, partnership learning or cooperative learning

EXISTING LEARNING	NEW CONTINUOUS LEARNING
Competency or skill-building for self-development	Self-development as appropriate and training/education/development for team teaching, resident expert, or train the trainer
Little written specific commitment to learning	Learning identified and added to policies, procedures, and all documents of the organization
Learning and training/education/development focus is primarily for the public	Focusing first on the employees
Secondary commitment of hardware and software for employee learning and teaching	Primary use and commitment
Ancillary and limited definitions of and commitment to training/education and development in budgeting	Defining and organizing training/education/development with program budget
Methods of teaching and learning chosen randomly, or not at all	Recognition and matching of staff learning styles

Index

About the Author

Julie Todaro has been a library manager for over thirty years and has experience in all types of libraries and library settings. She is a dean in a community college library, consults, presents workshops, and is an author and frequent presenter at association conferences and in organizational settings.

Todaro's work has included designing and delivering strategic planning processes and marketing initiatives for community leaders and public institutions for information services for all types and sizes of libraries, librarians, and library supporters. She has presented dozens of national workshops including: "21st Century Libraries," "Collaborating, Partnering, Cooperating: The Good, the Bad and the Future," "Staffing Issues for the 21st Century," "Integrating Learning with Work: Designing the 21st Century Learning Library," "Emergency Preparedness: The Human Factor, the Organization, and Resources in a 9/11 World," "21st Century Organizational Effectiveness," and "Cutting Edge Redux: New and 'Used' Programs and Services with a 21st Century Spin."

Her professional career includes: library manager for over thirty-five years including graduate school/doctoral educator (five institutions), and public librarian for seven years. Since 1990, Dr. Todaro has been closely involved with a variety of initiatives including the Texas White House Conference Program Planning (1989–1991) and the Texas Book Festival Steering Committee (1995 to present); project manager and president of the Board of Connections, a "Resource Center for Childcare Providers and Parents" (1992 to the present); chair of the Texas State Library and Texas Library Association Committee on Public Library Development Study (2003 to 2004); and chair of the Texas State Library and Archives Commission Committee to Develop Standard for School Libraries (1998 to 2001).

Todaro has authored many articles, columns, and editorials. Previous books include *Mentoring A to Z* (2014), *Public Library Advisory Board Manual* (2012), *Emergency Preparedness in Libraries* (2009), and *Extraordinary Customer Service* (coauthored with Mark Smith, 2006).

Todaro was awarded the 2012 Texas Library Association (TLA) Lifetime Achievement Award, was the 2007–2008 past president of the Association of College and Research Libraries, was the president of the American Library Association, was the 2000–2001 past president of the TLA, was the 2004–2006 chair of the TLA's Legislative Committee and chair of the TLA Public Relations Communications Committee. The TLA awarded her the 1996 Librarian of the Year Award, and she received the YWCA Austin Educator of the Year Award in 1999.

Todaro received her doctorate of library services from Columbia University and her masters of library and information science from the University of Texas at Austin.